Grief in Schools

Matthias Böhmer · Georges Steffgen
Editors

Grief in Schools

Basic Knowledge and Advice on Dealing with Dying and Death

Editors
Matthias Böhmer
Department of Behavioural and
Cognitive Sciences
University of Luxemburg
Esch-sur-Alzette, Luxembourg

Georges Steffgen
Department of Behavioural and
Cognitive Sciences
University of Luxemburg
Esch-sur-Alzette, Luxembourg

ISBN 978-3-662-64296-2   ISBN 978-3-662-64297-9 (eBook)
https://doi.org/10.1007/978-3-662-64297-9

This book is a translation of the original German edition „Trauer an Schulen" by Böhmer, Matthias and Steffgen, George, published by Springer-Verlag GmbH, DE in 2021. The translation was done with the help of artificial intelligence (machine translation by the service DeepL.com). A subsequent human revision was done primarily in terms of content, so that the book will read stylistically differently from a conventional translation. Springer Nature works continuously to further the development of tools for the production of books and on the related technologies to support the authors.

© Springer-Verlag GmbH Germany, part of Springer Nature 2022
This work is subject to copyright. All rights are reserved by the Publisher, whether the whole or part of the material is concerned, specifically the rights of reprinting, reuse of illustrations, recitation, broadcasting, reproduction on microfilms or in any other physical way, and transmission or information storage and retrieval, electronic adaptation, computer software, or by similar or dissimilar methodology now known or hereafter developed.
The use of general descriptive names, registered names, trademarks, service marks, etc. in this publication does not imply, even in the absence of a specific statement, that such names are exempt from the relevant protective laws and regulations and therefore free for general use.
The publisher, the authors, and the editors are safe to assume that the advice and information in this book are believed to be true and accurate at the date of publication. Neither the publisher nor the authors or the editors give a warranty, expressed or implied, with respect to the material contained herein or for any errors or omissions that may have been made. The publisher remains neutral with regard to jurisdictional claims in published maps and institutional affiliations.

This Springer imprint is published by the registered company Springer-Verlag GmbH, DE, part of Springer Nature.
The registered company address is: Heidelberger Platz 3, 14197 Berlin, Germany

Preface

"I always know what to do—that's what teacher Arne Ulbricht used to think. Then suddenly one of his students died, and he asked himself: what now?" (Ulbricht 2015). Yes, what now? What is to be done when a teacher is confronted with the death of a student? What is to be done in the case of an acute bereavement in a class and in the school? This book aims to answer these and other questions about dealing with death and grief in schools.

This book is the result of a seminar in the master's program in psychology: Psychological Intervention at the University of Luxembourg, which took place in the winter semester 2019/2020 and dealt with the topic of "Death and Grief in Schools." All authors are students of this master's program and present in the following chapters the current state of research on the topic of dealing with grief in schools.

Chap. 1 by *Ramona Czakon* and *Kim Harpes* introduces the topic. In Chap. 2, *Amna Skrozic* and *Dzenita Kijamet* give a definition of grief, describe gender differences, and identify cultural and religious influences in dealing with grief. The fact that children and adolescents grieve differently from adults is addressed in Chap. 3. *Tonie Schweich* and *Tamara Luxen* explain in Sect. 3.1 how children grieve and *Caroline Bell* and *Julia Federspiel* in Sect. 3.2 how adolescents grieve. The many causes of grief are described in Chap. 4. *Justine Hubertus* and *Katharina Schneider* deal with chronic illnesses in Sect. 4.1. Sudden deaths are discussed in Sect. 4.2, with *Katharina Barcatta* and *Anna-Lynn Schlund* discussing suicide (Sect. 4.2.1), *Lena Schwind* and *Vera Hilger* discussing accidents (Sect. 4.2.2), and *Jan Hamborg* and *Charlotte Ries* discussing acts of violence (Sect. 4.2.3). *Iris Cranfield* and *Maria Kohl* focus on appropriate interventions in Chap. 5. Finally, *Sam Bernard* and *Mario Scholer* point out the limits of grief work in Chap. 6.

We would like to express our sincere thanks to all authors for their extraordinary commitment to this project, which, after *Amok at Schools* (*Amok an Schulen*, Böhmer 2018) and *Bullying at Schools* (*Mobbing an Schulen*, Böhmer, and Steffgen 2019), is now the third book publication by students of the master's program in psychology: Psychological Intervention at the University of Luxembourg with Springer. We would therefore like to thank Springer in general and Joachim Coch in particular for their excellent cooperation.

Luxembourg
Summer 2020

Matthias Böhmer
Georges Steffgen

References

Böhmer, M. (Hrsg.). (2018). *Amok in schools: prevention, intervention and aftercare in school shootings* [*Amok an Schulen: Prävention, Intervention und Nachsorge bei School Shootings*]. Heidelberg: Springer.

Böhmer, M., & Steffgen, G. (Hrsg.). (2019). *Bullying in schools: measures for prevention, intervention and aftercare* [*Mobbing an Schulen: Maßnahmen zur Prävention, Intervention und Nachsorge*]. Heidelberg: Springer.

Ulbricht, A. (2015). I could hardly stand the pain [Ich hielt den Schmerz kaum aus]. Spiegel Online. https://www.spiegel.de/lebenundlernen/schule/tod-eines-schuelers-wie-lehrer-und-klasse-damit-umgingen-a-1009082.html

Contents

1 Introduction 1
Ramona Czakon and Kim Harpes
   1.1   Content and Aim of this Book 2
   1.2   Why Is the Topic of Grief Relevant in the School Context? 2
         1.2.1   Affected by Death and Grief: Children, Adolescents
               and Adults 2
         1.2.2   Taboo Subject 3
         1.2.3   Children and Grief 3
         1.2.4   Stages and Processes of Grief 4
         1.2.5   Healthy and Pathological Grief 4
   1.3   Potential Causes of Grief and General Prevalence Data 5
   1.4   Problems in Dealing with Grief in the School Context 10
   1.5   Status on Dealing with Grief in the School Context 11
   References 11

2 Definition of Grief, Gender Differences and Religious and Cultural Differences in Dealing with Death and Grief 13
Amna Skrozic and Dzenita Kijamet
   2.1   Definition of the Concept of Grief 13
         2.1.1   Grieving Vs. Being Sad 14
         2.1.2   Grieving Function and Situation 14
         2.1.3   Grieving Symptoms 16
         2.1.4   Grieving Intensity 17
         2.1.5   Definition of Grieving Terms 17
         2.1.6   Contradictory Grieving Reactions and Norms 18
   2.2   Gender Differences in Dealing with Death and Grief 19
   2.3   Cultural Influence in Dealing with Death and Mourning 20
   2.4   Religious Influence in Dealing with Death and Mourning 22
         2.4.1   Christianity 22

		2.4.2	Islam	23
		2.4.3	Hinduism	24
	References			24
3	**Grief in Children and Adolescents**			29
	Tonie Schweich, Tamara Luxen, Caroline Bell, and Julia Federspiel			
	3.1	Grief in Children		29
		3.1.1	Theory of Cognitive Development by Jean Piaget (1978)	30
		3.1.2	The Child's Understanding of Death	33
		3.1.3	The Infantile Mourning Process	40
		3.1.4	The Child's Grief Reactions	43
		3.1.5	The Child's Grief Tasks	46
		3.1.6	Pathological Grief	47
		3.1.7	Cultural Differences	48
	3.2	Grief among Adolescents		49
		3.2.1	Coping with Grief in Adolescents	50
		3.2.2	Somatization in the Grieving Process	52
		3.2.3	Adolescent Grief in the School Context	53
		3.2.4	Grief Via Social Media	56
		3.2.5	Grief within the Family Circle	56
		3.2.6	Accompanying Young People in their Grief	59
	Bibliography			61
4	**Causes of Grief**			69
	Justine Hubertus, Katharina Schneider, Katharina Barcatta, Anna-Lynn Schlund, Lena Schwind, Vera Hilger, Jan Hamborg, and Charlotte Ries			
	4.1	Chronic Diseases		69
		4.1.1	What Is it? And why Do we Talk about it?	69
		4.1.2	Interventions	72
		4.1.3	Conclusion	84
	4.2	Sudden Death		85
		4.2.1	Suicide	85
		4.2.2	Accidents	94
		4.2.3	Violence	103
	References			120
5	**Interventions**			135
	Iris Cranfield and Maria Kohl			
	5.1	Guide to the Delivery of the Message		135
	5.2	Individual and Group Interventions		137
		5.2.1	Individual Interventions	138
		5.2.2	Group Interventions	140

	5.3	Training of Teachers in Dealing with Grieving Pupils	142
	5.4	Conclusion	145
	References	145
6	**Limits of Grief Work**	147
	Sam Bernard and Mario Scholer	
	6.1	Limits of Grief Work by Teachers and Pedagogical Professionals	147
	6.2	Limits of Grief Counselling in the Institution School	149
	6.3	Limits of Grief Work with Affected Persons, Relatives and Fellow Sufferers	151
	6.4	Limits of Bereavement Work by Carers	152
		6.4.1 Compassion Fatigue and Secondary Traumatic Stress	152
		6.4.2 Relevance of Self-Care	154
	6.5	End and Closure of Grief Work	155
		6.5.1 Closure as Part of a Defined Intervention	156
		6.5.2 End of Grief Counselling as a Natural Process	157
	6.6	Conclusion	158
	References	159
Index		161

Introduction

Ramona Czakon and Kim Harpes

Case Study: Heart Attack

After a long and stressful day at work, Karl Müller (56 years old), a chemistry teacher at the Friedrich-Wilhelm-Gymnasium, goes to the school laboratory to prepare the material for the next day. As he unlocks the lab cabinet, he suddenly feels severe pain in his chest. Within seconds, this pain radiates down his left arm and into his lower jaw. He sits down on the floor and notices how his shortness of breath gradually increases. His skin becomes paler and cold sweat breaks out. Karl Müller is gripped by mortal fear. He immediately tries to call for help, but the shortness of breath reduces the volume of his call. After a few minutes, he passes out.

The next morning, the physics teacher, Franz Schneider (54 years old), enters the school laboratory and discovers the chemistry teacher on the floor. He rushes to him, kneels down, calls his name and shakes him. Karl Müller remains lying lifeless. Franz Schneider quickly checks Karl Müller's pulse. He cannot feel anything. He abruptly alerts the emergency services and the school secretary's office. Gradually, a commotion spreads through the school and the rumour mill is stimulated by the panic and the lack of knowledge.

R. Czakon (✉) · K. Harpes
Department of Behavioural and Cognitive Sciences, University of Luxembourg, Esch-sur-Alzette, Luxembourg
e-mail: ramona.czakon.001@student.uni.lu

1.1 Content and Aim of this Book

Deaths, such as sudden death due to a cardiovascular disorder as in the case study above, occur frequently. Young as well as older people can be directly or indirectly affected by a death. The actual reasons for death can be many and varied: chronic illness, suicide, accidents or violence. For some people the news of death is unexpected and surprising, for others it is not. Nevertheless, death and grief are rarely presented in school contexts. Yet it occurs there more often than not. Moreover, larger groups of people are usually affected by grief. Unfortunately, it often happens that people feel abandoned and helpless after a death of a teacher or a student. These points highlight two important aspects: the importance of the topic (i.e. dealing with grief) and the uncertainty about how to deal with the consequences.

Because of this, this book was written. The aim of this book is to educate those interested in the topic of dealing with grief in a school context. In addition, it is intended to offer practical support by providing information on how to act adequately after a death.

The aim of the introduction is to provide a general introduction and insight into the topic of grief in the school context and to present an overview of the relevance of the topic. For this purpose, the significance and necessity of the topic are discussed first. Then, possible causes of grief and the corresponding prevalence figures will be illustrated. Finally, some criticisms regarding the topic are addressed and the current state of knowledge is summarized. The remaining chapters of the book then clarify in detail what grief is, how grief processes differ among different age groups, and what interventions are available for this purpose. The book concludes with a discussion of when grief work in schools ends and when external help becomes necessary.

1.2 Why Is the Topic of Grief Relevant in the School Context?

The following sections illustrate the importance of the topic. Furthermore, a brief insight into the mourning processes will be given.

1.2.1 Affected by Death and Grief: Children, Adolescents and Adults

Death and mourning are important and current topics that everyone is confronted with at any age, and often several times in their lives (Brandl, 2015; Pesel, 2006). Be it through social platforms, media or personal experiences—the reasons for this confrontation can be of different nature. Therefore, it is important that children, adolescents as well as adults are informed in detail about death and grief and learn to deal with these topics in order to minimize short-term as well as long-term negative consequences. Overlooking these topoi can lead to short-term and/or also long-term negative consequences, such as personal and social harm and/or suffering, up to mental disorders (Barth et al., 2003; Lanzenberger, 2008; Znoj, 2016). Due to this, it is necessary to address, illustrate and thematize these issues.

1.2.2 Taboo Subject

Death and mourning seem to be taboo topics in German society. In many cases, death is repressed and denied in today's society (Brandl, 2015). The same view is held by Witt-Loers (2012), who assumes that death is a social taboo. Ortmann et al. (2014) confirmed this in a study: in various interviews it was found that this topic was not discussed with students who were seriously ill. A statement from one of the interviews illustrates this: "Well, I didn't talk to him about death in such a concrete and direct way" (Ortmann et al., 2014, p. 51). Terminally ill children feel the need to talk about death and grief in order to escape loneliness, their insecurity and their fears. Due to the taboo, those affected are not only left alone, but also abandoned (Ortmann et al., 2014).

This taboo also has an influence on the discussion of death and mourning in schools (Ortmann et al., 2014). Some teachers are not in a position to talk to the class about such a difficult topic as the illness of a pupil or a teacher and the potential fatal consequences. Some teachers additionally state that the parents of the affected, ill children make it difficult to address these issues. It happens that in the parental home the topic of death and mourning regarding the ill child is taboo. In other words, parents very often do not talk to the sick children about their illness and the possible consequences (Lanzenberger, 2008; Ortmann et al., 2014). This makes it difficult for teachers to work and communicate with the class on this topic (Ortmann et al., 2014).

1.2.3 Children and Grief

Children are part of society and are confronted with grief on a daily basis in a variety of ways, whether indirectly (e.g. adults' comments about the death of a person), directly (e.g. death of a pet) or fictitiously (e.g. death of a comic/fantasy character) (Pesel, 2006). However, in doing so, children are often excluded from grief processes by adults, largely parents, for perceived protection (Brandl, 2015). This can lead to children not having the opportunity to come to terms with death and grief, as well as learning to do so. This in turn can lead to children not being able to talk about their worries, fears and ideas about death, nor do they want to. Since these issues are also part of childhood—death is part of life and a problem of the living—the need for addressing this issue becomes apparent. Especially in the school context, different grief situations can occur, be it through fatal accidents, illnesses or suicide and violent crimes (Brandl, 2015; Vonderau, 2018).

Children receive a great deal of information, mostly from adults. This information serves as an orientation aid in order to be able to reflect realistically and critically on the world and to understand and cope with it. For this reason, children need help in dealing with death and grief. Unfortunately, in most cases they do not get this from their parents (Brandl, 2015). Parents, as mentioned earlier, often try to repress death experiences in order to protect their children. On the other hand, parents are often afraid of confronting death themselves. Therefore, teachers in particular play a central role in these issues. The school is an essential interaction and support system for children and due to this fact it is important that the school deals with the topic of death and grief. Children spend a large part of their time at school, where their cognitive and psychological development is also crucially influenced (Vonderau, 2018). Thus, teachers* could support their students with such issues and adequately assist them with death and grief. This could in turn minimize or even avoid factors such as fear, shame, loneliness as well as other negative experiences (Brandl, 2015; Pesel, 2006; Vonderau, 2018). This is why the need and urgency to develop teachers' professional and personal skills in knowing and acting on death and grief is so central (Witt-Loers, 2012).

1.2.4 Stages and Processes of Grief

Grief is a natural reaction to death, which manifests itself individually and in many different ways on a mental, physical and emotional level. Grief is a process that is not only different for adults, but also for children and adolescents. Children and adolescents, like adults, need time to deal with loss. However, there are differences in grief depending on age. The concept of death in children and adolescents is influenced by various factors, namely cognitive maturation processes, socialization influences, and adult experiences and dealings with this topic (Pesel, 2006). Thus, the grieving process is different for each person. It does not involve a fixed pattern. Nevertheless, typical patterns often emerge in coping with grief (Vonderau, 2018). More detailed information on grief coping concepts will be explained in the context of the book.

1.2.5 Healthy and Pathological Grief

Grief involves a temporary phase full of emotional fluctuations with different needs (e.g. need for support/help in coping with grief or will to cope alone), reactions (e.g. crying, screaming or laughing when the death news is announced) and behaviours (e.g. social withdrawal). Because of this, it is often difficult to distinguish between healthy and pathological grief, and likewise, appropriate definitions depend on how one describes grief or the grieving process (Lanzenberger, 2008; Vonderau, 2018). Grief always represents an individual process, so it is not the management of the different stages of grief as well as the mode of expression that should be considered, but rather the intensity and duration of the grief until the affected person is able to lead a content life again. During this time, individuals may exhibit depressive behaviors (e.g., constant fatigue, lack of energy, or disinterest). However, if these persist over a prolonged period of time and include passive (e.g. avoidance behaviour), regressive (e.g. defiance or withdrawal) and apathetic (e.g. apathy/indifference) behaviour, many cases are pathological grief reactions. In this case, the affected person is no longer able to cope with everyday situations on his or her own, and grief dominates his or her life. In such cases it is advisable to seek professional help, for example from psychotherapists. This professional help serves not only as support (Vonderau, 2018), but also as preventive care to prevent serious negative, long-term psychological consequences (e.g. alcohol or drug addiction, depression without or even with suicidal tendencies) (Lanzenberger, 2008; Vonderau, 2018).

1.3 Potential Causes of Grief and General Prevalence Data

There are multiple causes that lead to death and thus to grief reactions. In this book, the focus is specifically on causes of grief that can play a role in connection with schools, such as chronic illnesses or a sudden death due to an accident, a suicide, or a violent crime committed by a teacher or a student.

The prevalence figures for deaths vary depending on the time of measurement, age and cause of death. According to the Federal Statistical Office, in general, in May 2020, for ages 0 to 30, 638 deaths were recorded (Destatis, 2020c). For ages 30 to 50, these figures rise abruptly to 1838. Further general figures on deaths in the month of May 2020 can be seen in Table 1.1.

If we look at the annual deaths by age group, we obtain data as shown in Table 1.2. Table 1.2 shows general death rates from 2019 (*raw data) and 2018 (Destatis, 2020c).

As in Table 1.1, it can also be seen in Table 1.2 that the number of deceased increases with age. This can be attributed to many reasons. One obvious explanation is that stress levels often increase with age due to increasing responsibility, challenging working conditions, or other environmental demands and expectations. These, as well as other factors such as a high-fat and high-sugar diet or an increased lack of exercise, can influence the physical and mental condition and thus cause and/or promote various diseases. Ultimately, the most common causes of death are due to various diseases. This also becomes clear in the following table (Table 1.3).

Table 1.3 shows the number of deceased persons by cause of death and age group in 2018 (Destatis, 2020d). The actual database of the Federal Statistical Office contains a larger number of causes of death. However, some causes of death have been omitted to highlight the more relevant causes of death for the school context.

As already mentioned, Table 1.3 shows an extract from the Destatis database of the Federal Statistical Office. The detailed database can be accessed via the following link https://www.destatis.de/DE/Themen/Gesellschaft-Umwelt/Gesundheit/Todesursachen/_inhalt.html or by using various search engines such as Google under "Todesursachen in Deutschland—Statistisches Bundesamt" (Destatis, 2020d).

Table 1.1 Number of deceased in Germany in May 2020

Age from... to under... years	May 2020 [a] raw data
0–30	638
30–50	1838
50–55	1717
55–60	2955
60–65	4087
65–70	5136
Total	75,115

[a] Raw data may be slightly higher

Table 1.2 Number of deceased persons in Germany in 2019 and 2018

Age from... to under... years	2019 [a] raw data	2018
0–30	8293	7815
30–50	22,211	23,077
50–55	21,417	22,654
55–60	35,382	36,452
60–65	48,714	49,584
65–70	65,180	65,660
Total	936,591	954,874

[a] Raw data may be slightly higher

If you look at the data from 2018, it quickly becomes clear that the most frequent causes of death are due to physical diseases. The most common diseases are diseases of the circulatory system or malignant neoplasms (i.e. cancer). Günster et al. (2012) adds that 70% of all deaths in Germany are due to these chronic diseases. Finally, as in all other tables presented, Table 1.3 also shows that mortality rates increase with age.

Other interesting and noteworthy prevalence rates of the deceased target suicide and accidents. In 2018, as shown in Table 1.4, 8 boys and 5 girls aged 10 to 15 suicided (Destatis, 2020b). There were a total of 179 suicides between the ages of 15 and 20. Here, 132 males and 47 females were affected. Among older persons (55 to 60 years), there were far more suicides: 994. Of these, 739 were males and 255 females. The highest suicide numbers are found among people aged 50 to 55. Here, a total of 1055 persons died in 2018, of which 767 were men and 288 women (Destatis, 2020b).

Based on Table 1.4, it is clear that men are more affected by suicide than women—up to three times more. Although it is prominent that younger women are more likely to attempt suicide, it is usually men who successfully complete the suicide attempt. This may be because men use "harder" methods. For example, women who attempt suicide largely avoid disfiguring their faces (Callanan & Davis, 2011) and more often resort to "softer" suicide methods such as pill overdose. Men, on the other hand, do not shy away from "harder" methods, which can include facial disfigurement, to take their own lives. This refers to methods such as hanging, strangulation, suffocation, throwing oneself down,

Table 1.3 Number of deceased in Germany in 2018 by cause of death and age group

Cause of death	1 to 15 years	15 to 20 years	20 to 30 years	30 to 50 years	50 to 55 years	55 to 60 years	60 to 65 years	65 to 70 years
Total	666	1141	4172	22,964	21,488	34,344	45,769	58,762
Malignant neoplasms (BN)	137	68	234	2928	4348	8057	11,862	15,489
Malignant melanoma of the skin	1	1	8	109	86	105	143	178
Leukemia	38	18	46	121	98	175	271	399
Diabetes mellitus	–	9	16	246	282	464	647	1029
Mental and behavioural disorders	3	4	68	876	642	856	904	984
Mental and behavioural disorders caused by alcohol	–	–	12	498	480	678	707	633
Meningitis	1	–	2	6	4	4	2	10
Diseases of the circulatory system	21	22	147	2565	3174	5506	7905	10,968
Hypertension (high pressure disease)	–	–	6	118	163	336	454	714
Ischemic heart disease	–	–	21	1052	1576	2780	4086	5404
Acute or recurrent myocardial infarction	–	–	19	772	1107	1805	2351	2871
Other forms of heart disease	8	13	60	585	604	966	1251	1766
Cerebrovascular diseases	6	5	21	309	363	656	1059	1614
Diseases of the arteries, arterioles and capillaries	1	1	8	163	138	307	434	608
Diseases of the respiratory system	24	12	37	382	569	1266	2126	3241
Pneumonia	6	4	15	96	112	249	315	545
Chronic diseases of the lower respiratory tract	3	–	3	134	304	753	1365	2121
Asthma	2	–	1	29	21	33	28	29
Diseases of the digestive system	6	6	42	1295	1357	2041	2453	2552
Diseases of the liver	1	1	18	952	979	1472	1622	1604
External causes of morbidity and mortality	127	371	1299	3373	1568	1705	1547	1599

(continued)

Table 1.3 (continued)

Cause of death	Age groups							
	1 to 15 years	15 to 20 years	20 to 30 years	30 to 50 years	50 to 55 years	55 to 60 years	60 to 65 years	65 to 70 years
Accidents including late effects	112	217	626	1515	699	840	890	989
Transport accidents	46	154	385	581	230	255	217	173
Falls	7	7	35	192	147	182	296	429
Drowning and sinking	26	20	32	48	19	25	11	28
Exposure to smoke, fire and flames	2	–	6	33	17	20	22	20
Acid. Poisoning: Noxious substances (incl. Exp.)	4	9	86	380	91	55	56	31
Intentional self-harm	8	132	576	1566	767	739	558	508
Assault	5	4	16	48	12	22	12	11
Otherwise inaccurately designated and unknown causes of death	69	45	248	1755	1442	1895	2091	2130
Incidental event	2	18	79	237	89	97	84	85

1 Introduction

Table 1.4 Number of suicides 2018

Age groups From... to under ... years old	Total	Male	Female
Under 10	–	–	–
10 to 15	13	8	5
15 to 20	179	132	47
20 to 25	338	276	62
25 to 30	376	300	76
30 to 35	432	339	93
35 to 40	443	357	86
40 to 45	463	348	115
45 to 50	687	522	165
50 to 55	1055	767	288
55 to 60	994	739	255
60 to 65	733	558	175
65 to 70	667	508	159

being run over, or using a firearm or explosive (Wiesner, 2004). These methods also increase the success rate of the procedure.

Another observable feature concerns the increasing suicide rates. The suicide rate increases with age. More remarkable and perhaps incomprehensible at first sight are the quite high suicide rates at the age of 50 to 55. Some reasons for this can be attributed to changes in life circumstances (Hammer, n.d.). For example, illnesses or physical complaints increase at this age, which increases the fear of addiction and decreases the quality of life. In addition, relationships with other people often change or serious strokes of fate occur, such as the death of a partner, siblings or friends (Hammer, n.d.). These and other stressful factors can tempt people of advanced age to suicide.

Lastly, from Table 1.5, the rates of deaths due to various accidents can be taken. In total, in 2018, in the age group 5 to 15, there were 109 deaths, in the age group 15 to 25, 663 deaths and in the age group 55 to 65, 2039 deaths (Destatis, 2020a). As in the previous tables, also in this category, by and large, the prevalence figures increase with age. The mortality rates due to traffic accidents, domestic accidents and other accidents are the most pronounced.

One possible reason for the increasing mortality rates in older age is the decline in visual and muscular strength (Unfälle im Haushalt, 2017). Older people are particularly at risk of falling due to this. Another reason is the decrease in responsiveness. These points can promote as well as explain accidents such as road accidents or domestic accidents. Younger persons, on the other hand, show higher mortality rates in work/school accidents and especially in traffic accidents. This can be explained by the fact that younger persons, hormone-induced, overestimate their own abilities and limits or deliberately seek out riskier and adrenaline-stimulating moments. Factors such as recklessness, cockiness,

Table 1.5 Number of deceased persons by accident category in 2018

Age group (years)	Total	Work/school accident	Traffic accident	Domestic accident	Sports/games accident	Other accident
5 to 15	109	0	50	10	16	32
15 to 25	663	120	458	27	18	140
25 to 35	775	42	381	68	20	264
35 to 45	822	34	297	88	7	396
45 to 55	1386	74	455	234	26	597
55 to 65	2039	95	547	559	32	806

carefreeness, arrogance, or bragging often play a significant role in the basic attitude, which can lead to thoughtless and irresponsible behavior and actions.

In summary, the above prevalence rates show that the topic of grief is significant in the school context and should be urgently addressed. It becomes clear that both children and adolescents come into contact with death and grief not only through the media, but can also be confronted in real life by the death of a fellow student, a friend, a teacher or a family member.

1.4 Problems in Dealing with Grief in the School Context

Currently, many schools have very few, if any, support systems in place when a relative, teacher, or fellow student dies as a result of an accident, illness, suicide, or violent crime (Vonderau, 2018). When such a calamity occurs, dealing with death and grief in schools shows significant deficits. Even though a few programs are available, such as the project *Hospiz macht Schule* or *Leben bis zuletzt*, in which children as well as young people can creatively and actively deal with the topics of life, dying, mourning, comfort and consolation (Witt-Loers, 2012), there are serious deficiencies with regard to interventions in acute cases. Lack of knowledge of teachers in dealing with dying, death and mourning, as well as a low number of individual school projects regarding this topic, perpetuate this problem—dealing with grief. However, as these issues are of great importance, more schools should be encouraged to take up these factors in order to provide adequate education and help to all school stakeholders (Pesel, 2006).

A final point concerns the collection of specific prevalence rates. There is often a lack of such data. For example, after extensive research, one can learn what the crude death rates are in certain categories. However, no data, in response to specific questions, come up, such

1 Introduction

as "Which and how many states have implemented the topic of death and grief into the curriculum, how many students have dealt with this topic theoretically and practically, how many students are aware of the grieving process and possible support programs, or how many students (and at what age) have been confronted with the death of a teacher or student in school." This lack of information again indicates that this subject matter is not being addressed extensively. Additionally, it is clear that more specific data on frequency should be collected to gain a detailed insight and more thorough understanding regarding starting points as well as implementation of interventions.

1.5 Status on Dealing with Grief in the School Context

At present, as already mentioned, there is a great lack of knowledge and therefore many wishes for improvement in the matter of dealing with mourning. Nevertheless, there are a few federal states, such as Baden-Württemberg, Schleswig-Holstein or Bavaria, which have integrated this topic in subjects such as religion, German, ethics or philosophy (Witt-Loers, 2012). Furthermore, there is the possibility to inform oneself about numerous aspects of the topic with the help of the internet. Websites such as https://trauerseelsorge.de/jugendliche/ or https://www.trauerland.org/, as well as individual programs such as *Sinus,* a school-based crisis intervention, offer information and help on prevention, intervention and postvention (Sinus, n.d.). Even though some information is available on the Internet, there is currently a lack of specialist books that address this topic and summarize the most important points for teachers and students. This book is intended to remedy this situation.

References

Barth, S., Kerp, E. M., & Müller, M. (2003). *Trauer.* Accessed Jul 10, 2020, from https://psydok.psycharchives.de/jspui/bitstream/20.500.11780/332/1/beri157.pdf

Brandl, A. (2015). *Tod und Trauer als Thema für den Unterricht in der Sekundarstufe I.* Universität Wien.

Callanan, V. J., & Davis, M. S. (2011). Gender and suicide method: Do women avoid facial disfiguration? *Sex Roles, 65*(11–12), 867–879.

Destatis. (2020a). *Anzahl der Gestorbenen nach Unfallkategorien.* Accessed Jul 31, 2020, from https://www.destatis.de/DE/Themen/Gesellschaft-Umwelt/Gesundheit/Todesursachen/Tabellen/sterbefaelle-unfaelle.html

Destatis. (2020b). *Anzahl der Suizide 2018.* Accessed Jul 31, 2020, from https://www.destatis.de/DE/Themen/Gesellschaft-Umwelt/Gesundheit/Todesursachen/Tabellen/suizide.html

Destatis. (2020c). *Sterbefälle–Fallzahlen nach Tagen,* Wochen, Monaten, Altersgruppen, und Bundesländern für Deutschland 2016–2020. Accessed Jul 31, 2020, from https://www.destatis.de/DE/Themen/Gesellschaft-Umwelt/Bevoelkerung/Sterbefaelle-Lebenserwartung/Tabellen/sonderauswertung-sterbefaelle.html

Destatis. (2020d). *Tabelle: Gestorbene: Deutschland, Jahre, Todesursache, Altersgruppen*. Accessed Jul 31, 2020, from https://www.destatis.de/DE/Themen/Gesellschaft-Umwelt/Gesundheit/Todesursachen/_inhalt.html

Günster, C., Klose, J., & Schmacke, N. (2012). Versorgungs-Report 2012. In *Schwerpunkt: Gesundheit im Alter*. Schattauer.

Hammer, M. (n.d.). *Warum nehmen sich so viele ältere Menschen das Leben?* Accessed Jul 28, 2020, from https://www.stern.de/gesundheit/suizid-im-alter-warum-bringen-sich-vor-allem-aeltere-um-6452916.html

Lanzenberger, C. (2008). *Die Bedeutung von Trauer im Kontext Schule. Sonderpädagogische Aspekte zum Umgang mit trauernden Schülerinnen und Schülern in der Schule für Geistigbehinderte*. Wissenschaftliche Arbeit. Pädagogische Hochschule Ludwigsburg.

Ortmann, M., Jennessen, S., Bruns, C., & Uhrlau, K. (2014). *Schulpädagogisches Coping angesichts progredient erkrankter Kinder und Jugendlicher–zum pädagogischen Umgang mit Tod, Sterben und Trauer in der Schule (Bericht zum Forschungsprojekt)*. Carl von Ossietzky Universität Oldenburg.

Pesel, D. (2006). Die Thematisierung von Tod und Trauer. *Widerstreit Sachunterricht, 7*, 1–54.

Sinus. (n.d.). Accessed Jul 10, 2020, from https://www.schulische-krisenintervention.de/

Unfälle im Haushalt. (2017). Accessed Jul 28, 2020, from https://www.faz.net/aktuell/gesellschaft/senioren-besonders-gefaehrdet-fast-10-000-menschen-sterben-bei-unfaellen-im-haushalt-14848816.html

Vonderau, T. (2018). *Über die Enttabuisierung von Tod und Trauer in der Schule*. Universität Kassel.

Wiesner, G. (2004). *Suizidmethoden–ein Vergleich zwischen Ost- und Westdeutschland*. Accessed Jul 30, 2020, from https://edoc.rki.de/bitstream/handle/176904/1119/28hvS3LoVKX6g.pdf?sequence=1&isAllowed=y

Witt-Loers, S. (2012). Schulprojekte zum Umgang mit Sterben. Tod und Trauer. *Leidfaden, 1*(4), 10–17.

Znoj, H. (2016). *Trennung, Tod und Trauer*. Hogrefe.

Definition of Grief, Gender Differences and Religious and Cultural Differences in Dealing with Death and Grief

2

Amna Skrozic and Dzenita Kijamet

2.1 Definition of the Concept of Grief

What does it mean to feel grief when a loved one passes away? Is it the tears that one sheds after the loss of a person that define the grief? Is it the stabbing pain and the sudden surge of anger that one feels due to the loved one having been prematurely torn away from one's daily life? Or is it possibly the realization that one will never see the closed one again? What it means to grieve seems to be a rather simple, almost trivial question. However, it can hardly be answered with just a short definition. After all, grief may include all of the above listed emotions, thoughts, and behaviours, or in turn only include some or even none of the mentioned aspects. As is commonly known, each person grieves in their own way. While one person might be overcome with deep distress after the loss of a beloved friend or family member, another might happily revel in the precious memories of the deceased, albeit perhaps with a tinge of wistfulness.

Despite these inter-individual differences as to how people react to the death of a loved one, everyone intuitively knows what it means to grieve. For example, there is a general consensus that grieving is something natural—something which is even part of being human—and which is often associated with unpleasant and negative emotions. This presence of negative emotions is even emphasized in the thesaurus, where grieving is described as a feeling of deep emotional pain. Although human beings ultimately strive for the experience of pleasant and positive emotions, this feeling of sorrow can hardly be considered a pathological state of mind—particularly when it is seen as an essential part of human life. Similarly, it should not be interpreted as a weakness of character (Lammer,

A. Skrozic (✉) · D. Kijamet
Department of Behavioural and Cognitive Sciences, University of Luxembourg, Esch-sur-Alzette, Luxembourg
e-mail: amna.skrozic.001@student.uni.lu

© Springer-Verlag GmbH Germany, part of Springer Nature 2022
M. Böhmer, G. Steffgen (eds.), *Grief in Schools*,
https://doi.org/10.1007/978-3-662-64297-9_2

2014). The latter point in particular needs to be stressed, as this idea sadly continues to be propagated depending on a person's sex. After all, everyone, whether young, old, female, male or non-binary, goes through certain situations throughout life that can prompt grief, such as for example the loss of a relative. So why shouldn't someone grieve or be sad?

2.1.1 Grieving Vs. Being Sad

At this point, it must be specified that "grieving" is not necessarily on a par with "being sad". Some mourners are simply not able to feel sadness after the loss of a person (Znoj, 2005). Yet, this absence of sadness has often been equated with a complete lack of a grieving response, which only a few decades ago was even considered to be a pathological reaction and sometimes taken as an indication for an underlying personality disorder (Osterweis et al., 1984). After all, how else would one explain the absence of sadness after a child's death or after the loss of a beloved parent or a good friend? It must be said, however, that in the past years many researchers have stressed and even showcased that the absence of sadness is not an atypical reaction—on the contrary! For instance, while surveying the emotional state of widowed men and women three years prior to and four years after the death of their partners, Bonanno et al. (2008) showed that approximately half of their surveyed study participants were experiencing low levels of depression and showed only few grieving symptoms within their bereavement period. This might seem to be a surprising result for some, but it emphasises that the death of a person does not ultimately always trigger deep despair.

Having said that, the above-described absence of sadness is definitely not the only alternative reaction that can arise when a death occurs. Sometimes the death of a person can also be accompanied by positive emotions such as relief, peace, or even joy (Zisook & Shear, 2009). This may sound a bit grim at first. Yet, when this situation is considered in the context of a deceased person having battled with major health issues prior to their death and having suffered greatly because of them, this reaction does seem to be comprehensible. The same can be said for instance when experiencing such positive emotions when thinking of the happy memories that remain of the deceased. In fact, dealing with such fond memories can have an important coping function for the bereaved (Field et al., 1999). Thus, it can hardly be considered far-fetched that someone experiences pleasant moments after the death of a loved one; underlining once more that one does not only feel sadness or a void of emotions after the loss of a person.

2.1.2 Grieving Function and Situation

Whether or not someone expresses grief in a negative or a positive way or through a lack of an emotional response, what is interesting to point out is that the process of grieving is not only a normal one, but also a cross-cultural phenomenon. This phenomenon can, in fact, be found in different nations and cultures and is often—although not necessarily—expressed in the form of crying (Scherer et al., 2001). Likewise, grieving as a reaction to a death can not only be observed in humans but also in animals (Barth et al., 2003). Evidence that animals mourn the loss of a family or herd member in a similar fashion as humans for example do, can inter alia be found when looking into primate research. Here researchers have observed that grieving mother monkeys often carry along the bodies of their deceased offspring for up to several weeks after the death of their young ones (Watson & Matsuzawa, 2018). Similarly, specific behavioural patterns could also be observed in elephants after the death of a herd member (Douglas-Hamilton et al., 2006).

This experience of grief, whether done by humans or animals, has a significant background: the death of a loved often represents a major life event, sometimes even a threat to one's self seeing as the loss of such a person can lead to a non-compensable loss of important role models, life goals and self-value sources (Barth et al., 2003). Similarly, the death of an acquaintance or loved one can have various long-lasting consequences, which can require drastic life changes (Wagner, 2016). Sometimes these consequences can be so far-reaching that the mourner's world view is turned upside down and that their belief in a just world is called into question (Barth et al., 2003). Existential questions may arise, especially in the context of one's faith and raison d'être.

Based on Freud's definition of grieving as an expression of loss, Lammer (2014) summarizes grieving as "a normal reaction to a significant loss" (p. 2). In this context, grief is however not only understood to be the expression of one's loss and pain, but simultaneously also serves as a type of processing or a coping strategy for the bereaved (Lammer, 2014). As a result, similar to how each individual expresses grief in their own way, every individual ultimately also decides for themselves what can be considered a "loss" and how that person will deal with it. In this respect, Lammer (2014) underlines that experiencing a loss is not exclusively limited to the experience of a "final loss" i.e., the death of a person. Instead, grief can also occur after a separation, a divorce or, for example, after the loss of a job or one's health. Similarly, in certain instances a grieving response may also be absent—for example, if there was no meaningful or close relationship between the deceased and the surviving dependant. Accordingly, grief can be felt independently of a death. However, conversely, a death need not inevitably trigger feelings of grief. When trying to pinpoint in what instance someone may experience grief and when someone may not, it must be said that the past relationship with the deceased plays a significant role (Cooper, 2013). Whether grief is felt at all or whether feelings of loss arise and with what intensity this grief is manifested is often dependant on the relationship that one had with the deceased and whether this relationship was characterized by positive and/or negative feelings (Cooper, 2013). In this regard, it must however be underlined that negative emotions towards the deceased do not necessarily have to have been present if a bereaved person does not show any grieving response.

▶ Grief describes an emotional state of being or mood that can occur as a result of a loss (e.g., the death of a loved one) and can be accompanied by both negative emotions, such as sadness, or positive emotions, such as relief. An absent grief reaction following the death of someone is also possible.

2.1.3 Grieving Symptoms

Although it is difficult to objectively assess at what point someone begins to grieve and even harder to evaluate in which form a bereaved person "should" best express their grief (Metz, 2011), there are some general views as to what grief, particularly "normal" or healthy grief, entails. Seen to be a process rather than a static state (Wagner, 2016), Stroebe and Schut (1998) point out that grief is generally expressed with a wide variety of, which can play out on four different levels: an emotional level, a behavioural level, a physical/physiological level, and a mental level. Feelings of grief may inter alia include dejection, hopelessness, feelings of fear and guilt, or anger and hostility. Similarly, individuals who have lost a loved one may also experience a deep longing for the deceased, a pronounced separation pain or loneliness. An inability to feel joy may also be developed as a result of the death of a loved one. In this sense, some may even feel an emotional emptiness or coldness. These listed feelings may be expressed at the behavioural level in the form of agitation, nervousness, fatigue, apathy, hysteria, crying, as well as temporarily in social withdrawal or, in extreme cases, in social isolation. According to Stroebe and Schut (1998), the physical symptoms that can occur because of grieving are the loss of one's appetite or insomnia, eating and digestive disorders, or exhaustion. On the other hand, there can also be an increased susceptibility for developing illnesses, breathing difficulties and, in some extreme cases, even the appearance of heart problems. The thoughts that the bereaved can be left with are usually not only limited to the remaining memories of the deceased, but can also include self-reproach, denial, an absence of thoughts or conversely racing thoughts, as well as spiritual upheavals such as a loss of meaning and values or doubts about one's faith (Metz, 2011; Wagner, 2013; Znoj, 2016).

4 Levels of grief symptoms:	Examples
Emotional level	Dejection, hopelessness, anxiety, guilt, anger or hostility
Behavioural level	Agitation, nervousness, fatigue, apathy, hysteria, crying, social withdrawal or isolation
Physical/physiological level	Appetite and insomnia, eating and digestive disorders, exhaustion, increased susceptibility to diseases
Thought level	Self-reproach, denial, absence of thoughts or racing thoughts, doubts about one's faith

2.1.4 Grieving Intensity

Apart from being characterised by a multitude of different symptoms, grief is also qualified by another feature: namely, a grieving intensity which gradually decreases over time (Lammer, 2014). Yet, in the existing literature there seems to be no well-defined and clearly fixed time period, which might distinguish a normal mourning period from a pathological one. For example, some experts define a "normal" grieving period of 6 months (Prigerson et al., 2009), while other researchers have shown that people might still experience feelings of grief several years to even up to several decades after the death of a loved one—such may be the case after the loss of a spouse or a child (Carnelley et al., 2006; Lannen et al., 2008). Given these divergent opinions regarding the "acceptable" time window during which mourners might face intense negative and/or positive feelings, it hardly seems surprising that individual grieving processes and their time frames are often grossly underestimated (Bowlby, 1980; Znoj, 2016).

Yet, how long and how intensely someone is going to feel grief can ultimately vary from person to person, from death to death, and can even vary depending on an individual's current life situation (Zisook & Shear, 2009). In that regard, a wide variety of factors can influence the intensity and duration of a bereaved person's grief, such as for example the mentioned past relationship with the deceased, the griever's personality, and attachment styles, as well as their age, health status, and the circumstances surrounding the death of the deceased (Bonanno & Kaltman, 2001). The latter point appears to be particularly worth mentioning, seeing as there are some studies which support the idea that violent deaths can lead to particularly long-lasting and intense grieving symptoms (Pynoos & Nader, 1990).

> How long and to what extent someone is going to grieve is dependent on various factors. These factors may include, for example, an individual's personality and attachment style, the mourner's age and health status or the circumstances surrounding the death of the deceased.

2.1.5 Definition of Grieving Terms

Based on the described list of wide-ranging feelings, thoughts and reactions associated with grieving, it becomes clear that grief and the process of grieving are relatively complex and multi-faceted phenomena. This is further complicated by many existing terms used to describe certain stages in which someone might find themselves in following the loss of a person; easily leading to confusion. Thankfully, compared to other languages the English terminology offers some clarity. For instance, *grief,* which in some cases is synonymously also described as sorrow or woe, is generally understood to refer to the various emotional, but also cognitive and physical reactions to the loss or death of a loved one (Stroebe &

Schut, 1998; Zisook & Shear, 2009). *Bereavement*, on the other hand, describes the situation in which a mourner finds themselves in and the process they are going through in order to deal with their grief. In other words, a mood following the loss of someone and in which the bereaved might experience certain emotions or show certain behaviours. *Mourning* or grieving is understood to be the social expression of grief. This expression is often shaped by social and cultural norms as well as existing rituals within a society (Stroebe & Schut, 1998). By means of these terms, it hopefully becomes apparent that *grief* represents the inner reaction to a loss, while *mourning* represents the outer expression of the feeling of grief.

▶ Conceptualizations of grieving:

- grief [gri:v]: Emotional, cognitive and physical reactions to a loss
- bereavement [bɪˈriːvmənt]: Grieving period following the loss of a person
- mourning [ˈmɔː(r)nɪŋ]: Social expression of grief

2.1.6 Contradictory Grieving Reactions and Norms

Inner and outer grieving reactions do not necessarily have to be in sink in the event of a death (Metz, 2011). This explains why some people may inwardly be upset by the death of a loved one—even feel deep sadness and an intense pain of separation—but outwardly showcase (almost) none of these underlying emotions. Unfortunately, this discrepancy between inner grieving experiences and outward grieving behaviours can sometimes lead to misunderstandings and, in the worst-case scenario, lead to social rejection if the concerned individual is exposed to certain social behavioural norms, which their own displayed grieving behaviour does not abide by. As a result, the impression may arise that people, who do not outwardly express grief after the death of a loved one but who live in a society where openly dealing with grief is welcomed or even expected, are either emotionally cold or assumed to have had a dysfunctional relationship with the deceased. However, as we outlined earlier this does not need to have been the case. The aforementioned study by Bonanno et al. (2002) for example found no evidence that bereaved individuals, who exhibited low levels of depression and grief symptoms, had a more difficult relationship with their deceased spouses.

Interestingly, there are a number of very different grieving norms, which determine how someone "should" mourn. Yet, these norms can be in complete contrast to one another and, depending on the society, may also be practiced very differently (Jakoby et al., 2013). Such mourning norms relate not only to the appropriate expression of mourning, which may be lived out in silence or expressed openly, but also relate to the appropriate duration of the mourning period, with some societies accepting only a short period of grieving, while others accept much longer time periods (Walter, 1999). Similarly, there are norms regarding when, i.e., at what time and in what situations, it is appropriate to feel grief and when the feeling and the expression of grief is considered a socially frowned-upon reaction.

To better illustrate the complex diversity of some grieving norms, one can imagine the following example showcasing two types of societies: one where mourning is accepted following the death of a pet, and another where the overall public cannot relate to someone grieving the death of a deceased animal and thus rejects this reaction. Depending on the norms how one "should" feel in a given situation and how one "should" express that grief, the situation described above may vastly change: for example, there may be cases, where the overall public might understand—even relate—to feeling grief after the death of a pet but ultimately reject the idea of outwardly expressing such grief in the form of crying. As described above, there might also be societies where both the inner and outer expression of grief are rejected. Elsewhere, perceiving and expressing grief after the death of a pet might be equally well accepted, but perhaps not to the extent shown by the mourner. There might be some other societies, where the griever's peers ultimately accept both the inner and outer expression of grief as well as its intensity, but not in the chosen place or time (e.g., at work). As illustrated by these examples, existing grieving norms can not only differ in different societies but can also be different within the same society depending on the situation. In addition, norms regarding "appropriate" emotions and behaviours may differ among people of different cultural backgrounds and may vary according to gender, age, and religious affiliation (Hochschild, 1979).

2.2 Gender Differences in Dealing with Death and Grief

Dying and grieving are very individual and personal events, which—as addressed earlier on—can be influenced among other things by gender-specific characteristics (Lehner, 2013). For example, even today the idea is still being perpetuated that men must be strong beings and no "wimps". From an early age, boys are taught that one should not showcase any emotional weaknesses to the outside world (Althaus, 2017). Such pressure is not primarily exerted by parents, but rather constitutes a socialization pressure exerted by society itself. In this regard, men educate each other. That is, young boys learn from their peers or from older boys that they should be strong. Emotions must not be shown outwardly for too long as this might become dangerous since one may no longer be seen as reliable and powerful. This belief creates fear of losing one's control as well as leadership position and having to face judgments from others (Althaus, 2017). Women, on the other hand, have a strong desire to speak openly about their suffering. For this, they might seek out groups or decide to undergo psychotherapeutic treatment (Althaus, 2017). After the loss of a close one, women generally feel left alone by their husbands. They ask for an exchange, however, many men find it difficult to express their feelings. Women might interpret such behaviour as lacking emotion and empathy. In this context, men are overwhelmed by the duration and intensity of their partner's grieving reaction and, to not hurt their partner further, they try to hide their own wounds (Lehner, 2013).

Is it not then perhaps better for them to simply speak openly about their emotions? Why should a man be considered a wimp if he is open about his suffering? Would this then also mean that artists such as Ed Sheeran, who sings about the death of a friend in his song "We Are," are wimps? Some studies have measured grief while using various parameters such as for instance depression, anxiety and alcohol. They showed that while in the process of grieving women tend to suffer more from depression and anxiety, whereas men lean more towards excessive alcohol consumption (Lehner, 2013). These findings underscore that men undoubtedly grieve too, but differently from women. Instead of talking about their grief with friends or their partner, they (secretly) follow certain "male" coping strategies (Althaus, 2017). Such strategies include substance abuse as well as increased work and excessive physical activity, which are applied to regulate their own emotions and counteract the pain of loss (Althaus, 2017; Znoj, 2005). Thus, this shows that grief is expressed in different ways in men and women. Consequently, the comparison between women and men in terms of the intensity of grief is difficult to realize. Nevertheless, it should be noted that there are also men who showcase more "female" coping strategies during their bereavement period. In a similar sense, there are women who work harder to regulate their emotions and thus follow more typical "male" grieving reactions. In general, there are gender-specific needs and thus also gender differences with regard to experiences of loss (Althaus, 2017).

▸ Women and men differ in their grieving responses. While women are more likely to seek emotional escape from others, men tend to use distraction strategies (e.g., increased work or physical activity).

2.3 Cultural Influence in Dealing with Death and Mourning

Numerous cultures have left strong marks on planet earth with their rituals concerning various life events. Death is one such important life event, for which Neanderthals already had organized burials or Egyptians built tombs to say goodbye to their deceased people. Due to the modernization of our society, today it is even possible to arrange tree or space burials for a farewell (Frey, 2018). Attitudes towards death are determined by dynamic, changing interactions between the individual and the environment. The collective image of man, nature as well as society plays an essential role (Mischke, 1996). While in Western cultures the commemoration of the dead is predominantly undergone in silence, death is being celebrated in other cultures (Wehner, 2014). The latter may sound quite unimaginable to members of Western societies, but perhaps that open approach to death could help many people in our more Western societies to cope better with the loss of someone close and dear. It is certain that it can be helpful to deal with other cultures in order to better understand mourners from foreign cultures and to help them appropriately. Thus, before trying to comfort a person, one should first understand their grief (Dobrikova et al., 2015). In doing so, grief work in a cross-cultural context can help educate people in regard to the mourning habits of different cultures and perhaps also make one understand that it is a person's absence and loss rather than their death itself that leads to a period of mourning (Wehner, 2014). Certainly, more knowledge about the topic of death and grief is needed. But how to deal with such a topic when death has become a taboo in Western societies? Our performance, success and happiness mark our own life. In doing so, one hopes not to miss anything in life. The eternal avoidance of the topic of death explains the resulting fears in Western cultures (Ehring, 2015). In many Western cultures, fellow human beings who have died are remembered once a year on All Hallows' Day. In doing so, one is confronted with the memories of deceased loved ones and the topic of death. During this day of remembrance, the mood is often melancholic as mourners find it very difficult to accept death (Gül, 2019). In contrast, other cultures like to remember their deceased people. While Western society avoids confronting children with the topic of death, in Mexico, for example, children and adults dress up in colourful skeleton costumes to celebrate the Day of the Dead, which happens every year on November 1st. During "Día de los muertos," altars are set up around town for deceased loved ones who supposedly return to earth on this day. They are greeted with respect, love as well as merriment, and happy times of life are remembered together. Since people in Mexico are open about death and believe that the dead return once a year, death is more easily accepted by young and old alike (Gül, 2019). In Ghana, death is seen as a "gateway to eternal life" and funerals are celebrated in a big way. In India, mourning is also accepted, and death is not taboo, but rather seen as a redemption of the soul (Gül, 2019).

Why are children in Western cultures kept away from the topic of death, while other cultures consider it possible for children to deal with death? Death, grief, suffering and illness are without a doubt very stressful topics, but nevertheless they are part of our lives and should therefore be addressed openly in families as well as schools (Dobrikova et al., 2015). Especially in European societies, illness and death are hidden and misinterpreted in hospitals (Dobrikova et al., 2015). Life in Central Europe promises stability and security. This could not be promised, for example, 300 years ago. Children died at the age of 6 and childbirth was a risky event for expectant mothers. The regular confrontation with death and mourning forced people back then to develop a higher acceptance of death. In contrast, in modern times, death is very difficult to accept. A sudden loss of a close person is seen as a catastrophe during which many suffer and tend to break down (Althaus, 2017). In the private context, the same behaviours are exhibited in every culture after the death of a loved one, such as grief, fear, anger, and crying. In contrast, the public context is completely different. Especially in Western cultures, people are prevented from showing emotions openly, whereas a hundred years ago this was considered quite normal. In North America and Northern Europe, for example, grieving people are not welcomed in public and showing emotions in public is rather rejected (Laungani & Young, 2001).

▶ While in Western cultures death is dealt with in silence and the subject is partly tabooed, other cultures tend to celebrate death openly.

2.4 Religious Influence in Dealing with Death and Mourning

The fact that the practice of rituals, customs and traditions is found in a variety of cultures and religions and has a special significance for those religious followers or people of different cultural backgrounds—particularly, when it comes to the topics of life and death—probably surprises no one. After all, there are various ceremonies and traditions to welcome the birth of a child and thus the beginning of a new life. One only needs to think of the well-known "baby showers", which are organized in honour of expectant mothers, and which celebrate the arrival of a newborn. Why then, should there not be similar customs which are held after the death of a loved one to mark the end of that life? In this context, however, the question arises as to what mourning rituals exactly are? Often observed in religious contexts, such rituals involve certain actions that are performed according to a set of rules and procedures with the purpose to provide the practitioners with a sense of comfort and to create safety and security (Müller & Rechenberg-Winter, 2013). In the context of death and mourning, this definition underpins the fact that rituals are not only held as a sign of respect for the deceased, but often also have a coping function for the mourners to enable the bereaved to come to terms with their loss and to make it easier for them to say goodbye to the deceased.

Having said that, it is very interesting to observe how various communities can process the death of a loved one through very different means of practices and, thus, ultimately deal with their grief. Sometimes, large discrepancies can be observed between the mourning customs of certain religions, which can sometimes lead to customs or traditions being perceived as foreign and strange. However, this does not mean that one's own practices are therefore the "correct" ones and the foreign ones "wrong", but rather simply underpin the difference in the expression and handling of mourning in various cultures and different religions. Sometimes, there are even overlaps between the various religions in the way bereaved people say goodbye to their deceased relatives and acquaintances, and which followers of the various religions might not necessarily be aware of. Examples of such similarities and differences are going to be underlined below by comparing some practices observed in Christianity, Islam and Hinduism.

2.4.1 Christianity

In Christianity, death is not seen as something final, but rather as a transitional path between the earthly and eternal life. This belief is reflected in existing Christian rituals and customs. For example, services are held in honour of the deceased and candles are lit during church visits in memory of the dead to express joy that the deceased have passed on to the heavenly life (Dobrikova et al., 2015). Such services are important components in the Christian faith to give appropriate farewell to the deceased and to accompany them on their journey to eternal life (sicher gsund, 2018). Prayers as well as speeches delivered by the pastor and the singing of songs play an important role during these ceremonies. Apart from these customs, other mourning rituals can be found, which are mainly performed out of respect for the deceased. For example, some bereaved families refrain from eating right after the death of a loved one, to emphasise that a part of themselves has also been lost after the loss of a loved one. In addition, abstaining from sexual intercourse or wearing black clothing is also considered an expression of mourning (Heller, 2007). The latter point is even nowadays still a widespread custom. For example, bereaved families of Christian faith often wear black during the burial of a deceased person to express their grief and thus symbolize the death of a deceased person. Until the mid-twentieth century, this custom was not only limited to the burial of the deceased, but in the case of widows, could even last up to a year (Kolb, 2012). Other more forgotten customs include the washing and dressing of the deceased by relatives, which is nowadays mostly taken over by funeral homes (Lammer, 2014).

2.4.2 Islam

In Islam, death is something real. It is something which, similar to the beliefs in Christianity, represents the transition to eternal life and which should not be perceived as a threat or something frightening. One's life is a gift from Allah and therefore it is believed that only God decides when one's life will come to an end. As a result, it is commonly considered a sin in Islam to commit suicide or to wish for death (Mustafa, 2018). It is custom to visit the relatives of the deceased during the first seven days after the passing of a person to offer one's condolences. Following this, a so-called "Maulid" is held during which the life of Prophet Mohammad is commemorated. The first year after death is considered a year of mourning by most Muslims. During this time, celebrations or weddings are avoided and prayers are said for the soul of the deceased person. This includes reciting suras from the Quran and giving out donations (Mustafa, 2018). As is common among Christians, earth burials after the passing of a person also take place in Islam. Here the dead are placed in white cloths, carried for the community's prayer of forgiveness, and then taken to the cemetery. Interestingly, after the funeral prayer, the dead person is placed in the grave without a coffin and that in the direction of Mecca before it is covered with earth. Afterwards, close ones such as family, neighbours and friends gather at the house of the bereaved so that they are not left alone with their grief. They help the bereaved to return to reality by taking care of the mourners' meals, encouraging them to be patient and persevering, and wishing them a reunion with the deceased person in paradise. Children are part of the ceremonies and rites and are therefore allowed to participate everywhere except in the ritual ablutions.

2.4.3 Hinduism

Unlike Christians and Muslims, Hindus believe in reincarnation. They speak of a soul called "Atman" that persists after one's physical death and is reborn in another form of life (Battisti, 2019; Heller, 2012). Now the question arises: in what form is one reborn? According to the Hindus, this depends on the amount of karma accumulated through the good deeds one has committed. The more karma has been accumulated, the more likely one will return as a human being. Otherwise, one is reborn as an animal, a plant, or a stone (Battisti, 2019; Michaels, 2013). The Hindu intention is to dissolve the "samsara" cycle of living, dying, and rebirth and enter nirvana. Only then is there talk of salvation, "moksha" (Battisti, 2019; Stanford, 2011). When a Hindu is dying, the devout devote themselves to various religious rituals. First, the body is directed by the dying person with the feet towards the south, as that is where the god of the dead, Yama, is located (Battisti, 2019; Wujastyk, 2014). During this process, family or priests read from the sacred scriptures to the dying person and water is given to drink. Once the person has died, their body is cleansed exclusively by family members, then anointed with ghee and wrapped in plain as well as patternless cloths. Unlike in Christianity, jewellery on the dead body is usually a taboo as it might irritate the soul when it tries to leave the body (Battisti, 2019). Moreover, unlike in Christianity or Islam, in Hinduism, dead bodies are publicly cremated in the presence of male relatives (Ebeling, 2007). In this process, they circle the corpse five times to represent the five elements (water, fire, earth, air and space) that make up human beings. After that, the body is set on fire by the eldest son at the head end (Battisti, 2019). In order for the soul "Atman" to leave the body to return to God Brahma and to be reborn, the skull of the corpse is crushed (Ebeling, 2007). Such a ceremony can last around three days, as most Hindus claim that the spirit might be still present and needs to be provided with food during these days (Battisti, 2019). This is followed by the scattering of the ashes with garlands and flowers in a river, a sacred pilgrimage site, or they are buried in the ground. During the mourning period, which traditionally lasts thirteen days, the sons of a deceased person shave their heads. Unlike in Abrahamic religions, Hindu relatives are considered unclean (Wujastyk, 2014). Moreover, they are not allowed to cry and therefore isolate themselves from the society. They spend most of their time fasting at home and avoid any contact with other people (Battisti, 2019; Wujastyk, 2014).

References

Althaus, D. (2017). Frauen trauern-Männer arbeiten Ein Klischee? Ist gemeinsames Trauern möglich? *Agus-Schriftenreihe: Hilfen in der Trauer nach Suizid, 1*, 1–15.

Barth, S., Kerp, E.-M. & Müller, M. (2003). *Trauer*. (Berichte aus der Arbeitsgruppe "Verantwortung, Gerechtigkeit, Moral" Nr. 157). Trier: Universität Trier, Fachbereich I–Psychologie. Abgerufen am 30. Januar 2020, verfügbar unter https://psydok.psycharchives.de/jspui/bitstream/20.500.11780/332/1/beri157.pdf

Battisti, R. (2019, 23 Mai). *Von Reisbällchen und dem ewigen Kreislauf des Lebens*. Abgerufen am 30. Januar 2020, verfügbar unter https://www.asi-reisen.de/blog/totenrituale-hinduismus/

Bonanno, G. A., Boerner, K., & Wortman, C. B. (2008). Trajectories of grieving. In M. S. Stroebe, R. O. Hansson, H. Schut, & W. Stroebe (Eds.), *Handbook of bereavement research and practice: Advances in theory and intervention (pp. 287–307)*. American Psychological Association. https://doi.org/10.1037/14498-014

Bonanno, G. A., & Kaltman, S. (2001). The varieties of grief experience. *Clinical Psychology Review, 21*(5), 705–734. https://doi.org/10.1016/S0272-7358(00)00062-3

Bonanno, G. A., Wortman, C. B., Lehman, D. R., Tweed, R. G., Haring, M., Sonnega, J., ... Nesse, R. M. (2002). Resilience to loss and chronic grief: A prospective study from pre-loss to 18 months post-loss. *Journal of Personality and Social Psychology, 83*(5), 1150–1164. https://doi.org/10.1037//0022-3514.83.5.1150

Bowlby, J. (1980). *Attachment and loss: Loss, sadness and depression* (Vol. 3). Basic Books.

Carnelley, K. B., Wortman, C. B., Bolger, N., & Burke, C. T. (2006). The time course of grief reactions to spousal loss: Evidence from a national probability sample. *Journal of Personality and Social Psychology, 91*(3), 476–492. https://doi.org/10.1037/0022-3514.91.3.476

Cooper, R. (2013). Complicated grief: Philosophical perspectives. In M. Stroebe, H. Schut, & J. van den Bout (Eds.), *Complicated grief: Scientific foundations for health care professionals* (pp. 13–26). Routledge.

Dobrikova, P., Gebhardt, W., Giemza, G., Grajdian, V., & Kacian, A. (2015). *Trauerbegleitung in unterschiedlichen kulturellen, sozialen und religiösen Kontexten*. Wydawnictwo Warto. https://depot.ceon.pl/bitstream/handle/123456789/14388/Trauerbegleitung.pdf?sequence=1

Douglas-Hamilton, I., Bhalla, S., Wittemyer, G., & Vollrath, F. (2006). Behavioural reactions of elephants towards a dying and deceased matriarch. *Applied Animal Behaviour Science, 100*(1–2), 87–102. https://doi.org/10.1016/j.applanim.2006.04.014

Ebeling, K. (2007). *Weltreligionen kompakt: Zum Verständnis von Judentum, Christentum, Islam, Hinduismus und Buddhismus (Forschungsbericht 79)*. Sozialwissenschaftliches Institut der Bundeswehr.

Ehring, F. (2015, 13. Januar). *Na endlich!* Abgerufen am 27. Januar 2020, verfügbar unter https://www.fluter.de/na-endlich

Field, N. P., Nichols, C., Holen, A., & Horowitz, M. J. (1999). The relation of continuing attachment to adjustment in conjugal bereavement. *Journal of Consulting and Clinical Psychology, 67*(2), 212–218. https://doi.org/10.1037/0022-006X.67.2.212

Frey, D. (Ed.). (2018). *Psychologie der Rituale und Bräuche: 30 Riten und Gebräuche wissenschaftlich analysiert und erklärt*. Springer.

Gül, A. (2019, 19. Dezember). *Den Tod feiern: Wie andere Kulturen mit dem Sterben umgehen*. Abgerufen am 26. Januar 2020, verfügbar unter https://www.monda-magazin.de/leben/den-tod-feiern-wie-andere-kulturen-mit-dem-sterben-umgehen

Heller, B. (Ed.). (2007). *Tod und Ritual: interkulturelle Perspektiven zwischen Tradition und Moderne* (Vol. 2). LIT Verlag.

Heller, B. (2012). *Wie Religionen mit dem Tod umgehen: Grundlagen für die interkulturelle Sterbebegleitung*. Lambertus.

Hochschild, A. R. (1979). Emotion work, feeling rules, and social structure. *American Journal of Sociology, 85*(3), 551–575. https://doi.org/10.1086/227049

Jakoby, N., Haslinger, J., & Gross, C. (2013). Trauernormen: historische und gegenwärtige Perspektiven. *SWS-Rundschau, 53*(3), 253–274. Verfügbar unter https://nbn-resolving.org/urn:nbn:de:0168-ssoar-453371

Kolb, A. (2012). *In Memoriam: Müssen wir das Trauern neu lernen?*. Abgerufen am 30. Januar 2020, verfügbar unter https://www.mit-institut.de/assets/files/pdf/In%20Memoriam-BR-alpha-14-11-2012.pdf

Lammer, K. (2014). *Trauer verstehen*. Springer.

Lannen, P. K., Wolfe, J., Prigerson, H. G., Onelov, E., & Kreicbergs, U. C. (2008). Unresolved grief in a national sample of bereaved parents: Impaired mental and physical health 4 to 9 years later. *Journal of Clinical Oncology, 26*(36), 5870–5876. https://doi.org/10.1200/JCO.2007.14.6738

Laungani, P., & Young, B. (2001). Wnioski I: Wskazania dotyczące praktyki i polityki postępowania. In C. M. Parkes, P. Laugani, & B. Young (Eds.), *Przemijanie w kulturach. Obyczaje żałobne, pocieszenie i wsparcie*. Wrocław.

Lehner, E. (2013). Trauern Männer anders? Perspektiven aus Geschlechter-und Trauerforschung. *Leidfaden, 2*(2), 19–22. https://doi.org/10.13109/leid.2013.2.2.19

Metz, C. (2011). Die vielen Gesichter der Trauer: Anregungen zum Umgang mit Trauer und Trauernden. *Psychotherapie-Wissenschaft, 1*(3), 177–186. Verfügbar unter https://creativecommons.org/licenses/by-nc-nd/3.0/de/

Michaels, A. (2013). Im nächsten Leben wird alles anders. Erlösung aus Tod und Wiedergeburt. *Ruperto Carola, 2*, 104–111.

Mischke, M. (1996). *Der Umgang mit dem Tod. Vom Wandel in der abendländischen Geschichte* (Vol. 25). Reimer.

Müller, M., & Rechenberg-Winter, P. (Eds.). (2013). *Rituale–zwischen Pathos und Folklore: Leidfaden 2013*. Vandenhoeck & Ruprecht.

Mustafa, M. (2018). Islamischer Kulturkreis Tod und Trauer in der Schule. *«sicher! gsund!»*, Verfügbar unter https://nanopdf.com/download/aspekte-aus-sicht-des-islamischen-kulturkreises_pdf

Osterweis, M., Solomon, F., & Green, M. (Eds.). (1984). *Bereavement: Reactions, consequences, and care*. National Academy of Sciences.

Prigerson, H. G., Horowitz, M. J., Jacobs, S. C., Parkes, C. M., Aslan, M., Goodkin, K., . . . Bonanno, G. (2009). Prolonged grief disorder: Psychometric validation of criteria proposed for DSM-V and ICD-11. *PLoS Medicine, 6*(8), e1000121. https://doi.org/10.1371/journal.pmed.1000121

Pynoos, R. S., & Nader, K. (1990). Children's exposure to violence and traumatic death. *Psychiatric Annals, 20*(6), 334–344. https://doi.org/10.3928/0048-5713-19900601-11

Scherer, K. R., Banse, R., & Wallbott, H. G. (2001). Emotion inferences from vocal expression correlate across languages and cultures. *Journal of Cross-Cultural Psychology, 32*(1), 76–92. https://doi.org/10.1177/0022022101032001009

«Sicher!gsund!» (2018). Bestattungsrituale. *Tod und Trauer in der Schule*, Verfügbar unter https://www.sichergsund.ch/fileadmin/kundendaten/Hefte/Tod_und_Trauer/02_Dokumente/2018_Tod-u-Trauer_Bestattungsrituale.pdf

Stanford, P. (2011). Samsara. In P. Stanford (Ed.), *50 Schlüsselideen Religion* (pp. 132–135). Spektrum Akademischer Verlag.

Stroebe, M., & Schut, H. (1998). Culture and grief. *Bereavement Care, 17*(1), 7–11. https://doi.org/10.1080/02682629808657425

Wagner, B. (2013). *Komplizierte Trauer*. Springer.

Wagner, B. (2016). Wann ist Trauer eine psychische Erkrankung? *Psychotherapeut, 3*, 250–255.

Walter, T. (1999). *On bereavement: The culture of grief*. McGraw-Hill Education.

Watson, C. F., & Matsuzawa, T. (2018). Behaviour of nonhuman primate mothers toward their dead infants: Uncovering mechanisms. *Philosophical Transactions of the Royal Society B: Biological Sciences, 373*(1754), 20170261. https://doi.org/10.1098/rstb.2017.0261

Wehner, L. (Ed.). (2014). *Empathische Trauerarbeit: Vielfalt der professionellen Trauerarbeit in der Praxis*. Springer Verlag.

Wujastyk, D. (2014). Hinduistische Perspektiven zum Ende des Lebens. In H. Haker, G. Wanderer, & K. Bentele (Eds.), *Religiöser Pluralismus in der Klinikseelsorge* (pp. 123–142). LIT-Verlag.

Zisook, S., & Shear, K. (2009). Grief and bereavement: What psychiatrists need to know. *World Psychiatry, 8*(2), 67–74. https://doi.org/10.1002/j.2051-5545.2009.tb00217.x

Znoj, H. (2005). *Ratgeber Trauer: Informationen für Betroffene und Angehörige*. Hogrefe Verlag.

Znoj, H. (2016). *Komplizierte Trauer* (Vol. 23). Hogrefe Verlag.

3. Grief in Children and Adolescents

Tonie Schweich, Tamara Luxen, Caroline Bell, and Julia Federspiel

3.1 Grief in Children

Tonie Schweich and Tamara Luxen

The opinion that children are too young to understand what death means is widespread. Adults usually want to protect them from the reality of death and not burden them with something they believe they cannot yet grasp. In general, however, thoughts of death occur much earlier than most assume. Depending on their age, children have their own ideas about life and death (Fleck-Bohaumilitzky, 2004a, b).

In order for adults to understand children and their ideas about it, they need to deal with the topic of life and death themselves. It is important that they know what death can mean to children of different ages. However, it is also important to understand and keep in mind that children of the same ages are not always at the same stage of development. Children's ideas about death follow an ongoing maturation process. Thoughts about death have a great influence on the whole development as well as on the socialization process and the emergence of religion (Bürgin, 1981).

Children live in the present. This can be seen in the fact that moments of great sadness can follow happy play and vice versa. They experience the death of a close person as deep uncertainty, as they often lack the opportunity to obtain information that is important for them by asking questions. During this time, children are more dependent on the adults around them and on their support. Drawing pictures, inventing rituals, and re-enacting key scenes that have left a formative impression on the child can be very helpful for them to

T. Schweich (✉) · T. Luxen · C. Bell · J. Federspiel
Department of Behavioural and Cognitive Sciences, University of Luxembourg, Esch-sur-Alzette, Luxembourg
e-mail: tonie.schweich.001@student.uni.lu; caroline.bell.001@student.uni.lu

© Springer-Verlag GmbH Germany, part of Springer Nature 2022
M. Böhmer, G. Steffgen (eds.), *Grief in Schools*,
https://doi.org/10.1007/978-3-662-64297-9_3

express and process their extensive feelings. These ways of expressing their feelings are very important, as children tend to talk less about their feelings and grief, but rather use non-verbal ways of expressing them (Hirschberg, 2010).

Working with grief is a challenging task for children. As already mentioned, they can communicate their grief and the associated feelings in very different ways. As a result, children's reactions to grief are not the same, but differ individually from child to child. It is important that adults listen to such situations, respond to feelings and needs and react appropriately to children's grief behaviour (Nindler, 2014).

3.1.1 Theory of Cognitive Development by Jean Piaget (1978)

The conceptions of death at different ages are always related to the different developmental stages of the child and should be considered together (Piaget, 1970).

Therefore, we will first take a closer look at child mental development from Jean Piaget's (1936) point of view. He postulates that thinking errors in children reveal certain forms and structures of thinking. According to him, from birth, thinking becomes increasingly detached from sensory perception (i.e., sight, hearing, smell, taste, and touch) and over time allows for increasingly sophisticated performance on an abstract-conceptual basis. According to Piaget, the changes in human thinking are age-related and involve both quantitative (more) and qualitative (different) changes (Piaget, 1936). Increasingly, thinking changes from the concrete to the abstract and from the simple to the differentiated. This is referred to as an integrated, systematic, flexible as well as adapted interactionist constructivist approach. From this, Jean Piaget developed a model of four successive stages (the sensorimotor, preoperational, concrete operational, and formal operational periods) to illustrate the limitations and abilities of children at different ages (Piaget, 1936). The different periods are briefly presented below.

3.1.1.1 The Sensorimotor Period (0–2 Years)

He gave this period its name because it is in the sensory perceptions and motor activities that the infant's intelligence shows itself earliest. The infant increasingly learns to pay attention to his environment, perceives other people as well as his own environment and objects that exist independently of himself. Intelligent performance already exists before thinking (in the sense of internal operation with ideas, symbols, etc.) is possible. According to Piaget, this period is divided into 6 stages of sensorimotor development. The first stage, practice of innate mechanisms, is devoted to the practice of the innate behavioural repertoire. This refers to sucking, grasping, swallowing reflexes, etc. Learning success becomes apparent when reflex behaviors occur without the need for a trigger stimulus. The second stage, Primary Circular Reactions, refers to the repetition of an activity. The child repeats actions that are experienced as interesting or pleasant, and are thus perceived as rewarding. These effects, however, are limited to the child's own body and do not involve the environment at this stage. This changes, however, between the fourth and eighth month of life, with the beginning of the third stage, the secondary circle reactions. From 4 months onwards, activities that affect the environment now become "means to an end". The infant is now able to recognize that a particular action always leads to the same result. For example, banging on a mobile seems interesting and is repeated to make a difference in the environment. The initial nudging is unintentional and is not done intentionally until between 8 and 12 months of age. The infant has now gained experience of how to achieve certain goals and has an understanding of elementary cause-effect relationships (e.g. an object disappears under a cloth, the infant pulls the cloth away). The fourth stage involves coordinating the acquired action schemas and applying them to new situations. Several action schemata are applied to the same object, according to the principle of "trial and error". For example, a rattle is tapped, shaken, put in the mouth, and more. In this way, the child can try out everything that can be done with the object. Accordingly, the action patterns are differentiated and adapted to the objects. In addition, the respective action patterns (e.g. grasping and throwing) are coordinated. The fifth stage is the tertiary circle reaction and takes place between the 12th and 18th month of life. During this period, new action schemas are discovered through active experimentation. The child uses creative means to reach his goal. For example, he pulls the tablecloth towards him in order to reach his toys that are out of reach. The child develops what is called an exploratory character and throws different objects in order to perceive the different sounds. The sixth and therefore final stage represents the transition from the sensorimotor act of intelligence to imagination. This occurs in the middle of the second year of life and represents the end of the sensorimotor phase. Actions are mentally internalised, practical trying is therefore no longer necessary, because actions are now internally comprehended and the result of the action is anticipated. The transition represents a structural change with the "awakening of intelligence".

3.1.1.2 Pre-Operational Period (2–7 Years)

This stage is characterised above all by egocentric thinking, which is expressed in animism, artificialism, realism and magical omnipotence (see box for explanations) (Pulaski, 1975). According to Piaget, at this stage the child is still unable to put himself in the place of another, to see his own point of view as one among several possibilities, or to take the point of view of another person.

Definition

Explanation of terms:	
Animism (Lat.: anima = soul) The child's belief that everything in nature is filled with life and purpose, like itself (e.g. the sun accompanies it to shelter it, the wind blows to cool it down) (Pulaski, 1975). According to Piaget, this is a kind of "false consciousness" and lasts until	*Realism* The child's belief that everything that is real to him, such as dreams, feelings, or imaginings, has objective reality and is shared by others (Pulaski, 1975). *Magic omnipotence* (lat.: Omnipotenta = omnipotence) during the

(continued)

Explanation of terms:	
about the time of puberty (Piaget, 1978, p. 143) *Artificialism* (Lat.: artifex = creator) The child's belief that human beings produce natural phenomena, such as the sun, moon, lakes, rivers, mountains (Pulaski, 1975).	third year of life, the "magic phase" begins for children, according to which everything is possible in the imagination of the child. Thus, everything the child wishes for and thinks could happen, both beautiful and "terrible" (kindergesundheit-info.de). *Egocentrism* Inability to put oneself in another's place, to take another's point of view, or to understand one's own current point of view as one among several possibilities (Pulaski, 1975)

In this phase, thinking is strongly bound to perception and the ability to form mental representations of the world (of states and events) is already present. However, the children are not yet able to perform operations on the mental representations. At this age they make inappropriate generalizations and errors in thinking. For example, they attribute mental properties, such as a will or a consciousness, to objects or objects *(animistic interpretations of nature)*.

Example Example at 4.3: *"These are small stones, the mountains, which have become very big. They remained small for a long time, then they became big, bigger and bigger (...)"* (Montada, 1987, p. 419).

In addition, natural phenomena are interpreted as if humans had created them *(artificialistic interpretations of nature)*.

Example Example at 4.2: *"They put them there, the rocks. They are very strong people who put them there. (...)"* (Montada, 1987, p. 419).

In addition, natural phenomena are explained from their purpose.

Example Example: *"Stones are there so that houses can be built; trees are there so that they give us shade"* (Montada, 1987, p. 419).

Children at this stage of development make these erroneous interpretations because they use the concepts they know when trying to solve new problems. For example, if the child knows the concept of growing, it explains the formation of the mountains.

3.1.1.3 Concrete Operational Period (7–11 Years)

This stage is characterized by logical and reversible thinking. More precisely, Piaget means that children can now operate in thought with concrete objects or their ideas. Operations of mass, quantity, and volume invariance thus become possible.

3.1.1.4 Formal Operational Period (from Age 11 or 12)

In this stage, which begins in early adolescence, the person begins to "operate with operations". This means that he can now think not only about concrete things, but also about thoughts. This implies second-order operations, or thinking about thoughts and theories rather than just concrete realities. The young person is now able to assess possible consequences or conclusions from a hypothesis, to follow the form of an argument and to abstract from the content.

3.1.2 The Child's Understanding of Death

The trigger for children to think about death is often the death of a beloved animal or also direct experiences with the death of important attachment figures such as parents or grandparents. Sometimes it is also the confrontation with one's own near death that triggers thinking about it. Observations by Gesell and Ilg (1962) show that the question of the limitation of life at different ages is sometimes triggered by the birth of a baby in the family. Children thus seem to contemplate a state of non-existence. Through similar statements by Stern (1983), the assumption of non-existence is associated with an "innate potential" of the notion of death. It seems that the question of the origin of life also entails the question of the future, the end and the limitation of life. This is illustrated by an utterance of a four-year-old boy: *"Isn't it true that you're already dead when you're not even in the world yet?"* (Zlotowicz & Redie, 1983, p. 109). After this, the boy showed an increasing interest in questions about death and dying: *"I would like to see someone die; not how people look when they are dead, but when they are just dying, and then I would also like to see how it is when they are dead"*.

In general, it can be assumed that children have a more unbiased attitude towards death than adults. On the one hand, children do not yet follow a corresponding taboo, and on the other hand, many studies indicate that at least young children do not yet have realistic ideas about death (Gebhard, 2009). Many of the studies dealing with children's conceptions of death date back to the 1980s and 90s. However, research on children's conceptions of death has intensified in recent decades (summaries in Speece & Brent, 1984; Stambrook & Parker, 1987; Wittkowski, 1990). Nevertheless, there are still many questions about infant understandings of death that are considered unresolved (Kenyon, 2001; Plieth, 2001a, b). This will be shown more clearly as we proceed. There is disagreement among researchers about the age at which children can form a concept of death. Some authors claim that children already have their own concepts of *animate* and *inanimate* in the first year of life (Keil, 1991). During this time, the child tries to compare the process of the death of plants and animals with experiences he has had so far. Interest in the transition from the animate to the inanimate is often very strong at this age, but then changes to greater disinterest. This is because the child himself is afraid or senses that the subject is causing discomfort in his environment (Bürgin, 1981). In general, it is important to understand that ideas about death cannot be separated from those about life (Fleck-Bohaumilitzky, 2003).

Like Piaget, Corr (1995) asserts that children move from concrete intellectual operations to more abstract or conceptual ways of thinking during their development. Children are not elevators that function uniformly in three-story buildings. Development in children is more complex, variable, and individualized than a stage-based metaphor might suggest (Corr, 1995). The more subtle children's understandings of death (and life) become, the better they are able to manage their experiences and concerns (Corr, 1995).

3.1.2.1 The View of Nagy

Nagy (1948) postulates that distinct "stages" can be distinguished in the development of children's understanding of death. He identifies three stages in this process:

1. In the first phase, children do not yet understand the finality of death, they usually compare it more with a journey or sleep.
2. In the second phase, children understand that whenever death occurs, it is also final. However, they also believe that it can be avoided (e.g. by outwitting death; it is often seen as an external force).
3. Then, in the third and final stage, children understand that death is both final and inevitable, that is, irreversible and universal.

3.1.2.2 Piaget's View

As early as 1926, Piaget investigated in his animism studies which ideas children associate with the concept of life. In general, it can be stated that they regard objects as alive that have a consciousness or to which they attribute a consciousness. In his research, Piaget asked children whether certain objects are alive and why. Piaget excludes children under the age of 3 in his research because according to his findings, children up to the age of six to seven are given everything with consciousness. However, children do not explicitly attribute consciousness to things, but they do not make distinctions between their own thinking and the external world.

The results found were divided into four stages, which are briefly explained below (Piaget, 1978):

Stage 1 (between the ages of three and six):
  The children consider everything to be alive that is somehow active or useful in their eyes with regard to the human being. Because of their egocentric view of the world at this stage, they think in final terms. Thus, as it were, an inner force is attributed to objects, which strives for a certain goal useful to man. Accordingly, all existing things were created

for a specific purpose. Accordingly, "life" concerns the notion of *"a force at once material and imbued with purpose"* (Piaget, 1978, p. 165).

Example Example: *Is the sun alive? - Yes. - Why? - It gives off light. Is a bicycle alive? - No, if it's not moving, it's not alive. If it rides, it's alive. - Is a tree alive? - No; if it has fruit, it's alive. If it has none, it is not alive* (from Piaget, 1978, p. 163).

Stage 2 (approximately between the ages of six and eight):
In this stage, life is defined almost exclusively by movement. Piaget sees this stage as a transition to the next stage.

Example Example: *Is a cat alive? - Yes. - A snail? - Yes. - A fish? - No. - Why not? - It doesn't move. - Is a bicycle alive? - Yes. - Why? - It rolls. - Is a lizard alive? - Yes. - A nail? - No. - A flower? - No. - A tree? - No. - Is the sun alive? - Yes. - Why? - It works when it needs to* (from Piaget, 1978, p. 166).

Stage 3 (approximately between eight and twelve years of age):
From this point on it is possible for the child to distinguish between its own and received movement. From this point on, everything that has a spontaneous movement of its own is considered to be alive. This is, according to Piaget, the most important period within the phase of infantile animism.

Example Example: *Is an earthworm alive? - Yes, it can walk. - Is a cloud alive? - No, because the wind pushes it. - Is a bicycle alive? - No, it is moved by us. - Is fire alive? - Yes, it moves itself* (from Piaget, 1978, p. 168).

Stage 4 (from about the age of twelve):
With the onset of adolescence, only plants, animals, and humans are considered alive (Piaget, 1978).

However, these stages should not be regarded as a rigid frame of reference, but rather as an approximate reference. Although the logic of the stages and Piaget's assumptions have been confirmed in follow-up studies, the ages must nevertheless be regarded as rather uncertain or variable, since children of one age group can differ greatly from one another (see Dennis, 1957). In this respect, it is important to always take these variation potentials into account.

Laurendeau and Pinard (1962), using a similar experimental design and questioning to that of Piaget, arrived at comparable results in terms of age structure (500 subjects between 4 and 12 years of age). However, no significant differences were found here between the first two stages. However, motility as a criterion for aliveness was also observed by Hofmeister et al. (1982) in a study of primary school pupils.

3.1.2.3 Opposing Views

However, there are also findings that contradict the above. Accordingly, some studies claim that even younger children are already able to distinguish quite reliably between living and dead (Klingberg, 1957; Klingensmith, 1953). Studies by Keil (1991) seem to show that children already possess an ability to distinguish between animate and inanimate environments in the first months of life. One even speaks of corresponding innate cognitive structures (Keil, 1991).

Several studies have shown that even newborns distinguish between humans and inanimate objects (Dornes, 1993; Gelman, 1990; Mandler, 1992; Premack, 1990; Trevarthen, 1974). Newborns attempt to communicate with living people but not with inanimate objects (Wellman & Gelman, 1992). Accordingly, there would be naïve thinking about the biological world and, by association, an early concept of life (Inagaki & Hatano, 2002; case studies of related conceptual shifts in Venville, 2004). While one-year-olds are amazed at the seemingly active behavior of inanimate objects, the activity of living things is considered quite normal (Poulin-Dubois & Shultz, 1990). Similar findings are provided by the study of Bertenthal et al. (1985). Here, 5-month-old infants could already distinguish biological from non-biological movement.

3.1.2.4 The View of Fleck-Bohaumilitzky

According to Fleck-Bohaumilitzky (2003), death is not something final for most children **before the age of five,** but is rather compared to sleep from which one wakes up again or a journey from which one returns.

Example Example: *Little Jasmin got terribly upset when her mother did not mention her deceased friend Lukas when listing her birthday guests. She explained that Lukas would be back from heaven by her fourth birthday, because being dead cannot last that long* (Fleck-Bohaumilitzky, 2003).

At this age there is also often an unconscious parallelisation of death and separation, which in turn often leads to unpleasant and painful feelings. It can therefore also be like death for a child when the father or mother goes to work. Emotionally, death for younger children primarily means deprivation or withdrawl of something important and is closely related to the fear of being abandoned by parents. This fear of loss begins at the age of one and can continue into the seventh or eighth year. For example, after a death in the family or among friends, children may cling strongly to their parents and no longer want to be left alone. They are afraid that something will happen to them or their parents if they are separated (Grollman, 1991).

Children of this age find it difficult to imagine that death is an irreversible and not a temporary phenomenon. This is mainly because the concept of time is very limited at this stage of development (Fleck-Bohaumilitzky, 2003).

Example Example: *Little Sandra, when she was three years old, said shortly after her grandfather died: "Is grandpa dead now? Did he die? When is he coming back?" The mother replies, "Grandpa just died, he's not coming back."*

It is quite possible that little Sandra did not exactly understand the answer. The fact that you cannot simply exchange death and life is difficult to explain to a child. Tales in which grandpa lives in heaven with the angels, as well as comic series in which characters are torn into a thousand pieces one moment and look the same the next, make it even more difficult for the child to understand that death is irrevocable. At this age level, death tends to be understood as something accidental. You die when the evil robber comes or you get hit by a car. However, with a little luck, it is possible to live forever (Grollman, 1991).

It is not until the **age of four that** a cognitive understanding of death sets in. However, for the four to five year old child, their own death does not exist emotionally, it only happens to others. At this age, children often play at being dead with their peers, avoid dead things or kill small animals such as ants or flies (Fleck-Bohaumilitzky, 2003).

From school age, i.e. after the **age of five,** a child develops a realistic idea of death. At this stage of development, the child learns to empathise and sympathise with situations and therefore also associates death with affect. Gradually the finality of death is accepted. However, children still believe that they are not affected by it themselves and do not understand that every living being is affected by it. In their eyes, it is still possible to escape death. At this age level, some of the children personify death. This, according to their imagination, is either the dead person himself or his own separate person. Often the children have an idea of an angel living in heaven in human form or a skeleton who serves as an accomplice to the devil in hell. It leaves footprints and is silent. The being is able to turn invisible, dance with spirits, operate in darkness, and send harbingers. They believe that you can escape death if you are good, fast, and skilled. For death only comes for the wicked and disobedient. The view of a personified death can also be influenced by social environment and cultural factors (for example: religion, horror movies, fairy tales). Children of this age group live in the present. They find it difficult to imagine that they did not exist in the past and that one day they will no longer exist (Fleck-Bohaumilitzky, 2003).

Around the **age of six**, children begin to have partly concrete ideas about death (dead people lie in a coffin under the ground; they can no longer breathe, have their eyes closed) and show increasing interest in what becomes of the dead. However, there is little emotion attached to these ways of thinking. They realize at this time that there may be other causes of death besides old age, such as illness or accidents. Children start expressing death wishes out of anger at this time, both to their mother, father and siblings. They may also look for a replacement in case one of the closest family members would die (Fleck-Bohaumilitzky, 2003).

The **seventh year of life** is the beginning of a more differentiated sense of time. Children now consciously perceive events and temporal relationships. However, the inkling of being affected by death themselves one day is still ignored. They show great interest in all things associated with death, the cemetery, grave, coffin or even the funeral. In fact, children are most concerned with the phenomenon of death before the **age of seven.** This could be related to the detachment from home and the process of self-discovery.

Most children realize by the **age of eight** that all people, including themselves, must die one day. Their interest now becomes focused on what happens after death (Bürgin, 1981).

Example Example: *"I imagine that when I am dead and lying in the coffin, that it is completely dark. And whether I'm already lying on another coffin or whether there's only sand under my coffin. What my parents would do and my grandmas would do. How long they would mourn"* Andrea K., 8 years (Brocher, 1985).

Normally, by this time it is already known that the body decays after death. Due to intolerability of these thoughts, children begin to believe in immortality. This happens regardless of the particular religion to which they belong. Usually, this remains upright until the age of 13 or 14 and then drops significantly, depending on the religious affiliation (Brocher, 1985).

During the **ninth year of life,** the child slowly begins to deal with the issue of the detachment of the soul from the body (Bürgin, 1981).

Example Example: *"I first lie in bed at home and then in bed outside. Maybe it's very cold in winter, and then it doesn't freeze me because the coffin has a thick white blanket. In the coffin I think my grandma and grandpa have to wait for the dear God, because he still has to work so much with the other dead people. Because he counts the souls"* Andreas Sch., 9 years (Brocher, 1985).

Children now accept the fact that death is a natural phenomenon. It is also recognized that all living beings, including themselves, are affected by death and cannot avoid it. These ideas are realistic and based on experience and observation of biological and physiological processes. *"When you no longer have a pulse, a temperature, or the ability to breathe"* (Rudolph, 1979), the organs begin to fail and death occurs (Bürgin, 1981).

Children begin to search for their own identity at the age of nine; death, as the end of life, can thus be perceived as a frightening and painful fact (Grollman, 1991). Sometimes children find comfort in the belief that after death the soul detaches itself from the body and lives on (Bürgin, 1981).

Example Example at the age of 9: *"What is death? Well, I think it is a part of a person's life. Like school. Life has many parts. Only one part of it is earthly. It's like school when we go on to another class. To die is to start a new life. Everyone must die once, but the soul lives on* (Reed, 1972).

Between the ages **of nine and eleven**, interest in death decreases. In puberty, the interest then emerges again more strongly. Fleck-Bohaumilitzky (2003) assumes that the more self-confident and secure someone feels in their role, the less they care about death.

In clinical observations it is doubted to what extent the child's understanding of death also applies to the sick or terminally ill child. In a study by Bluebond-Langner (1977), with three- to nine-year-old children suffering from leukaemia, it was shown that the finality and irreversibility of death is already clearly seen by the younger children. Thus, the assertion that the meaning of death cannot be understood by the child even when it concerns his or her own dying cannot be sustained (see Larbig, 1974). The notion of the reversibility of death usually begins to falter around the age of five. Children begin to consider what becomes of the dead. In addition, they take over, even if only vaguely and not yet completely convinced, their parents' ideas about death.

3.1.2.5 Summary

In summary, it can be generally stated that in our society younger rather than older children assume that death is not universal, preventable, or will only occur in the distant future. Moreover, death is seen as temporary and reversible in spontaneous, magical, or medical situations. Death is perceived as a state in which the dead and their bodies can still engage in various activities. Ultimately, death is seen by younger children as the result of unrealistic, specific, concrete, or external causes. Younger children are quite familiar with day-to-day experiences, such as going to sleep (and waking up again) or leaving (and coming back). These activities are time-limited and reversible events (Corr, 1995). In our society, older children are more likely to understand the main elements of death (such as that everyone will die once, that death is inevitable and often unpredictable) but also the finality of death in terms of irreversibility and the cessation of bodily functions (Corr, 1995). According to Fleck-Bohaumilitzky (2003), after the age of five, children begin to question the reversibility of death and worry about what will become of the dead. The parents' ideas about death are adopted for the time being, although not with complete conviction and vaguely. In this context, Nagy (1948) also defined that children in the third and final stage of development perceive death as both final and inevitable, irreversible and universal. According to Wittkowski (1990), the development of the concept of death is thus related to both cognitive development and age.

Since there are other significant factors influencing a child's understanding of death besides biological age (such as family, social environment, etc.), it can be assumed that children's cognitions about death and dying do not develop as rigidly as they might seem to and as many authors assume.

3.1.3 The Infantile Mourning Process

Grief is an emotional reaction to separation, loss, but also to the death of a loved one. Grief can be very painful on the one hand because of the finality of the loss and the difficulty of accepting it. On the other hand, however, the process of mourning is also necessary in order to be able to come to terms with the loss suffered. Only by means of these two aspects is it possible for the mourner to engage in new relationships. There is, however, one prerequisite for mourning: there must have been an emotional bond between the two persons (see Bojanovsky, 1984; Wendt, 1984a, b). Although mourning takes time, it passes after a while and the mourner is able to bear the loss without having to repress or forget the deceased (Gebhard, 2009).

Children, like adults, go through several different stages during their grieving process. One cannot predict and determine the duration of a person's grieving process.

The mourning process and thus the individual phases of mourning are actively gone through by the mourner. Through the active role, the grieving person has the possibility to influence the process (Attig, 1991).

3.1.3.1 Model Concepts

Although each person expresses his or her grief differently and very individually, one can nevertheless recognize some recurring patterns and processes in different mourners. Based on these processes and patterns, some models of the grieving process have been developed. The models can be divided into two categories: those that assume a linear conception, and those that assume a cyclical conception. Linear conception in this case means that the stages of grief are lived through sequentially by the mourner. It is assumed that after all the phases have been gone through, reorganization and recovery will occur. In contrast, the cyclical conception assumes that individual phases are completed again and again.

The two model conceptions are strongly criticized by various researchers. The main criticism is that each person has a different, quite variable way of grieving. For this reason, critics argue, phase models of grief do not do justice to individuals (Attig & Attig, 1996; Biondi & Picardi, 1996; Clegg, 1988). They criticize model representations that would lead to generalizations and simplifications of grief responses (e.g., Levang, 2002). Furthermore, specific criticisms of linear models are that grief does not proceed like a straight line. Phases may overlap, for example, the griever may skip phases or regress to earlier stages of grief (Goldbrunner, 1996; Mittag, 1992). However, authors such as Znoj (2004) or Buijssen and Polspoel (1997) explain in this context that these models should be understood as heuristics. They are intended to help grieving people to find their way through their mourning process and thus to be able to orient themselves.

The general model of grief and loss (Katz & Florian, 1986/87; Kelley, 2001; Lev & McCorkle, 1998; Schmied, 1988) is divided into three phases. First, shock sets in, which is then followed by the mourning phase. Finally, the mourner is in the phase of adjustment and reorganization.

3.1.3.2 The Bowlby Model

Bowlby (1987) also wrote a model to more accurately illustrate and explain the grieving process through the stages. He distinguishes between four different phases:

1. Phase of numbing and shock
    Bowlby describes that states of numbness alternate with panic attacks as well as with initial outbursts of emotion. The exact expression of the emotions varies greatly from individual to individual, as this is directly related to the personality of the grieving person. The duration of this first phase is usually estimated from a few hours to a week.
2. Phase of yearning and searching for the deceased person
    In this second phase, the longing for the deceased dominates. The desire for a reunion with the deceased person is very pronounced during this time. This second phase can last a few months, but sometimes also a few years.
3. Phase of disorganization and despair
    This phase is one of upheaval. The mourner tries to reorganize the present while accepting that the loved one is not coming back.
4. Reorganisation phase
    In the best case, it is possible for the person to take on new roles in this phase, but also to take up old resources again. The resumption of the social role always leads to a simultaneous rediscovery and redefinition of the self in the grieving person.

3.1.3.3 Kast's Model

Another model of the stages of grief is that of Kast (1985, 1990, 1992). Here she borrows from Bowlby's (1987) stages of grief and the "five stages of dying" formulated by Elisabeth (1969). However, Kast bases the development of her model primarily on the observation of mourners and their dreams. Namely, in her view, dreams initiate the different stages of grief. She also described four different phases:

1. Phase of denial
2. Phase of bursting emotions
3. Searching, finding and separating phase
4. Phase of the new reference to the self and the world

However, difficulties can also arise in each of the four phases, leading to a stagnation of the grieving process. However, this can often be prevented with appropriate support.

Concrete observations of children have shown that children often experience longer and more intense grief than adults (Kliman, 1980). Bowlby also reported cases of 6-month-old babies grieving as early as 1960. However, the loss response of young children, more specifically children up to 4 years of age, is referred to by Bowlby as "grief" rather than "mourning" (Bowlby, 1987). Furman (1977) also believes that loss is more severe for children than for adults. She explains her view by saying that adults divide their love among several relationships. Thus, an adult loves his children, spouse, and friends, as well as his leisure pursuits and work. The young child, on the other hand, invests all his feelings in his parents. Thus, when the parents die, all the possibilities of living as well as being loved are suddenly destroyed for the toddler.

As has already been mentioned, there are very contradictory assumptions about children's ability to grieve. It may be that there are children as young as 3 who already have an understanding of death and are therefore able to grieve, but on the other hand there are also nine-year-olds who still lack this understanding. It should be noted that there are also adults who are unable to grieve. Gebhard (2009) points out that this does not mean that the adult population should be denied the ability to grieve, as is sometimes done with children.

> **Overview**
> Infobox 1: Mourning process model ideas.

General model of grief and loss (Katz and Florian 1986, 1987; Kelley, 2001; Lev & McCorkle, 1998; Schmied, 1988).

- 3 phases:
    - Shock phase
    - Mourning
    - Adaptation and reorganisation phase

Bowlby's model (1987)

- 4 phases:
    - Phase of numbing and shock
    - Phase of yearning and searching for deceased persons
    - Phase of disorganization and despair
    - Reorganisation phase

Kast model (1985, 1990, 1992)

- 4 phases:
    - **Phase of denial**
    - Phase of bursting emotions
    - Searching, finding and separating phase
    - Phase of the new reference to the self and the world

3.1.4 The Child's Grief Reactions

In addition to stages of grief, it is also possible to identify some specific, but individually variable, grief responses in children (Charlton & Dolman, 1995; Kaffman & Elizur, 1996).

Grief Grief is felt by children as well as adults in every age category (Altschul, 1988; Kaffman & Elizur, 1984, 1996; Samuels, 1988; Silverman & Worden, 1992; Wayment & Vierthaler, 2002). Grief is most apparent in the first few months after loss through repeated crying. Researchers found that the older children and adolescents are, the longer and more intensely they cry (Bowlby, 1987; Garber, 1989). However, grief cannot and should not be reduced merely to crying, for that would mean that children who do not (no longer) cry do not experience grief. Crying is not a necessary characteristic of grief, for it can also manifest itself through (intense) preoccupation with the deceased. This includes recurring thoughts, such as memories, conversations and actions. Although grief is primarily very pronounced in the first year after the death of a loved one, it can also persist over a long period of time, but without being classified as pathological (Winkel, 2002).

Longing and Desire for Reunification Losses such as the loss of a parent lead to grief and pain in children. Mainly in the first months, there is an intense longing for the deceased person, therefore the desire to be reunited with this person is often in the foreground (Balk, 1997; Bowlby, 1987; Burnett et al., 1994; Samuels, 1988; Zerbe & Steinberg, 2000). Similar to grief, children become intensely preoccupied with the deceased, which inevitably affects their behaviors and thoughts. For example, grieving children can be observed trying harder to remember the deceased by using certain objects or pictures. Certain places associated with the deceased are also visited more frequently (Weiß, 2006).

Guilt If a person feels responsible for the death of the deceased for any reason, feelings of guilt may arise. In such cases, the mourner often reflects and thinks back on the past and thus on potential complicity (Boelen & van den Bout, 2002). Guilt is one of the grief characteristics that are present in children, adolescents, as well as young adults at all ages, but may have different causes depending on age. The cause of guilt in young children is often due to magical thinking. As has already been explained, young children believe that they are capable of wishing death on people. If this actually occurs, the child may experience extreme feelings of guilt (Baker & Sedney, 1996; Gardner, 1983; Lamers, 1995; Lord, 1999).

Regression Regression is understood, also in children and adolescents, as falling back to earlier developmental stages. This can be the result of too much stress or excessive demands on the situation. Due to the extreme stress, all resources as well as the child's strength have been used up, which in turn leads to various abilities being discontinued in order to thereby save strength (Schweitzer & Niedermann, 2000). In young children, such regressive behaviors may include baby talk, thumb sucking, wetting, as well as defecation.

Teeth grinding, nail biting, and skin scratching are examples of regressive behaviors in older children (Furman, 1984; Hummer, 1988; Koocher & Gudas, 1992; Parnes, 1975; Wessel, 1996).

Anger, Rage and Fury Like many grief reactions, anger, rage and rage are also part of the grieving process at any age. This makes itself felt through outbursts of anger and rage, but also through mild irritability (e.g. Hirschberg, 2010).

Somatic Symptoms The grieving process of children, adolescents and adults is often accompanied by somatic and/or psychosomatic symptoms (Clark et al., 1994; Garber, 1989; Kalter et al., 2002/03; Raphael, 1983; Sood et al., 1992; Wessel, 1996). The most common symptoms reported by mourners are headaches, shortness of breath, gastrointestinal complaints, exhaustion and allergic reactions. However, stress-related heart complaints, severe pain syndromes or asthma may also occur. In addition, a reduced resistance to infections has also been found in all age groups. In the first year after the loss experience, such physical symptoms and complaints are considered normal. However, they can also last much longer than a year. Franz (2002) explains that grief symptomatology can shift from the psychological to the physical level when the mourner represses the loss of a loved one. In addition, several studies conclude that the loss of a parent in childhood places such a high physical stress on children's bodies that they are still susceptible to illness and health complaints years later (Bendiksen & Fulton, 1975; Brähler et al., 2000; Luecken, 1998, 2000a, b; Ryan-Wenger, 1990).

Fear Anxiety as well as specific and non-specific fears can be observed in all age groups as a grief reaction. In addition, fear is one of the grief reactions that occur most frequently in children, adolescents and young adults. Separation anxiety, in particular, is often prominent in grieving children. For example, the fear here may be that after the death of one parent, children fear losing the other parent as well (Bowlby, 1987; Donders, 1993; Garber, 1989; Koocher & Gudas, 1992; Sanchez et al., 1994). Children may also exhibit fear of the dark, of being alone, or phobic fears.

Idealization Sometimes children may tend to idealize the deceased. The process of idealization, which occurs primarily after the death of a parent, becomes apparent fairly quickly in the period following the loss of the loved one, but can also be found years later (Garber, 1985; Iskenius-Emmler, 1988; Moebius, 1985). In this process, the focus is almost exclusively on the positive qualities of the deceased person; negative qualities often fade into the background or are even pushed out of the mourner's consciousness. Idealization serves as a protective mechanism for the griever, as memories of the deceased's positive qualities somewhat dull the pain of separation. As already mentioned, the idealization can persist for years, but usually a realistic image of the deceased is created (Weiß, 2006).

Other Grief Reactions There is a whole range of other grief reactions. For example, *social withdrawal* can also be observed in children, which manifests itself as apathy and silence (Buirski & Buirski, 1994; Raphael, 1983). Another grief reaction, *sleep disturbances,* can be observed at all ages. Sleep disturbances are expressed in the same way at all ages, i.e., from young children to adults. Bereaved people complain of nightmares, which are often related to the deceased, but also of problems falling asleep as well as sleeping through the night (Altschul, 1988; Menke, 2002; Zerbe & Steinberg, 2000). *School* children also experience *difficulties* in connection with grief. It is not uncommon for concentration problems to occur, which impair the ability to learn and thus usually inevitably lead to a deterioration in school performance. In many cases there is also a decline in interest in school activities or in school matters in general (Abdelnoor & Hollins, 2004; Felner et al., 1975, 1981; Smilansky, 1987; Wessel, 1996).

Overview
Infobox 2: Childhood grief reactions.
Grief

- Possible features: repetitive crying, recurrent thoughts

Longing and desire for reunification

- Especially during the first months
- Objects and places are visited in order to remember the deceased person

Guilt

- Mourning characteristic of all ages
- Cause in younger children often lies in magical thinking

Regression

- Result of too much stress or overstraining with the situation
- Symptoms of younger children: baby talk, thumb sucking, wetting and defecation
- Symptoms of older children: teeth grinding, nail biting and skin scratching

Anger, rage

- Mourning characteristic of all ages
- Symptoms: anger and rage outbursts and mild irritability

(continued)

Somatic symptoms

- Mourning characteristic of all ages
- Symptoms: including headache, shortness of breath, gastrointestinal complaints as well as exhaustion and allergic reactions

Fear

- Mourning characteristic of all ages
- Occurs most often in children, adolescents and in young adults

Idealization

- Predominantly after the death of a parent
- Serves as a protective mechanism

3.1.5 The Child's Grief Tasks

The mourning process is exhausting and painful, which is why Freud introduced the term "grief work" (Freud, 1917). Grief work helps to accept the irreversible change in reality caused by the loss. It may also be reliving and acknowledging the ambivalence of the relationship. This leads to a process of change that the grieving person goes through. Thus, the grieving person matures during the grieving process and gains a greater ability to bear reality (Mitscherlich & Mitscherlich, 1967).

Grief tasks are the interpretation of coping and adjustment processes as processes that the grieving person must have successfully completed in order to process this loss in an effective manner. Fox (1988) described tasks for children to ensure coping with loss and grief so that "grief work" is in fact equivalent to "good grief". He explained the following four tasks:

1. understand what has happened and make sense of what has happened (cognitive)
2. show emotional reactions to the loss (affective)
3. ritually commemorate the deceased (related to behaviour)
4. learn to live on (in terms of values)

Much of this grief work depends on the child's understanding of death, the circumstances of the loss for the child, and what all that has happened means for the child's life (Corr, 1995). Predominantly, it has been pointed out that the focus as well as the relative importance of these tasks may shift over time. For this reason, it is important to consider that there are differences between early, middle and late tasks in children's bereavement (Baker et al., 1992).

Culture has a high impact on the nature of the grief task, as well as on its "completion". Not every grieving person is able to complete all grief tasks. Grief tasks bear a strong resemblance to the stage models of grieving, some of which have been discussed in more detail above (Wittwer et al., 2010).

3.1.6 Pathological Grief

It is not always clear where and when normal grief ends and pathological grief begins (Charlton & Dolman, 1995). There are many difficulties in making this distinction and there is much disagreement (e.g. Rando, 1993; Znoj, 2004). This disagreement is already evident in the term itself, because in addition to the term *pathological grief,* there is also talk of *complicated grief.* It is only in recent years that there have been official criteria for recording as well as diagnosing pathological grief. In 1997, based on empirical findings, a panel of experts came to the conclusion that pathological grief is an independent disorder category. Pathological grief signifies a clinically relevant psychological impairment and is diagnostically distinct from anxiety disorders and depressive disorders. Separation stress and traumatic stress define the consensus criterion for pathological grief according to the expert panel (Wagner, 2014). Loneliness, a strong longing for the deceased, and a continuing mental preoccupation with the deceased person are symptoms of separation stress. Traumatic pain includes feelings of uselessness and emptiness, a negative outlook on the future, avoidance of memories of the deceased, shock and anger, and disbelief regarding the person's death (Wagner, 2014). In order to identify dysfunctional grief patterns and grief reactions, different grief reactions have been studied and compared (Arnette, 1996). It was only a few years ago that the criteria of pathological grief, which serve to define and diagnose it, were published (Horowitz et al., 1997; Jacobs, 1999). To answer the question of how common complicated grief is, there is little epidemiological data. There is no estimate for children and adolescents, but for adults it is thought to affect up to 40% of all bereaved people. However, it must be added that the estimates are generally far apart (Znoj, 2004).

There are hardly any publications on pathological grief in children and adolescents, which is why we can only fall back on isolated theses and presentations for a description. Siegel et al. (1996) are of the opinion that pathological grief is rarely observed in children, even in the case of the death of a parent. According to them, dysfunctional grief reactions occur mainly when there were already difficulties before the loss. This is understood to include family difficulties as well as pre-existing mental illness. Diagnosing pathological grief in children is also more difficult because, depending on their stage of development, they have a different concept of death than, for example, adolescents or adults. Because the grief response is related to developmental stage, children are said to have abnormal grief when their grief results in behaviors and reactions to loss that are inconsistent with their developmental stage (Bürgin, 1989; Dilworth & Hildreth, 1997/98; Schepker et al., 1995; Steck & Bürgin, 1996). Such reactions include, for example, striking behaviors that persist for a long time and various anxiety disorders. Other reactions indicative of abnormal grief include: Hyperactivity, aggressive behavior, hypochondria, and compulsions. In addition, it should be noted that persistent denial of reality, that is, of the death of the loved one long after the loss, may also be a possible indication of abnormal grief (Bird et al., 1996). According to Paulley (1983), it should also not be ignored that older children may not begin their grieving process immediately after the loss for a variety of reasons. Some possible reasons for this are, for example, because they have to continue to go to school or because they (have to) comfort siblings. Thus, older children may try to suppress their grief in order to support others by going easy on them and hiding their own pain. Permanent repression of loss leads to a failure to mourn the deceased. This can result in massive effects on the child's physical as well as mental health. These consequences can also show up years later or persist for years.

3.1.7 Cultural Differences

However, there are not only differences between different age groups in dealing with the topic of death and mourning, but cultural differences must also be taken into account. Studies have found significant differences in the understanding of life and death among children of different cultures. Hatano et al. (1993) found that for Japanese children, more phenomena are *animate,* such as mountains, than for American children, while for Israeli children, on the other hand, fewer things are considered *animate.* In a study of the concept of life in four- to ten-year-old children in a cross-cultural comparison, Anggoro et al. (2005) found that the language system (English/Indonesian) influences the concept of life. For example, from the age of 6, the term "living thing" includes animals and plants, whereas the term "alive" often does not include plants. The term "living thing" is also consistently associated with death, need for food, and growth.

Bowlby (1983) also looked at cultural differences regarding death and grief. He stated that the reactions of people across cultures are very similar after a serious loss. The difference is mainly in the way the situation is handled, such as social customs. Bowlby further defined three types of rules and rites that are found in different cultural patterns of dealing with grief: The first type of rites and rules determine a predetermined way of relating to the deceased. Second, he mentioned those that represent a norm, such as where mourners are allowed to express their anger, or where accusations are appropriate. Finally, as a third he named those that give the mourners a time frame how long they should mourn the deceased (Bowlby, 1983).

In this context, Langenmayr (2013) noted that across different eras and cultures, mourners were, and are, offered the opportunity to express common emotions, such as anger, crying and fear, in response to death. However, according to Langenmayr, only Western culture deviates from this.

In Western cultures, it is more accepted for women and girls to express their grief through crying than men and boys (Barth et al., 2003; Lenhardt & McCourt, 2000; Versalle & McDowell, 2005). The social norm in Western cultures has taught men and boys not to show their pain outwardly, to bear their pain silently and alone (Ecker, 1999; McGoldrick, 1992; Wolf, 1991).

With regard to the cultural dimension of mourning, the religious approach to death and mourning rituals cannot be disregarded, as this has a significant influence on mourning behaviour (Jackson, 1979). Thus, the development of a child's concept of death depends, among other things, on the parents' attitudes towards the subject of death, as well as how they deal with it. Again, religious and cultural backgrounds are also decisive here and thus extremely shape the child's concept of death (Bürgin, 1989, 1991; Morin & Welsh, 1996; Specht-Tomann & Tropper, 2001; Stillion & Wass, 1979).

The cultural background has an influence on the handling of death and mourning in various ways. In addition to customs and rites that often make mourning an integral part of social life in many other cultures, the expression of mourning and the accompanying feelings is also deeply rooted in the culture and thus plays an essential role in the mourning process.

3.2 Grief among Adolescents

Caroline Bell and Julia Federspiel

▶ **Adolescence** ... is defined as the developmental phase between childhood and adulthood. There are no uniform age limits, but the literature usually refers to the beginning of the first phase of adolescence at the age of **12** or **14**, and the onset of puberty is commonly associated with the beginning of adolescence (Kessels, 2013).

From an age of about 10 to 14 years, adolescent girls and boys are assumed to have a realistic concept of death. However, the actual age limits, individual assumptions and beliefs vary from person to person. According to experience, there is reason to believe that a realistic understanding of the finality and irreversibility of death is discernible for the first time at this stage of development. Along with this, the question of the meaning of death and a possible life after death plays an important role for adolescents (Fleck-Bohaumilitzky, 2004a, b; Witt-Loers, 2009).

Adolescence is characterized by **numerous developmental steps,** particularly with regard to psychological, physical, biological, social and cultural further development. The development of sexual maturity, for example, goes hand in hand with the establishment of an individual gender role and a possible first partnership. Adolescents face the big step of exploring and developing their own personality under the influence of social possibilities and limits. Often they experiment with their own identity and different personality accentuations become recognizable in the course of development. In addition to the development of one's own values, norms and convictions, the increasing turning towards and the accompanying increasing contact with peers is also considered completely normal, indeed it is perceived as a further important developmental step. Thus, adolescence broadly denotes **a phase of self-discovery** in life. An immense challenge for parents and guardians is to determine up to what point one allows one's own children to gather precisely these new experiences, to try themselves out and to form as well as reject different life plans on the way to finding one's identity. In this context, however, not only parental feelings play a decisive role, but also social norms and expectations, which usually have a decisive influence on parents in terms of their limits and rules (Göppel, 2005).

3.2.1 Coping with Grief in Adolescents

> **The Four Tasks of Grief Work**
> 1. Task: **Accept the loss as reality.**
>   Accept that the loss is final and that a reunion with the dead person will not happen in this life.
> 2. Task: **To deal with the pain.**
>   The grief pain that accompanies loss—whether physical, cognitive, emotional, or behavioral—must first be recognized, accepted, and processed.
> 3. Task: **Adapt to a world without the deceased person.**
> 4. Task: **Assign a new place to the deceased person and learn to move on with your own life.**
>   Without losing the bond with the deceased, a suitable place should be found for the person, while allowing space for others.
>   (Worden, 2018)

Objectively, grievers are faced with coping with the four demands mentioned above. According to American psychologist and leading grief researcher William J. Worden (2018), any grieving process takes a long time. The process of "proper grieving" by a bereaved person not only deals with one's own thoughts and feelings, but further consists in the requirement of having to reorder the now changed world. Whether this very process has been "successfully" gone through, can be recognized by the fact that a person no longer feels the need to remember the deceased in everyday life to an exaggerated extent, has discovered a new meaning in life and finally, in the best case, is able to use the loss experience for their own further development (Bundesarbeitsgemeinschaft Trauerbegleitung, 2019; Worden, 2018).

Objectively speaking ... but don't we all know—given our own experiences with death—that grief and the associated processing cannot simply be viewed in such a "cool" and "sober" way? **Everyone grieves differently, uses different strategies** to process the loss, and **takes different amounts of time.** Some feel they have processed the death of a loved one after one year—the so-called year of mourning—whereas others feel such a sense only after years—if ever. Sometimes it seems simply impossible to accept the loss of a close person. There are **no hard-and-fast rules** about how the grieving process should work or a fixed point in time at which it must end. Although adults, unlike children, have a realistic concept of death and realize a loss as such, most people are very reluctant to deal with this issue and do not seem to accept that life is finite. Not only that of others. But how does the whole thing behave with regard to young people? (Bundesarbeitsgemeinschaft Trauerbegleitung, 2019; Der Sonntag/Harringer, 2017).

Adolescents grieve differently. Nowadays, adolescents are often expected to be small adults. This is not the case and they also differ significantly in their way of grieving. Death does not fit into their view of the world, to discover life with ease and carefree, to savour it and enjoy it to the fullest in a carefree way. A death shakes this world view and puts it to the test. Often young people find themselves walking a tightrope, so to speak, between the desire to enjoy life and the sudden death and the ever-present thoughts of loss associated with it. Young people's reactions to death often seem incomprehensible to outsiders. Going on dates with friends even though a loved one has just left forever? Laughing? Go to the cinema? Doing what you had planned to do anyway before the death seems to shatter everything? Adults often find these behaviors of young people difficult to comprehend, as it is simply not appropriate to have fun after the death of a loved one. Rather, one should be in a subdued mood, close relatives should appear dressed in black, and mourning should be expressed openly, not just within the family circle. Some behaviors of young people do not fit into this picture at all. And yet they are normal, the result of being torn between the two.

Statements such as "You don't seem to be interested in the whole thing at all!" or "You obviously don't care much for the deceased person!" from adults are not uncommon, as they see these behaviours as a slight. They sometimes find it difficult to recognise young people for what they are—adolescents, no longer children, but not yet adults either. Seemingly inappropriate behaviour of children is accepted or even considered normal ("After all, it is still a child"). Adolescents, on the other hand, are no longer granted this; they have to behave "correctly" according to the situation (Bundesarbeitsgemeinschaft Trauerbegleitung, 2019; Der Sonntag/Harringer, 2017).

However, it is important to recognise that young people find their own ways of grieving and expressing it. Grief can take many different forms. Being loud, laughing, testing boundaries are all ways in which a grief response can take place. Such behaviours may sometimes seem disturbing, as they are in contrast to the socially widespread subdued mood of mourning (Bundesarbeitsgemeinschaft Trauerbegleitung, 2019; Der Sonntag/Harringer, 2017).

Adolescents often tend to hide their grief from the outside world. In addition, they often take on new roles in the family circle, for example in the form of responsibility for younger siblings. In order not to cause more grief and problems for relatives, they cover up their tears and instead feel compelled to show strength or even offer a shoulder to lean on. This leads many adolescents to grow up unnoticed in the grieving process within the family circle (Diebold, 2013). Often, adolescents are internally grieving for a person while engaging in such seemingly out-of-place behaviors. In other words, a mourning reaction may well take place at the same time as the "usual" life of an adolescent, characterized by joie de vivre and energy.

> **Notice!** It is of great importance to understand these reactions and behaviors and to communicate acceptance as an adult. Under no circumstances should adolescents be left alone with their grief. Grieving adolescents should be met with empathy, openness, and understanding without imposing or forcing conversations. Whether young people seek conversations with their own parents, siblings, friends, teachers or other people varies from person to person. Friends of the same age are usually an important support to give stability and support.Finally, it should be said that grief reactions of adolescents should be accepted by their (adult) environment (as long as no self-destructive action tendencies are feared), no matter how different and incomprehensible they may turn out to be. Adolescents grieve differently—but, just as with adults, there are no right or wrong ways to do so (Bundesarbeitsgemeinschaft Trauerbegleitung, 2019; Der Sonntag/Harringer, 2017).

3.2.2 Somatization in the Grieving Process

Since teenagers consequently face quite different everyday demands than children or adults, the predominant needs in the context of grief counselling vary accordingly. Teenagers are very busy developing their own identity and finding a place in life, they are, as described above, in the middle of a nerve-racking development process. Grief usually represents an additional challenge for them, a completely new and unexpected feeling, which they are often **overwhelmed** to **cope with** (Röseberg & Müller, 2014). Often, similar to children, adolescents are in a kind of **state of shock** immediately after the death of a known or close person. To the outside world, the behaviour sometimes continues to appear completely normal and the impression may be given that nothing has happened. Adolescents try to act habitually "cool" even though the pain behind the facade runs deep. **Silly or seemingly inappropriate behaviors** may also occur during the individual's state of shock and are generally considered **normal.** Whether certain behaviors have a calming, pain-relieving effect or tend to be more counterproductive varies from person to person. By and large, the majority of individual action tendencies serve as a form of numbing the pain experienced and are considered a healthy protective mechanism of one's soul. While the behavior of affected adolescents may appear **outwardly normal**, it is not uncommon for emotional pain **to** express itself in **physical complaints** known as somatization (Becker & Shah, 2008).

▶ **Somatization—What is it?** Somatization describes the phenomenon that psychological, often unconscious conflicts and difficulties express themselves in physical signs. Stressful life events that could not be processed express themselves in various disease-like symptoms. Somatization is therefore to be understood as a defense mechanism, so to speak. The consideration of psychological factors therefore represents an important component in the research into the causes of unexplained physical complaints.
   Possible physical complaints.
   → Headache, abdominal pain, sleep disturbances, loss of appetite, fever, etc.
   Kriebel et al. (1996).

After a while, according to experience, the initial state of shock is usually followed by **intense anger**. To a certain extent, this is a form of **protest against death** and can be directed against anyone in principle. Often the anger is directed at the deceased, the doctors treating him or her, or at God. Young people in mourning usually find themselves in a kind of emotional chaos and, in addition to feelings of guilt and fear, also experience withdrawal tendencies or a feeling of listlessness. Not infrequently, there is also excessive counteracting, so-called overcompensation, or a drop in performance in school (Becker & Shah, 2008).

3.2.3 Adolescent Grief in the School Context

School is an important place of mourning for young people. Especially when a classmate or teacher has died, there is a close connection with everyday school life. Therefore, it is of great importance to be able to grieve in such a case in the context in which the relationships were lived, in this case at school, be it in the classroom or in a larger setting.

It is essential to talk **openly and honestly** with the adolescents about death, but only to communicate verified facts. Even a case of suicide should not be an exception or covered up, but details should be left out. **Providing information** not only prevents rumours among adolescents, but is also a way of containing any feelings of guilt that may arise. Rumors about the event quickly arouse fears through **adolescent fantasies,** which can lead to stress. Young students also tend to feel guilt easily and, especially in the case of a suicide, tend to believe that they acted wrongly and should have recognized signs that suicide was imminent. Likewise, bereaved young people are quick to blame themselves if they have argued with the deceased person or suddenly recall other seemingly unforgivable behaviours.

Preventively, teenagers can be made aware of warning signals and offers of help in the school context. It is especially important to make clear that there is always a way out of a crisis situation, even if it is not obvious to the person concerned. Telephone counselling or other psychological counselling centres can be a first point of contact and should be introduced in order to reduce uncertainty and fear of contacting them. It should be encouraged to make use of such an offer of help oneself not only when one is feeling bad, but also to turn to an institution when one notices that a fellow student is feeling very bad (Becker & Shah, 2008).

Just like children, young people are also allowed to grieve and yet also show happy light-hearted behaviour. Adolescents should be involved in saying goodbye to the deceased and be given the opportunity to say goodbye in a specific place and to be able to stay there later. The mourning process and saying goodbye can be facilitated and symbolically supported by various mourning rituals (Becker & Shah, 2008).

> **Grief rituals . . .**
> . . . are loving signs to say goodbye to. . .
> . . . should be designed individually for each person.
> . . . give comfort and support to the grieving, provide a pillar of strength. . .
> . . . enable the control of emotions, the acting out of feelings.
> **Suggestions . . .**
> . . . sing favourite songs of the deceased together.
> . . . write a book of condolence.
> . . . plant a tree together.
> . . . a walk on the (common) favourite path.
> . . . **in the school context.**
> . . . circle of chairs with a cloth in the middle and a candle.
> . . . devotion that finds words of comfort.
> . . . commemorative minutes, long-term commemorative events (e.g. anniversary).
> . . . classmates can make something and/or write a farewell letter.
> . . . signs of remembrance/hope (e.g. planting a tree in the schoolyard).
> (Becker & Shah, 2008)

According to Sieck (2010), mourning is on the one hand hard work for the body and the soul, but on the other hand also a **healthy and vital as well as creative reaction to loss and grief.** Death and the need to say goodbye are unfortunately almost everyday events and regularly recurring challenges in our society today. It is assumed that the older, more mature and mentally healthier a young person is, the better they can cope with grief (Fleck-Bohaumilitzky, 2004a, b). Accepting personal loss as a reality means reliving grief pain each time and adapting to a new environment in which the deceased is missing. Over time, a new place is assigned to the deceased person in order to have the opportunity to invest in new relationships elsewhere (Worden, 2018). However, this does not automatically mean that the deceased person is replaced, as a **lifelong emotional connection** can also be perfectly normal depending on the personality (Klass et al., 2014). According to experts, the intensity of grief in adolescents usually tapers off after about a year. Such a temporal pattern is similar to a grief cycle that also occurs in adults. In general, however, it is not possible to define a clear point in time at which grief should begin to fade into the background, as each grieving process is individually different. The loss of a loved one usually accompanies a lifetime. In particular, drastic events such as one's own wedding, the birth of one's first child or other comparable developmental steps often evoke memories (Röseberg & Müller, 2014).

A particular **challenge for school bereavement work** is when an individual pupil loses a parent or sibling and has to come to terms with this loss in the normal classroom setting. In most cases, young people not only have to cope with their own grief, but also feel that they have to support their own family members and offer a strong shoulder. The belief that they **must continue to "function"** so as not to cause additional grief to their parents **stresses students immensely.** This is not an uncommon phenomenon, as many adolescents withhold their grief within the family circle in order to protect others. Such behaviour should be recognised at an early stage in order to **offer** the adolescent an opportunity and a **place for** their **grief.** There are numerous alternatives to talking to relatives in order to learn how to deal with the situation. **Creative activities** such as painting, writing a diary or sporting activities can provide an outlet. Depending on the age, **computer games** or **partying** can also be important in the process of dealing with grief. It should be kept in mind that **everyone benefits from something different** and there is **no one-size-fits-all recipe for coping.** Everyone grieves in a different way and therefore benefits from different activities. The decisive factor is always the particular situation, the day, the specific moment and the actual closeness of the other person. An important piece of advice when interacting with those affected is **to ask directly how best to behave and deal with the situation in** order to provide support that is accepted and does not drive the person affected into a corner. Be it as a friend, acquaintance, classmate or teacher (Röseberg & Müller, 2014).

In order to better support an affected individual in everyday school life, secure information should be passed on to classmates. Together, teachers and students should consider what help might look like. Consideration should be given to obtaining prior consent from the affected family to discuss the death in the classroom. It seems important, on the one hand, to convey to the affected class member that you are listening and are there, but on the other hand, not to impose a conversation and allow normality. **Asking how the person is doing** and being **gentle and patient with them** are important aspects of helpful support. In addition, one can try to provide young people with practical help and, especially in the initial phase, facilitate relief through individual arrangements regarding school requirements (Röseberg & Müller, 2014).

In addition to school support, some grieving young people find help in **grief counselling** in conversation with outsiders. Even in such a setting, there is no uniform standard programme from which all young people benefit equally. Rather, it is important to listen and build a trusting foundation for deep conversations. Serious topics such as fears, worries, pain and despair are addressed in the conversation, but there is also room for fond memories of the deceased as well as one's own future. In general, the aim is usually to **help people to help themselves** and the aspect of support is at the forefront of such offers of help (Diebold, 2013). It is important to find out what exactly the grieving young person needs in terms of support and what exactly he/she can and wants to allow at the moment in order to cope with personal grief in his/her own way.

3.2.4 Grief Via Social Media

Nowadays, there is another important component regarding **young people's grief processing.** Social media are an important part of the everyday life of young people and the internet opens up completely **new dimensions** for grieving. Via **Facebook, Instagram, WhatsApp and Co.** not only can feelings seemingly be articulated more easily, there is also the possibility of exchanging experiences with other affected persons whose experiences may be similar to one's own. However, it should be said that online social media also have their limits and can only provide support up to a certain point. There is no substitute for human care, closeness and support. Existing memorial sites and grief blogs are not a helpful tool for everyone in the processing process. Again, individual needs vary widely. It is also important to remember that (anonymous) virtual exchange can always bring negative experiences, for example in the form of bullying (think of the increasing problem of cyberbullying), insults or lack of understanding. In general, previous online experiences show that people need a **concrete place in the real world** where they can mourn the deceased (Luthe, 2016; Offerhaus et al., 2013).

The option of online grief management can usually be practiced as a supplement to offline grief processing, mostly from the point of view if offline grief options are not sufficient for effective grief management (Rimé, 2009).

Grief on Social Media
- Facebook, Instagram, WhatsApp and Co.
   → Young people can write about their own grief with a little distance

   - Exchange with others is important to process the loss
   - Confrontation and confrontation with death (e.g. RIP statements on the occasion of the death of prominent persons)

3.2.5 Grief within the Family Circle

Within the family circle, young people can be affected by losses of various kinds. Be it through the age-related death of grandparents or a loss through illness or accident. Again, **honesty** with adolescents about what has happened is highly relevant. This also includes informing adolescents about terminal illnesses within the family in order to have the opportunity to spend remaining time with the affected person.

Often, the sudden death of a close family member leads to young people not being sufficiently considered in their grief. This usually results in a **feeling of being alone** with all the grief and sorrow, although this is not intended. Rather, parents, siblings, uncles or aunts, etc. also have to struggle with the loss. Especially when a child dies, parents are often unable to offer sufficient support and stability to siblings because they are shaken by their own grief. The assumption of many parents that it is better not to talk about the death in the presence of the children in order to protect them reinforces the young person's feeling of loneliness (Witt-Loers, 2014).

Whether and how mourning takes place within the family circle varies from person to person. In accordance with the guiding principle that everyone grieves and deals with loss in a different way, there are families who find their way back into everyday life quite quickly and, in turn, those who are unable to return to routine for a long time. Everyone realizes in different ways after the loss of a family member how much the deceased is missing and what place he/she has taken in one's life. Be it through the tasks taken over by the deceased or through the emotional affection. If, for example, the father with whom one was always fooling around or the sister with whom one could talk about everything is suddenly missing, one's own world seems to be shaken in a fundamental way.

In a family structure, grief is rarely expressed in a uniform way, but rather varies individually from family member to family member. It **is essential for parents to know that they cannot take the grief and the associated pain away from their child.** The knowledge that familiar people are aware of the suffering experienced and always have a **sympathetic ear** when there is a need to talk is immensely valuable and comforting to an adolescent. It can be very stressful for adolescents to witness the grief of others. Feelings of loneliness, guilt or despair can arise (Witt-Loers, 2014).

If a parent dies, young people usually experience little support from their mother/ father, as the loss of their own partner means the loss of a central support. Grandparents also feel great sorrow and usually do not offer the adolescent sufficient support and security. Such fundamental changes in the life of an adolescent can reinforce the feeling of helplessness, since one's own existence seems to be endangered. The direct assumption of new roles and tasks previously held by the deceased should be urgently avoided. Sentences such as "You're the man in the family from now on!" can have stressful consequences. Young people should not be pressured to take responsibility for the rest of the family (Witt-Loers, 2014). Other changes usually consist of **financial and structural adjustments.** The loss of an income can result in financial constraints, which contribute to additional dissatisfaction and frustration in the stressful situation. Career reorientations of the remaining parent result in even less time and support being available for grief counseling. Dealing with one's own grief, the fundamental changes brought about by the shared loss and the numerous new demands that come with it easily cause a feeling of being overwhelmed, which once again illustrates **the importance of the remaining family members sticking together** (Witt-Loers, 2014).

The **death of a sibling** is another bad scenario that upsets the family's previous daily routine and the seemingly "normal sequence" of life. Due to deep grief and pain, all family members are preoccupied with themselves that they mostly cannot provide sufficient care and security to the adolescent. Siblings experience a close bond, they grow up together and usually know each other inside out. Numerous memories and shared childhood experiences are associated with such a loss. Death may appear in a different, threatening light, as it is perhaps only now that they really become aware that it is not age-related. In addition to grief, adolescents must reorder previous assumptions and habits. The relationship with parents and their behavior usually changes greatly. The latter distance themselves from the adolescent in their grief, so that eventually not only the loss of the sibling, but to a certain extent also that of the parents must be processed. Often siblings do **not** want to **be a further burden for** the parents **and simply "function"** in an attempt to continue everyday life by taking over important tasks (Witt-Loers, 2014).

The **loss of a person outside the family circle,** such as a friend or classmate, also requires special handling within the family. After all, grief does not simply end at the front door. Parents should not simply overlook it and go on with everyday life. It is of great importance to be aware of the young person's grief and to offer appropriate support. There should always be the possibility to express the grief, to talk about what happened and to **involve** the **family in the grieving process** (Witt-Loers, 2014).

Adult family members should be aware of their **role as role models**. Hiding one's own feelings, withholding information, or sparse communication about shared loss and grief can be copycat behaviors. Appropriate grief management by the adolescent(s) may be impaired. As a general rule, an **empathetic family culture** in which feelings are expressed and exceptional situations are overcome together is conducive to coping with bereavement. The **cohesion of the remaining family members** can be strengthened by such an emergency situation (Witt-Loers, 2014).

In conclusion, a loved one who has died will **often** remain **part of the family** for the adolescent(s). Regular conversations together in specific places or days in memory of the deceased and the loss experienced are generally helpful not only for adolescents. The deceased is inextricably linked to the adolescent's childhood and own life story and thus always a part of their self, which is why **memories** are **usually of particular value.** Young people inevitably have to say goodbye and come to terms with and process loss and grief. However, this does not mean that memories of the deceased should completely disappear from one's life from now on (Witt-Loers, 2014).

Mourning within the Family Circle
- Young people should be trusted to deal with loss
- Basic assumption that adolescents grieve after the death of a family member, but that grief may be inappropriate and not directly recognizable
- Family members grieve and go through adjustment processes to the new situation differently
- No close relationship: Death of a person can nevertheless mean considerable stress for the adolescent(s), insecurities and fears regarding their own existence.

- Young people's needs, feelings and wishes for family members should be respected and permitted

(Witt-Loers, 2014)

3.2.6 Accompanying Young People in their Grief

At first glance, young people are not so different from adults in their understanding of grief. However, some important aspects should be taken into account in grief counselling: Adolescents are not yet as emotionally mature and stable as adults.

> **Notice!** Apparently inappropriate or absent grief reactions can occur (see Section 3.2.1 Coping with grief in adolescents/3.2.2 Somatisation in the grieving process). One challenge in grief counselling for young people is that on the one hand they are still dependent on the **help, closeness and support** of adult caregivers, but at the same time they are in a phase of detachment and **increasing independence.** The accompaniment from "outside", however, is an essential aspect of successful grief management. It is assumed that each adolescent finds his or her own way through grief, but support and stability are nevertheless indispensable in view of the acute threat to the previous world view. Since young people often initially withdraw in exceptional situations, supportive persons should **approach those who are grieving.** In principle, anyone can take on this role. Parents or other family members, as long as they are not too busy coping with the grief themselves, neighbours, but above all friends. For young people, the peer group of familiar people often plays a central role (Fig. 3.1).

Fig. 3.1 Hierarchy of needs according to Maslow, 1943

Following the hierarchy of needs (Maslow, 1943), it is important to promote the basic need for security in order to meet the desire for **normality and daily routine.**

Providing assistance, offering support, ... that sounds simple at first. However, many people are actually overwhelmed in the role of grief counsellor and do not really know what to say or do. Some try to express their own dismay at the loss and understanding for the griever(s) by drawing comparisons from their own lives or recounting similar experiences. Others show themselves to be overprotective and shower the adolescent(s) with care. As individual as each person is in mourning, so **individual** should the grief **counselling** be. What is good for one person in this exceptional situation does not help the other. On the contrary, especially with young people, excessive care and support can even be undesirable. Consequently, grief counselling is individual, and here too the following applies: **there is no right or wrong** (Diebold, 2013). In their own overwhelmingness or helplessness, those providing support should **simply ask directly** how they can best help and what the young person wants.

▶ **Tips for dealing with grieving young people**

- Inquiries
- Taking a step back
- Death is not a contagious disease
- Laughter is also allowed
- It does not need gifts
- Just "be there
- Avoid hectic
- Separate professional from private life
- Supports
- Do not compare
- Ask again

(Riedeberger, 2016)

Engaging with young people sometimes requires a great deal of sensitivity. **Encouraging and supporting** adolescents in their individual response and coping to find and live through their own way of grieving is essential. Even if an adolescent has just been on a date with friends and laughed a lot, he or she can fall into serious and deep mourning shortly afterwards. Therefore, it may **not always** be **easy** for a companion to deal honestly and sincerely with the grieving person. However, these two qualities are indispensable in coping with grief. **One** should also **admit to being overwhelmed** by the situation. In general, there should be a **willingness** to **listen to** the bereaved person, **to accept him** or her **as he or she is at the moment and to accept him** or her **as he or she is.** It should not matter how much time the mourner spends doing this. The accompanying person does not have to speak or explain much, since for many **physical closeness,** such as hugs, is most helpful anyway.

▸ **Remember!** It is essential to give support and simply be there.

However, not everyone wants to be continuously comforted and supported, so one should not impose. The mourner should be able to choose when support or someone to talk to is needed. While male adolescents often want to be alone, girls often show a greater need to talk (Diebold, 2013). It can also be helpful to maintain some level of daily habits to keep in mind the desire for stability and routine. Sports, writing, painting, spending time with pets, and more can alleviate grief (Diebold, 2013).

▸ **Notice!** Coping with grief is different for each individual and there is no right or wrong way. Young people do not need to be "wrapped in cotton wool" and should be supported in their way of grieving.

Bibliography

3.1 Grief in Children

Abdelnoor, A., & Hollins, S. (2004). The effect of childhood bereavement on secondary school performance. *Educational Psychology in Practice, 20*(1), 43–54.

Altschul, S. (1988). Trauma, mourning, and adaptation: A dynamic point of view. In S. Altschul (Ed.), *Emotions and behavior monographs, no. 8. Childhood bereavement and its aftermath (p. 3–15)*. International Universities Press.

Anggoro, F. K., Medin, D. L., & Waxman, S. R. (2005). The effects of naming practices on children's understanding of living things. In *Proceedings of the annual meeting of the cognitive science society* (Vol. 27, p. 27).

Arnette, J. K. (1996). Physiological effects of chronic grief: A biofeedback treatment approach. *Death Studies, 20*(1), 59–72.

Attig, T. (1991). The importance of conceiving of grief as an active process. *Death Studies, 15*(4), 385–393.

Attig, T., & Attig, T. W. (1996). *How we grieve: Relearning the world*. Oxford University Press.

Baker, J. E., & Sedney, M. A. (1996). How bereaved children cope with loss: An overview. In C. A. Corr & D. M. Corr (Eds.), *Handbook of childhood death and bereavement (p. 109–129)*. Springer Publishing.

Baker, J. E., Sedney, M. A., & Gross, E. (1992). Psychological tasks for bereaved children. *American Journal of Orthopsychiatry, 62*(1), 105–116.

Balk, D. E. (1997). Death, bereavement and college students: A descriptive analysis. *Mortality, 2*(3), 207–220.

Barth, S., Kerp, E. M., & Müller, M. (2003). *Trauer [Hausarbeit]*. Universität Trier.

Bendiksen, R., & Fulton, R. (1975). Death and the child: An anterospective test of the childhood bereavement and later behavior disorder hypothesis. *OMEGA-Journal of Death and Dying, 6*(1), 45–59.

Bertenthal, B. I., Proffitt, D. R., Spetner, N. B., & Thomas, M. A. (1985). The development of infant sensitivity to biomechanical motions. *Child Development, 56*(3), 531–543. https://doi.org/10.2307/1129742

Biondi, M., & Picardi, A. (1996). Clinical and biological aspects of bereavement and loss-induced depression: A reappraisal. *Psychotherapy and Psychosomatics, 65*(5), 229–245.

Bird, H. R., Green, A. H., Kranzler, E. M., Rubinstein, B., & Wasserman, G. A. (1996). Belastungen und Traumen in der Kindheit. In F. I. Kass, J. M. Oldham, & H. Pardes (Eds.), *Das große Handbuch der seelischen Gesundheit. Früherkennung und Hilfe bei sämtlichen psychischen Störungen* (pp. 308–325). Weinheim.

Bluebond-Langner, M. (1977). Meanings of death to children. In H. Feifel (Ed.), *New meanings of death*. McGraw Hill.

Boelen, P. A., & van den Bout, J. (2002). Positive thinking in bereavement: Is it related to depression, anxiety, or grief symptomatology? *Psychological Reports, 91*(3), 857–863.

Bojanovsky, J. (1984). Einführung in die Problematik und einige wichtige Ergebnisse zum Forschungsbereich Trauer. In J. Howe & R. Ochsmann (Eds.), *Tod–Sterben–Trauer (S. 330–337). Bericht über die 1. Tagung zur Thanato-Psychologie vom 4.-6. November 1982 in Vechta*. Fachbuchhandlung für Psychologie.

Bowlby, J. (1960). Rief and mourning in infancy and early childhood. *The Psychoanalytic Study of the Child, 15*(1), 9–52.

Bowlby, J. (1983). *Attachment: Attachment and loss* (Vol. Bd. 1, 2nd ed.). Basic Books.

Bowlby, J. (1987). *Verlust, Trauer und Depression*. Frankfurt a. M.: Fischer Taschenbuch (Originalarbeit erschienen 1980: Loss, sadness and depression, Vol. III: Attachment and loss).

Brähler, E., Schumacher, J., & Strauß, B. (2000). Leiden vaterlos Aufgewachsene im Erwachsenenalter häufiger unter psychischen Beeinträchtigungen? *PPmP-Psychotherapie· Psychosomatik· Medizinische Psychologie, 50*(07), 287–291.

Brocher, T. (1985). *Wenn Kinder trauern* (Vol. Bd. 1). Rowohlt.

Buijssen, H. P. J., & Polspoel, A. R. M. (1997). Trauer. In H. P. J. Buijssen & R. D. Hirsch (Hrsg.), *Probleme im Alter. Diagnose, Beratung, Therapie, Prävention* (S. 67–106). Weinheim: Beltz (Originalarbeit erschienen 1994: Psychologische hulpverlening aan ouderen. Diagnostiek, therapie, preventie).

Bürgin, D. (1981). *Das Kind, die lebensbedrohende Krankheit und der Tod*. Huber.

Bürgin, D. (1989). Trauer bei Kindern und Erwachsenen. *Zeitschrift für Psychoanalytische Theorie und Praxis, 4*(1), 55–78.

Bürgin, D. (1991). Kinder und der Tod. In R. Battegay & U. Rauchfleisch (Eds.), *Das Kind in seiner Welt* (pp. 82–95). Vandenhoeck & Ruprecht.

Buirski, C. K., & Buirski, P. (1994). The therapeutic mobilization of mourning in a young child. *Bulletin of the Menninger Clinic, 58*(3), 339–354.

Burnett, P., Middleton, W., Raphael, B., Dunne, M., Moylan, A., & Martinek, N. (1994). Concepts of normal bereavement. *Journal of Traumatic Stress, 7*(1), 123–128.

Charlton, R., & Dolman, E. (1995). Bereavement: A protocol for primary care. *British Journal of General Practice, 45*(397), 427–430.

Clark, D. C., Pynoos, R. S., & Goebel, A. E. (1994). Mechanisms and processes of adolescent bereavement. In R. J. Haggerty, L. R. Sherrod, N. Garmezy, & M. Rutter (Eds.), *Stress, risk, and resilience in children and adolescents. Processes, mechanisms, and interventions* (pp. 100–146). Cambridge University Press.

Clegg, F. (1988). Bereavement. In S. Fisher & J. Reason (Eds.), *Handbook of life stress, cognition and health* (pp. 61–78). Wiley.

Corr, C. A. (1995). Children's understandings of death-striving to understand death. In *Children mourning, mourning children* (pp. 3–15). Hospice Foundation of America.

Dennis, W. (1957). Animistic thinking among college and high school students in the near east. *Journal of Educational Psychology, 48*(4), 193.

Dilworth, J. L., & Hildreth, G. J. (1997/98). Long-term unresolved grief: Applying Bowlby's variants to adult survivors of early parent loss. *Omega–Journal of Death and Dying, 36*(2), 147–159.

Donders, J. (1993). Bereavement and mourning in pediatric rehabilitation settings. *Death Studies, 17* (6), 517–527.

Dornes, M. (1993). *Der kompetente Säugling. Die präverbale Entwicklung des Menschen* (Bd. 13). Frankfurt/M.: Fischer.

Ecker, G. (1999). Trauer zeigen: Inszenierung und die Sorge um die anderen. In G. Ecker (Ed.), *Trauer tragen–Trauer zeigen. Inszenierung der Geschlechter* (pp. 9–25). München.

Felner, R. D., Stolberg, A., & Cowen, E. L. (1975). Crisis events and school mental health referral patterns of young children. *Journal of Consulting and Clinical Psychology, 43*(3), 305–310.

Felner, R. D., Ginter, M. A., Boike, M. F., & Cowen, E. L. (1981). Parental death or divorce and the school adjustment of young children. *American Journal of Community Psychology, 9*(2), 181–191.

Fleck-Bohaumilitzky, C. (2003). *Wenn Kinder trauern*. Südwest-Verlag.

Fleck-Bohaumilitzky, C. (2004a). *Wie Kinder Tod und Trauer erleben*. Das Familienhandbuch des Staatsinstituts für Frühpädagogik (IFP).

Fox, S. S. (1988). Helping a child Deal with death teaches valuable skills. *Psychiatric Times*, 10–11.

Franz, M. (2002). *Tabuthema Trauerarbeit. Erzieherinnen begleiten Kinder bei Abschied, Verlust und Tod*. München.

Freud, S. (1917). Mourning and Melancholia. *The Standard Edition of the Complete Psychological Works of Sigmund Freud, Volume XIV (1914–1916): On the History of the Psycho-Analytic Movement, Papers on Metapsychology and Other Works*, 237–325.

Furman, E. (1977). *Ein Kind verwaist. Untersuchungen über Elternverlust in der Kindheit* (1st ed.). Klett-Cotta.

Furman, E. (1984). Children's patterns in mourning the death of a loved one. In H. Wass & C. A. Corr (Eds.), *Childhood and death* (pp. 185–203). Hemisphere Publishing Corporation.

Garber, B. (1985). Mourning in adolescence: Normal and pathological. *Adolescent Psychiatry, 12*, 371–387.

Garber, B. (1989). The child's mourning: Can it be learned from the parent? In K. Field, B. J. Cohler, & G. Wool (Eds.), *Learning and education: Psychoanalytic perspectives* (pp. 355–376). International Universities Press.

Gardner, R. A. (1983). Children's reactions to parental death. In J. E. Schowalter, P. R. Patterson, M. Tallmer, A. H. Kutscher, S. V. Gullo, & D. Peretz (Eds.), *The child and death* (pp. 104–124). Columbia University Press.

Gebhard, U. (2009). *Kind und Natur: die Bedeutung der Natur für die psychische Entwicklung*. Springer.

Gelman, R. (1990). First principles organize attention to and learning about relevant data: Number and the animate-inanimate distinction as examples. *Cognitive Science, 14*(1), 79–106.

Gesell, A., & Ilg, F. L. (1962). *Säugling und Kleinkind in der Kultur der Gegenwart: Die Förderung d. Entwickl. in Elternhaus u. Kindergarten*. In Zsarb. mit Janet Learned u. Louise B. Ames. Hrsg. vd Hochschule f. Internat. Pädagog. Forschung. Frankfurt/Main: Christian-Verlag.

Goldbrunner, H. (1996). *Trauer und Beziehung. Systemische und gesellschaftliche Dimensionen der Verarbeitung von Verlusterlebnissen*. Matthias-Grünewald.

Grollman, E. A. (1991). *Mit Kindern über den Tod sprechen*. Ein Ratgeber für Eltern.

Hatano, G., Siegler, R. S., Richards, D. D., Inagaki, K., Stavy, R., & Wax, N. (1993). The development of biological knowledge: A multi-national study. *Cognitive Development, 8*(1), 47–62.

Hirschberg, C. (2010). *Wie Kinder trauern Kinder in ihrer Trauer begleiten. Wie Kinder trauern Kinder in ihrer Trauer begleiten*. Diakonisches Werk der Evangelischen Kirche in Deutschland e. V.

Hofmeister, H., Miehe, D., Hapke, C., & Schilling, B. (1982). Lebendig oder nicht? *Unterricht Biologie, 6*, 15–20.

Horowitz, M. J., Siegel, B., Holen, A., Bonanno, G. A., Milbrath, C., & Stinson, C. H. (1997). Diagnostic criteria for traumatic grief disorder. *American Journal of Psychiatry, 154*(7), 904–910.

Hummer, K. M. (1988). Johnny: mobilizing a child's capacity to mourn by means of psychotherapy. In S. Altschul (Ed.), *Childhood bereavement and its aftermath*. Emotions and Behavior Monographs, No. 8. Madison/CT: International Universities Press.

Inagaki, K., & Hatano, G. (2002). *Young children's naïve thinking about the biological world (essays in Developmental Psychology)*. Psychology Press-Taylor and Francis Group.

Iskenius-Emmler, H. (1988). *Psychologische Aspekte von Tod und Trauer bei Kindern und Jugendlichen*. Europäische Hochschulschriften, Reihe VI, Psychologie, Bd. 263. Frankfurt a. M., Bern, New York, Paris: Peter Lang.

Jackson, E. N. (1979). Bereavement and grief. In H. Wass (Ed.), *Dying. Facing the facts* (pp. 256–281). Hemisphere Publishing Corporation.

Jacobs, S. (1999). *Traumatic grief. Diagnosis, treatment, and prevention*. Brunner/Mazel.

Kaffman, M., & Elizur, E. (1984). Children's bereavement reactions following death of the father. *International Journal of Family Therapy, 6*(4), 259–283.

Kaffman, M., & Elizur, E. (1996). Bereavement as a significant stressor in children. In C. R. Pfeffer (Ed.), *Severe stress and mental disturbance in children* (pp. 591–628). American Psychiatric Press.

Kalter, N., Lohnes, K. L., Chasin, J., Cain, A. C., Dunning, S., & Rowan, J. (2002/03). The adjustment of parentally bereaved children: I. factors associated with short-term adjustment. *Omega–Journal of Death and Dying, 46*(1), 15–34.

Kast, V. (1985). *Trauern. Phasen und Chancen des psychischen Prozesses*. Kreuz.

Kast, V. (1990). Verlust, Ablösung und Trauer im therapeutischen Prozess. *Integrative Therapie, 3*, 174–190.

Kast, V. (1992). Unfähig zu trauern? In R. Schmitz-Scherzer (Ed.), *Altern und Sterben* (pp. 105–115). Hans Huber.

Katz, S., & Florian, V. (1986/87). A comprehensive theoretical model of psychological reaction to loss. *International Journal of Psychiatry in Medicine, 16*(4), 325–345.

Keil, F. C. (1991). The emergence of theoretical beliefs as constraints on concepts. *The epigenesis of mind*, 237–256.

Kelley, P. (2001). *Trost in der Trauer. Ein Begleitbuch*. München: Droemersche Verlagsanstalt (Originalarbeit erschienen 1997: Companions to grief).

Kenyon, B. L. (2001). Current research in Childrens conceptions of death: A critical review. *OMEGA–Journal of Death and Dying, 43*(1), 63–91. https://doi.org/10.2190/0x2b-b1n9-a579-dvk1

Kliman, G. (1980). *Seelische Katastrophen und Notfälle im Kindesalter*. Frankfurt a. M.

Klingberg, G. (1957). The distinction between living and not living among 7–10-year-old children, with some remarks concerning the so-called animism controversy. *The Journal of Genetic Psychology, 90*(2), 227–238.

Klingensmith, S. W. (1953). Child animism: What the child means by "alive". *Child Development, 24*, 51–61.

Koocher, G. P., & Gudas, L. J. (1992). Grief and loss in childhood. In C. E. Walker & M. C. Roberts (Eds.), *Handbook of clinical child psychology* (2nd ed., pp. 1025–1034). Wiley.

Elisabeth, K.-R. (1969). *On death and dying* (1st ed.). The Macmillan Company.

Lamers, E. P. (1995). Helping children during bereavement. In I. B. Corless, B. B. Germino, & M. A. Pittman (Eds.), *A challenge for living. Dying, death, and bereavement* (pp. 203–220). Jones & Bartlett.

Langenmayr, A. (2013). *Einführung in die Trauerbegleitung*. Vandenhoeck & Ruprecht.

Larbig, V. W. (1974). Zum Kindlichen Todeserleben Und Zur Situation Des Todkranken Kindes Im Krankenkaus. *Praxis der Kinderpsychologie und Kinderpsychiatrie, 23*(7), 245–255.

Laurendeau, M., & Pinard, A. (1962). *Causal thinking in the child: A genetic and experimental approach*. Int.

Lenhardt, A. M., & McCourt, B. (2000). Adolescent unresolved grief in response to the death of a mother. *Professional School Counsell, 3*(3), 189–196.

Lev, E. L., & McCorkle, R. (1998). Loss, grief, and bereavement in family members of cancer patients. *Seminars in Oncology Nursing, 14*(2), 145–151.

Levang, E. (2002). *Männer trauern anders*. Freiburg im Breisgau: Herder (Originalarbeit erschienen 1998: When men grieve. Why men grieve differently & how you can help).

Lord, J. H. (1999). *Nicht einmal ein Abschiedswort. Trauer nach einem unerwarteten Todesfall*. Zürich: Kreuz (Originalarbeit erschienen 1998: No time for goodbyes: coping with sorrow, anger, and injustice after a tragic death).

Luecken, L. J. (1998). Childhood attachment and loss experiences affect cardiovascular and cortisol function. *Psychosomatic Medicine, 60*(6), 765–772.

Luecken, L. J. (2000a). Parental caring and loss during childhood and adult cortisol responses to stress. *Psychology and Health, 15*, 841–851.

Luecken, L. J. (2000b). Attachement and loss experiences during childhood are associated with adult hostility, depression, and social support. *Journal of Psychosomatic Research, 49*(1), 85–91.

Mandler, J. M. (1992). How to build a baby: II. Conceptual primitives. *Psychological review, 99*(4), 587.

McGoldrick, M. (1992). Verluste im Kontext verstehen. In J. Schweitzer, A. Retzer & H. R. Fischer (Hrsg.), *Systemische Praxis und Postmoderne* (S. 118–135). Frankfurt a. M.: Suhrkamp.

Menke, E. M. (2002). Handling children's grief at the first anniversary. *Journal of Pediatric Health Care, 16*(5), 267–271.

Mitscherlich, A., & Mitscherlich, M. (1967). *Die Unfähigkeit zu trauern Grundlagen kollektiven Verhaltens*. R. Piper &.

Mittag, O. (1992). Psychologische und psychotherapeutische Aspekte der Trauer. *Psychotherapie, Psychosomatik, Medizinische Psychologie, 42*(5), 150–157.

Moebius, M. (1985). Trauer. Die bittere Zeit des Leidens. *Psychologie Heute, 12*(11), 48–55.

Montada, L. (1987). Kapitel 8-Die geistige Entwicklung aus der Sicht Jean Piagets.

Morin, S. M., & Welsh, L. A. (1996). Adolescents' perceptions and experiences of death and grieving. *Adolescence, 31*(123), 585–595.

Nagy, M. (1948). The child's theories concerning death. *Journal of Genetic Psychology, 73*, 3–27.

Nindler, A. (2014). Wenn eine Welt zusammenbricht .... *Zeitschrift Für Psychodrama Und Soziometrie, 13*(1), 51–66. https://doi.org/10.1007/s11620-014-0217-1

Parnes, E. (1975). Effects of experience with loss and death among preschool children. *Children Today, 4*, 2–7.

Paulley, J. W. (1983). Pathological mourning: A key factor in the psychopathogenesis of autoimmune disorders. *Psychotherapy and Psychosomatics, 40*(1–4), 181–190.

Plieth, M. (2001a). *Kind und Tod*. Zum Umgang mit kindlichen Schreckensvorstellungen und Hoffnungsbildern.

Piaget, J. (1926). *The language and thought of the child (M. Warden, Trans.)*. New York.

Piaget, J. (1936). The origins of intelligence in children. Trans. M. Cook. New York: WW Norton.

Piaget, J. (1970). *Epistémologie des sciences de l'homme*.

Piaget, J. (1978). *Das Weltbild des Kindes* (Vol. 35.004). Klett-Cotta.

Poulin-Dubois, D., & Shultz, T. R. (1990). The infant's concept of agency: The distinction between social and nonsocial objects. *The Journal of Genetic Psychology, 151*(1), 77–90.

Pulaski, M. A. S. (1975). *Piaget: Eine Einführung in seine Theorien und sein Werk*. Otto Maier Verlag.

Premack, D. (1990). The infant's theory of self-propelled objects. *Cognition, 36*(1), 1–16.

Rando, T. A. (1993). *Treatment of complicated mourning*. Research Press.

Raphael, B. (1983). *The anatomy of bereavement*. Basic Books.

Reed, E. L. (1972). *Kinder fragen nach dem Tod.*. Quell Verlag.

Rudolph, M. (1979). *Wie ist das, wenn man tot ist?: mit Kindern über das Sterben reden*. Ravensburg.

Ryan-Wenger, N. M. (1990). Children's psychosomatic response to stress. In L. E. Arnold (Ed.), *Childhood stress* (pp. 109–140). Whiley.

Samuels, A. (1988). Parental death in childhood. In S. Altschul (Hrsg.), *Childhood bereavement and its aftermath*. Emotions and Behavior Monographs, No. 8. Madison: International Universities Press.

Sanchez, L., Fristad, M., Weller, R. A., Weller, E. B., & Moye, J. (1994). Anxiety in acutely bereaved prepubertal children. *Annals of Clinical Psychiatry, 6*(1), 39–43.

Schepker, R., Scherbaum, N., & Bergmann, F. (1995). Zur pathologischen Trauer bei Kindern nach frühem Tod eines Elternteils. *Kinderanalyse, 3*(3), 260–280.

Schmied, G. (1988). *Sterben und Trauern in der modernen Gesellschaft*. R. Piper.

Schweitzer, R., & Niedermann, A. (2000). Wenn Kinder dem Tod begegnen. (Heil)-Pädagogische Hilfestellungen für trauernde Kinder. *Vierteljahresschrift für Heilpädagogik und ihre Nachbargebiete, 69*(2), 111–128.

Siegel, K., Raveis, V. H., & Karus, D. (1996). Pattern of communication with children when a parent has cancer. In L. Baider, C. L. Cooper, & A. K. De-Nour (Eds.), *Cancer and the family* (pp. 109–128). Wiley.

Silverman, P. R., & Worden, J. W. (1992). Children's reactions in the early months after the death of a parent. *American Journal of Orthopsychiatry, 62*(1), 93–104.

Smilansky, S. (1987). *On death. Helping understanding and cope*. Lang.

Sood, B., Weller, E. B., Weller, R. A., Fristad, M. A., & Bowes, J. M. (1992). Somatic complaints in grieving children. *Comprehensive Mental Health Care, 2*(1), 17–25.

Speece, M. W., & Brent, S. B. (1984). Children's understanding of death: A review of three components of a death concept. *Child Development, 55*, 1671–1686.

Specht-Tomann, M., & Tropper, D. (2001). *Zeit zu trauern. Kinder und Erwachsene verstehen und begleiten*. Patmos.

Stambrook, M., & Parker, K. C. (1987). The development of the concept of death in childhood: A review of the literature. *Merrill-Palmer Quarterly, (1982-)*, 133–152.

Steck, B., & Bürgin, D. (1996). Über die Unmöglichkeit zu trauern bei Kindern trauerkranker Eltern. *Kinderanalyse, 4*(4), 351–361.

Stern, M. M. (1983). *Death and the child. Schowalter, JE ua (Hrg.): The child and death (S. 9–26)*. Columbia Univ. Press.

Stillion, J., & Wass, H. (1979). Children and death. In H. Wass (Ed.), *Dying. Facing the facts* (pp. 208–235). Hemisphere Publishing Corporation.

Trevarthen, C. (1974). Conversations with a 2-month-old. *New Scientist, 22*, 230–235.

Venville, G. (2004). Young children learning about living things: A case study of conceptual change from ontological and social perspectives. *Journal of Research in Science Teaching: The Official Journal of the National Association for Research in Science Teaching, 41*(5), 449–480.

Versalle, A., & McDowell, E. E. (2005). The attitudes of men and women concerning gender differences in grief. *OMEGA–Journal of Death and Dying, 50*(1), 53–67. https://doi.org/10.2190/R2TJ-6M4F-RHGD-C2MD

Wagner, B. (2014). Diagnose der komplizierten Trauer. In *Komplizierte Trauer* (pp. 13–32). Springer Medizin.

Wayment, H. A., & Vierthaler, J. (2002). Attachment style and bereavement reactions. *Journal of Loss and Trauma, 7*(2), 129–149.

Weiß, S. (2006). *Die Trauer von Kindern, Jugendlichen und jungen Erwachsenen um den verstorbenen Vater* (dissertation).

Wellman, H. M., & Gelman, S. A. (1992). Cognitive development: Foundational theories of core domains. *Annual Review of Psychology, 43*(1), 337–375.

Wendt, W. (1984a). Trauerarbeit. In *Tod, Sterben, Trauer* (S. 352–357). Frankfurt.

Wessel, M. A. (1996). When children mourn a loved one. In H. M. Spiro, M. G. M. Curnen, & L. P. Wandel (Eds.), *Facing death. Where culture, religion, and medicine meet* (pp. 77–80). Yale University Press.

Winkel, H. (2002). Trauer ist doch ein großes Gefühl . . . . In *Zur biographiegenerierenden Funktion von Verlusterfahrungen und der Codierung von Trauerkommunikation*. UVK Verlagsgesellschaft.

Wittkowski, J. (1990). *Psychologie des Todes*. Wissenschaftliche Buchgesellschaft.

Wittwer, H., Schäfer, D., & Frewer, A. (2010). Trauer (kulturhistorisch und psychologisch). In *Sterben und Tod. Ein interdisziplinäres Handbuch* (S. 192–202). J.B. Metzler.

Wolf, D. (1991). *Einen geliebten Menschen verlieren. Vom schmerzlichen Umgang mit der Trauer*. PAL Verlagsgesellschaft.

Zerbe, K. J., & Steinberg, D. L. (2000). Coming to terms with grief and loss. *Postgraduate Medicine, 108*(6), 97–106.

Zlotowicz, M., & Redie, R. (1983). *Warum haben Kinder Angst?*. Klett-Cotta.

Znoj, H. (2004). *Komplizierte Trauer*. Hogrefe.

3.2 Grief among Adolescents

Becker, U., & Shah, H. (2008). *Vom Umgang mit Trauer in der Schule. Handreichung für Lehrkräfte und Erzieher/innen* (S. 6–37). Stuttgart: Ministerium für Kultur, Jugend und Sport Baden-Wüttemberg.

Bundesarbeitsgemeinschaft Trauerbegleitung (BAT). (2019). Trauer und Trauerphasen. Accessed Nov 23, 2019, from https://www.trauerbegleiten.at/trauernde-trauer

Der Sonntag, & Harringer, A. (2017). Jugendliche trauern anders. Accessed Nov 23, 2019, from https://www.erzdioezese-wien.at/site/servicehilfe/werhilftmir/trauer/article/60745.html

Diebold, R. (2013). *Trauerbegleitung von Jugendlichen: Bausteine professionellen Handlungswissens in der offenen Jugendarbeit*. Springer VS. https://doi.org/10.1007/978-3-658-02057-6_4

Fleck-Bohaumilitzky, C. (2004b). Wie Kinder Tod und Trauer erleben. *Das Familienhandbuch des Staatsinstituts für Frühpädagogik (IFP).*. https://link.springer.com/chapter/10.1007/978-3-642-20934-5_15

Göppel, R. (2005). *Das Jugendalter: Entwicklungsaufgaben, Entwicklungskrisen, Bewältigungsformen*. Kohlhammer.

Kessels, U. (2013). Jugend. In S. Andresen, C. Hunner-Kreisel, & S. Fries (Eds.), *Erziehung*. Metzler.

Klass, D., Silverman, P. R., & Nickman, S. (2014). *Continuing bonds: New understandings of grief*. Taylor & Francis.

Kriebel, R., Paar, G. H., & Stäcker, K. H. (1996). Somatisierung. *Psychotherapeut, 41*(4), 201–214. https://doi.org/10.1007/s278-1996-8107-x

Luthe, S. (2016). Trauerarbeit online. Facebook als Generator für Erinnerungen. In T. Klie & I. Nord (Hrsg.), *Tod und Trauer im Netz. Mediale Kommunikationen in der Bestattungskultur*. Stuttgart: Kohlhammer.

Maslow, A. H. (1943). A theory of human motivation. *Psychological Review, 50*(4), 370.

Offerhaus, A., Keithan, K., & Kimmer, A. (2013). Trauerbewältigung online: Praktiken und Motive der Nutzung von Trauerforen. *SWS-Rundschau, 53*(3), 275–297.

Plieth, M. (2001b). *Kind und Tod. Zum Umgang mit kindlichen Schreckensvorstellungen und Hoffnungsbildern*. Neukirchener Verlag.

Riedeberger, S. (2016). 11 Tipps für den Umgang mit Trauernden. *Edition F*. Accessed Jun 29, 2020, from https://editionf.com/11-tipps-fuer-den-umgang-mit-trauernden/

Rimé, B. (2009). Emotion elicits the social sharing of emotion: Theory and empirical review. *Emotion Review, 1*(1), 60–85. https://doi.org/10.1177/1754073908097189

Röseberg, F., & Müller, M. (2014). *Handbuch Kindertrauer. Die Begleitung von Kindern Jugendlichen und ihren Familien*. Vandenhoeck & Ruprecht GmbH & KG.

Sieck, A. (2010). *Trauer bewältigen: Tod und Trauer verstehen. Wieder ins Leben zurückfinden. Mit der Erinnerung leben*. Hannover: Schlütersche.

Wendt, W. (1984b). Trauerarbeit. In J. Howe & R. Ochsmann (Hrsg.), *Tod–Sterben–Trauer* (S. 352–357). Bericht über die 1. Tagung zur Thanato-Psychologie vom 4.-6. November 1982 in Vechta. Frankfurt a. M.: Fachbuchhandlung für Psychologie.

Witt-Loers, S. (2009). Sterben, Tod und Trauer in der Schule. In *Eine Orientierungshilfe*. Vandenhoeck & Ruprecht GmbH & KG.

Witt-Loers, S. (2014). *Trauernde Jugendliche innerhalb der Familie*. Vandenhoeck & Ruprecht GmbH & KG.

Worden, J. W. (2018). *Grief counseling and grief therapy: A handbook for the mental health practitioner*. Springer Publishing Company.

Causes of Grief

Justine Hubertus, Katharina Schneider, Katharina Barcatta, Anna-Lynn Schlund, Lena Schwind, Vera Hilger, Jan Hamborg, and Charlotte Ries

4.1 Chronic Diseases

Justine Hubertus and Katharina Schneider

This chapter deals with serious chronic illnesses among students and what effects and consequences these have for the school. In this context, the school not only bears a great responsibility for paying attention to these problems, but also offers an optimally suitable framework for psychological interventions in dealing with grief.

In the following, we will explain what is meant by a chronic or serious chronic illness and why the topic of chronic illness plays a role, especially in the context of schools, and what teachers or parents can do to support the affected children and adolescents.

4.1.1 What Is it? And why Do we Talk about it?

A chronic disease is a long-lasting, possibly even lifelong, serious or incurable disease.

According to the "Chroniker-Richtlinie" of the Joint Federal Committee (Gemeinsamen Bundesausschusses, G-BA) of physicians, psychotherapists, hospitals and health insurance funds in Germany (n.d.), a disease is severely chronic if it requires long-term treatment (for at least one year, at least once per quarter) and one of the following three criteria is also met:

J. Hubertus (✉) · K. Schneider · K. Barcatta · A.-L. Schlund · L. Schwind · V. Hilger · J. Hamborg · C. Ries
Department of Behavioural and Cognitive Sciences, University of Luxembourg, Esch-sur-Alzette, Luxembourg
e-mail: justine.hubertus.001@student.uni.lu; katharina.barcatta.002@student.uni.lu; lena.schwind.001@student.uni.lu; jan.hamborg.001@student.uni.lu

© Springer-Verlag GmbH Germany, part of Springer Nature 2022
M. Böhmer, G. Steffgen (eds.), *Grief in Schools*,
https://doi.org/10.1007/978-3-662-64297-9_4

1. Specified minimum degree of need for care,
2. Some degree of disability, consequence of injury or reduction in earning capacity,
3. Expectation of a life-threatening exacerbation, reduced life expectancy, or permanent impairment of quality of life without ongoing care (medical, psychotherapeutic, nursing, and/or medication).

At this point it should be noted that chronic diseases can be both somatic and psychological in nature, whereby the psyche and the body can influence each other. It is assumed that the majority of chronic diseases are congenital, i.e. inherited or acquired prenatally. In the majority of cases, a chronic impairment is diagnosed at birth or in early childhood and thus already plays a role in kindergarten and school age. For this reason, they cannot be ignored in the context of school. It is therefore unavoidable to deal with the topic in the field of school.

4.1.1.1 Disease Progression

An acute illness may be accompanied by a temporary loss of autonomy, social participation and capacity to act. However, this phase tends to be short-lived if the ill person is resting and/or taking therapeutic measures (e.g. medication). In contrast, chronically ill patients experience a very dynamic course of the disease. Table 4.1 shows the typical stages that characterize the course of chronic diseases with a fatal outcome.

A serious chronic disease can remain continuously in one stage, e.g. infantile cerebral palsy, a movement disorder caused by early childhood brain damage. However, a disease can also be chronic-recurrent, i.e. it can flare up again and again in episodes, which is the case with chronic inflammatory bowel diseases, or, as in cystic fibrosis, it can take a progressive course, i.e. it progressively worsens. However, consistent therapy can slow down the course of the disease and thus increase the quality of life and life expectancy of people suffering from cystic fibrosis.

The presentation of the course of a chronic disease makes it clear that the patients, their relatives and their everyday lives are permanently affected. The dynamic course of the disease demands a great deal of patience and adaptability from all involved.

4.1.1.2 Frequency

Physical chronic diseases in childhood and adolescence are functional disorders of the metabolism (e.g. diabetes or cystic fibrosis), of an organ system (e.g. cardiovascular system, muscles, bones or sensory organs) and/or of the immune system (e.g. allergies, inflammatory bowel diseases or tumours). Definitions of chronic disease vary with respect to the duration of the disease and the curability aspect.

If we look at the figures of current epidemiological studies, we can assume that, depending on the diagnoses to be included and the methodological precision in the recording of the diseases, on average 5 to 40% of all children and adolescents can be diagnosed with a chronic physical disease and/or a disability, whereby the frequency distributions vary internationally due to environmental factors and a different genetic

Table 4.1 Course of disease (Haslbeck et al., 2015)

Onset of the disease (gradual or acute phase)	– First signs and symptoms of a chronic disease – First contact with doctors/other specialists – Diagnosis (can take months/years) – Physical and mental impairments – Complications due to illness, if any – Medical treatments or longer hospital stays
Crisis	– Partially life-threatening situations – Active shaping of everyday life not possible – Frequent states of shock and disorientation
Normalization	– Usually after acute crisis situations – Physical and emotional recovery – Goal of the patients: recovery of physical well-being and functional capacity – After overcoming the state of shock and confusion → Attempt to regain balance in everyday life
Disease state: stable and unstable	Stable phases (compensated state) – The course of the disease does not change for the better or for the worse (persistence in one stage) – Malfunctions can be compensated by appropriate therapeutic measures – Objective to maintain this state	Unstable phases (decompensation) – Disease progression and symptoms can no longer be kept under control – Characterize course of disease (illustrate erratic character), but do not necessarily occur
Deterioration and dying	– Course of the disease slowly or quickly becomes significantly worse – Increasingly difficult to control pace and extent of deteriorating disease state – Hardly any active action possible – Dealing with the question of preparation for death – Dying phase: hours/days/weeks immediately before death

background. According to the Federal Centre for Health Education (Bundeszentrale für Gesundheitliche Aufklärung, BZgA), 5 to 10% of all children in Germany are affected by a chronic disease.

If one looks at the values collected on the time axis, it can also be seen that the number of chronic diseases in the western industrialized countries has increased significantly in recent years. This applies above all to allergies and autoimmune diseases. Crohn's disease is also being diagnosed with increasing frequency. The incidence of inflammatory bowel disease is approximately 25–50: 100,000 (Hoß & Maier, 2013). Cystic fibrosis, one of the most common congenital metabolic diseases, has a frequency of 1: 2500. This means that chronic diseases in childhood and adolescence are rarer but more varied than in adults.

4.1.2 Interventions

4.1.2.1 Guide to the Delivery of the Message

With the diagnosis of a serious chronic disease (e.g. cystic fibrosis, inflammatory bowel disease, cancer), the grieving process begins for the children and adolescents as well as their family and environment. It is to be expected that the announcement of the diagnosis of a serious or incurable illness triggers a psychological stress reaction that is not necessarily expressed verbally. After a first and second phase of shock that can be characterized by insensibility, a feeling of emptiness, the impression of dreaming or denial of the problem ("phase of shock" and "phase of denial"), different reactions such as fear, shock, pain, anger or despair can occur and be perceived (Mehmke, 2016; Adler et al., 2003). In this third phase ("outburst of intense feelings"), different thoughts may arise such as the search for someone to blame ("Why me?"), fearful thoughts of death, abandonment or no longer being loved, up to suicidal thoughts (Mehmke, 2016; Adler et al., 2003). At the same time, parents are burdened with the diagnosis. New fears and uncertainties arise regarding the child's or adolescent's coping with the disease (Mehmke, 2016). In this situation, doctors strive to encourage those affected to open up and express their feelings and thoughts and, if necessary, can refer them to professional support services such as hospital chaplains or psychooncologists (Adler et al., 2003). In this difficult phase, it is also important to strengthen the feeling of hope. In this case, one speaks less of hope in the prolongation of life expectancy, which inevitably decreases in the case of an unfavourable course of the disease, but rather of hope in maintaining the abilities, integrity and integration in the community of the person (Adler et al., 2003), which in the case of children and adolescents means that school also plays an important role in maintaining "normality" for those affected. Thus, in addition to the affected family, teachers are also faced with the question of how to deal with the diagnosis at school. It is essential that the teacher agrees with the family on how to communicate the diagnosis and the illness. The way in which the diagnosis is communicated to the class can vary (Etschenberg et al., n.d.):

1. Inform the classmates that the sick person cannot participate in everything for health reasons (in the future) and that he/she should not or cannot make an effort, and that the sick person decides what measures will be taken and that the classmates must stay out of it. The illness is not mentioned by name.
   Advantages:
   - Small time expenditure
   - If the class is satisfied with the vague information and the behaviour towards the sick person works as discussed, the teacher does not have to do anything more.
     Disadvantages:
   - Speculation among children/young people and in parents' homes about the possible diagnosis, which can lead to misinformation or rumours
   - Rumours and misinformation can be even worse for the ill person than the disclosure of the diagnosis (e.g. exclusion up to bullying).

2. Another way of breaking the news to the class would be, in addition to communicating the diagnosis and some rules of conduct, to plan a lesson in which something can be said about the nature and development of the disease. This lesson is then not intended for the person with the disease, as in most cases he is well informed about his disease.

Advantages:
- For the classmates and indirectly the corresponding parents, a simple explanation of the illness can counteract rumours and lead to the desired contact with the ill person.
- Students understand why new behaviors need to be integrated into the school day.
- Sick person can decide whether he or she wants to share his or her experiences orally or whether the teacher presents the illness in a general way

Disadvantages:
- The teacher must be well acquainted with the subject matter and adapt the way in which knowledge is imparted to the age group of the class.
- Greater expenditure of time

Some points should be considered when communicating the diagnosis (Etschenberg, n.d.; DHPV, 2017):

Regarding the sick child or adolescent:
- The overall atmosphere of the class is very crucial in deciding whether the person with the illness wants to talk about the diagnosis,
- it is important to discuss with the child or young person concerned which way of imparting knowledge is most comfortable,
- one is allowed to express one's own speechlessness and to perceive and communicate one's own limitations,
- attentively distinguish between compassion and pity

Regarding classmates:
- It is helpful to establish rules of conversation before the class discussion, such as: "treat each other with respect", "let each other finish", "issues raised remain in the group", so that openness can be encouraged in the class,
- A wide range of emotions of grief can occur, similar to those of the person affected. It is therefore important to provide a space where students can ask questions or express their feelings and thoughts. It is therefore very important to listen carefully,
- Communicate with the students at eye level,
- It is also a good idea to give the students the opportunity to collect topics or questions related to the disease over a certain period of time and then discuss them together in the class, as they might be overwhelmed by the news at first.

General notes:
- The diagnosis may not be made public without the written consent of the parents,
- Avoid statements about the prognosis of the child/adolescent's chronic illness,
- "Embellished" statements should be avoided, as affected children and adolescents then do not feel that they are being taken seriously,
- No derogatory or critical remarks regarding the use of medication,

- Discussions about forms of therapy in the class are prohibited. If the teacher has doubts about the chosen form of therapy, then this should only be discussed with the parents, if at all.

4.1.2.2 School Psychological Coping

A child or adolescent with a life-threatening chronic disease often represents an additional burden for educators. Very rarely are teachers prepared to deal with such a situation. What is stressful in this context is that they feel and partly are co-responsible as long as the child or adolescent is in their care. Furthermore, they have to make additional considerations regarding the school day, the scheduling of lessons and an individually fair assessment of performance. Another stressful point is that the affected child or young person needs a certain amount of observation, but this should not be perceived as too overprotective of the affected person. In order to meet these additional needs, it is very important to deal with the illness and its symptoms in detail in order to be prepared for illness- or therapy-related behavioural peculiarities and to find an appropriate limit for the physical and mental demands on the child or adolescent (Etschenberg, n.d.).

In the following section, the focus is on the difficulties of the dynamic course of the disease before the subsequent part deals with the preparation for the final phase of the disease.

After receiving the diagnosis, a difficult time begins for the children and adolescents with a life-shortening illness, in which they learn to deal with the loss of abilities and dreams for the future and must come to terms with their own dying and death. After diagnosis, support through hospice-directed and palliative treatment and accompaniment, as well as their integration into the everyday life of the ill person, can lead to a better quality of life (DHPV, 2017). These services are divided into outpatient hospice services, palliative care units, specialized outpatient palliative care (SOPC) and inpatient hospices (Table 4.2), all of which can be used from the time of diagnosis and can often last for years (DHPV, 2017).

The German Hospice and Palliative Association (Deutscher Hospiz- und Palliativ Verband e. V.) has set itself the task of encouraging parents, teachers and educators to expand their competencies in order to deal with the topics of dying, death and mourning with children and adolescents through their project "Learning Hospice". As shown in previous chapters, loss, serious illnesses, dying and death of a close person or of fellow students and teachers have an impact on one's own life situation as well as on the common school community, and can possibly lead to a crisis. The DHPV demands support for action competences and strategies, as it has been determined that similar to the social attitude towards death and mourning, day care centres and schools also tend to avoid and taboo. This support is made possible by a preventive approach that systematically imparts knowledge, skills and attitudes.

Table 4.2 Hospice and palliative treatment (Hospizverein Bamberg e. V., 2020)

Outpatient hospice service	– Accompaniment of seriously ill, dying and grieving people – Counselling of affected persons and their relatives – Hospice companions are trained volunteers who are committed to their work. – Accompanies people in their own homes, in institutions for the elderly and disabled, clinics and palliative care wards.
Palliative care unit	– Admission by medical referral in the case of a life-limiting illness with distressing concomitant symptoms – Medical and nursing treatment – Relief of agonizing concomitant symptoms and individual support to improve the quality of life – Accompaniment and counseling regarding pain relief, discharge planning to the home, and the dying situation.
SOPC Specialized outpatient palliative care	– Prescription by general practitioner or hospital practitioner on discharge in the case of life-limiting illness with distressing concomitant symptoms – Team of palliative trained nurses and doctors – 24-hour on-call service – Look after people at home or in facilities for the elderly and disabled – "Palliative care on wheels"
Inpatient hospice	– People in the final stages of a disease – Enabling a dignified, self-determined life to the end – Work follows the principles of palliative care, i.e. palliative care to achieve the best possible quality of life and to make pain more bearable.

4.1.2.2.1 Individual and Group Interventions and Training of Teachers

In the following, the offers of the DHPV are presented in more detail. These support the educators, the fellow students and the sick person in dealing with death and grief in an age-appropriate way after the announcement of the diagnosis. They make it possible to create a framework in which the children and young people can talk about the subject without fear of judgement.

Daycare and school projects for children and adolescents—"Give me a little bit of security"—Hospice projects with children and adolescents (GmS).

This concept was developed in 2011 by the Malteser Hospizprojekte and offers on the one hand information with experience reports on dying and mourning and on hospice work and on the other hand elaborated project days (–weeks; –cycles) on which knowledge and self-experience parts on the topic of dying, death and mourning are worked out. This offer can be adapted to local conditions and takes place in consultation with kindergartens, primary schools, secondary schools, parishes, e.g. as project days in connection with parents' evenings, teacher training or as visits in individual lessons.

"Hospice makes school"—a concept for primary school pupils in the third and fourth grade.

This project was initiated in 2005 by the hospice movement Düren-Jülich e. V. as part of the federal model program "Intergenerational Volunteer Services" with the DHPV. The

Table 4.3 Structure of the project days (Bayerisches Staatsministerium für Bildung und Kultus, Wissenschaft und Kunst, 2015, p. 70–71)

Day one: Becoming and passing away (transformation experience)	– Get to know the course of the week – Introduction of a ritual that is observed throughout the week at the beginning and end (ribbon tying and singing). – Finding access to the theme of the week: Reading text—Zaira's journey to heaven – Based on the development of caterpillar-doll-butterfly deal with transformation experiences – Identify their own development and the development of the hospice companions on the basis of the photographs they have brought with them and recognise as a person's development that dying is part of life
Day two: Sickness and suffering	– Feedback on the previous day – Report about own experiences with diseases – Be able to name diseases – Pantomime diseases – Prepare questions for a visit to a doctor – Working out what is good for a sick person and what everyone can do for it
Day three: Dying and death	– Feedback on the previous day – Using a sequence of pictures to find access to the dying process ("is grandpa wearing a suit?"- Amelie fried) – Discuss experiences and questions about death and dying – Through the film Willi will's Wissen (Willi wants to know), learn about voluntary care for the dying and the work of a funeral director. – Getting to know one's own idea of the afterlife and that of different cultures
Day four: From being sad	– Feedback on the previous day – Perceive feelings of grief – Depicting and describing feelings of grief – Recognize that mourning means saying goodbye in order to start anew (plants are repotted)
Day five: Comfort and consolation Graduation	– Feedback on the previous day – Developing awareness and sensitivity to forms of consolation – Write comfort letters – Developing what the class community can do when a classmate is not well – Visit to a cemetery – Experience togetherness in celebration (celebration of life prepared by parents and relatives) – Children present the week to their parents using the posters on the themes of

aim of this offer is to accompany the children in dealing with dying, mourning and death. This preventive project runs over five days and deals with the themes of becoming and passing away, illness and suffering, dying and death, being sad, comfort and consolation (Table 4.3). Five qualified volunteers and the class teacher introduce these topics to the pupils in a playful way through small groups, creative design, making music, dialogical interaction, quiet work and movement. During these five days, the children keep a learning diary in which they can collect their impressions, among other things. Before the five project days, a parents' evening takes place in which family structures are taken into account.

"At last—Dealing with dying, death and mourning"- A concept for pupils in grades 9 to 13.

This concept was developed in 2009 in the Centre for Palliative Medicine at the University Hospital of Cologne (Uniklinik Köln). It is continuously discussed, evaluated and further developed with experts from the federal, state and local authorities. In the so-called project lessons, the students exchange ideas about dying, mourning and suicide with each other using different methods and action strategies. In addition, they are introduced to the professional and voluntary support services for seriously ill people. In the so-called multiplier training, teachers from all types of schools and employees from psychosocial teams (e.g. school social work, school psychology, pastoral care or employees from the hospice and palliative sector) receive a qualification that authorizes them to conduct the project lessons at the schools.

Training and Further Education for Educators
On life, illness, dying, death, mourning and loss—"Life, dying, death and mourning in school"—further training for teachers.

Since 2004, teachers, school staff, school social workers and school psychologists have been able to participate in seminars to understand that death and mourning are part of the school culture. The focus of the seminar is to sensitize and strengthen the school staff so that they can support the chronically ill children and adolescents in the phase before death and in the mourning situation. The seminar will therefore discuss the life situation of children and adolescents with life-threatening chronic illnesses and their families. It will also be discussed how the grief of children and adolescents with disabilities differs from other children without disabilities, which supportive rituals and symbols can be used meaningfully for classes and school communities and how the deceased can be remembered and commemorated at school. Another essential aspect of the seminar is the topic of parental work.

The ultimate goal of this seminar is to make the topic of death and mourning less fearful and to give educators the confidence to perceive and support children and young people appropriately.

In their manual, Sitte and Stöbener (2017) provide further didactic possibilities for entering into the topic of death and dying in the classroom. For example, they suggest using story cubes to pursue an associative approach. The story cubes are cubes that have a symbol on each side that can be associated with the topic of dying and death (e.g. shooting star, scales, sad face). Other methods for teaching include using pictures, mind maps and flash rounds to gather different opinions on the topic as a class. They also suggest more creative approaches, such as using and creating quotes or even pavement painting to express thoughts and feelings about the topic of dying and death. For education about hospice work and palliative care, they suggest cloze texts and offer templates for these. To stimulate discussion, in addition to flashlight rounds, materials can also be used for an "opinion poll" in which students can state their opinions on various topics related to dying and death on a scale from "strongly agree" to "strongly disagree". Example questions are "It makes me uncomfortable to think about the topic of dying and death" or "I have personally had to deal with this topic in the last five years (e.g. death of a relative)". In addition, interviews with seriously ill children and adolescents can be found in the manual, so that it can be used to work out what emotions ill children and adolescents are confronted with and what their opinion is on topics such as euthanasia and hospices or palliative care, which is a good way of gaining an insight into the life of a chronically ill person in school classes in which there is no ill child.

4.1.2.2.2 Dealing with Difficulties in Everyday Life

For children and adolescents, attendance at daycare or school is firmly integrated into everyday life. For those who are ill, this daily routine changes due to hospital stays and poor physical and mental health (DHPV, 2017). As a result, they cannot always pursue their urge to move, play and learn or discover new things together with their peers. In most cases, children and adolescents with life-shortening illnesses are required to be more independent and to take on additional tasks. Goals that lie in the future are questioned by the person with the illness, with individual plans and dreams having to change, as the altered reality means that wishes and needs have to be adapted to the physical and psychosocial condition (DHPV, 2017). Most affected children and adolescents have a long course of illness ahead of them, in which they steadily lose abilities and life functions, leading to a great deal of grief for those affected and those around them. Therefore, it is important to pay attention to the age-appropriate life impulses and to support a creation of meaning (DHPV, 2017).

▶ **Special features in adolescents (Dachverband (DLFH) & Deutsche Krebsstiftung,** 2014)

Older adolescents find themselves in a time in which they are actually detaching themselves from home, pushed by the disease back into the role of the child with greater dependence and also realize how much they need parental care. Here it is important for the parents to strike the right balance between love, security and courage and at the same time to leave room for the independent personality of the person concerned and to let them participate in important decisions. When dealing with adolescents, it is very important to be honest and to inform them about the disease, the therapy and its consequences. At this age, changes in appearance (e.g. hair loss, stroma, weight fluctuations, amputations, etc.) can also be very stressful for young people. Psychological support is particularly important here. In this context, educators can strengthen the affected adolescents' sense of self-worth and belonging by allowing them to participate in school activities, if their health permits.This includes topics such as school, pursuing a professional activity, living independently of parents, partnership and sexuality. In contrast to healthy children and adolescents, those suffering from the disease cannot separate themselves from their parents due to the progression of the disease. The children and adolescents should therefore be enabled by their environment to perceive and express their own needs in order to promote their autonomy development and to enable the detachment process as far as possible (Zernikow et al., 2013).

▸ **Important** Siblings/"shadow children" (Jurack, 2009).

The siblings are also burdened by the situation and should therefore also be taken into account. Often their needs are pushed into the background due to the illness of their siblings ("shadow children").

1. Role change: younger siblings take care of older siblings
2. Care for the sick sibling
3. Siblings may no longer be available as discussion, play, conflict and coalition partners against the parents.
4. If applicable, envy and aggression
5. "Abandonment" of own development
6. fear for one's own well-being
7. Fear for the sick sibling

Throughout the course of the disease, it is important to give the child or adolescent the opportunity to express his or her grief reactions (e.g. anger, sadness, despair) (Droste & Hartekopf, 2013). Children and adolescents ask themselves how long they will live, whether they will be in pain, whether they will be alone when they die, what will happen after death, whether they will be missed and who will look after the bereaved when they are no longer there ("may I die?") (DHPV, 2017).

Depending on the progress of the disease, maintaining social contacts becomes more difficult, which can be attributed to the time restrictions due to hospital stays, for example, or to the fear of contact on the part of outsiders. However, many families also experience that friends and loved ones from the environment are an important support (DKHV, 2015) and that contact with people in similar situations can strengthen those affected (Jennessen et al., 2011). School in particular can promote social contact. However, questions arise for the ill person such as: "Can I still continue to go to school?", "Is my lifespan sufficient to complete my degree?", "Why do I still have to go to school if I am dying?", "Does everyone at school understand if I sometimes don't feel like learning or am aggressive because of my illness?", "Are there people at school I can talk to about death if I want to?", "How will I be remembered at school if I am dead?" (DHPV, 2017, P. 32). Parents are also concerned about whether teachers will be able to deal with the child and their illness, especially in the event of an emergency or whether there is any point at all in their child continuing in nursery or school (DHPV, 2017). These concerns of parents and, in some cases, children or adolescents can be alleviated by participating in hospice training and services (as presented), and the school can take steps to ensure appropriate management of the serious chronic illness (e.g., Crohn's disease, cystic fibrosis, cancer). This includes reminding and tolerating the taking of medication, allowing visits to the toilet during the lesson, tolerating missing homework, allowing participation in physical education taking into account physical deficits and tolerating when the student cannot participate in physical education (regular consultation with parents and the student is advised in this regard), compensation for disadvantages and understanding during longer hospital stays (Schönekerl, 2009).

4.1.2.2.3 Hospitalisation

As already mentioned, the children and young people suffer from the fact that they have to go to hospital more often, which is a frightening event for many (Blatt 2018). Also with regard to school, the question arises how to deal with absences due to the stay and how a disadvantage compensation can be handled when missing class work.

The following options were listed for cancer patients in the source used (Dachverband (DLFH) and Deutsche Krebsstiftung, 2014). However, they are also generally applicable to all diseases that lead to increased absenteeism due to longer periods in hospital (Hedderich & Tscheke, 2013), such as chronic inflammatory bowel diseases or cystic fibrosis (Table 4.4).

Compensation for disadvantages (Sticker & Grosser, 2016):

1. The compensation for disadvantages takes place both for certificates of achievement and for lessons in general.
2. Request for a disadvantage compensation is submitted to the school management by means of an (informal) written application by the legal guardian or the teaching pedagogue.
3. Design of the disadvantage compensation is individually adapted to the needs of the child or adolescent
4. Compensation for disadvantages should be designed according to the motto "as much normality as possible, as much support as necessary" (Sticker & Grosser, 2016, p. 11).
5. Compensation for disadvantages can take place at different levels:
    i. Technical level: e.g. provision of special working and auxiliary aids (e.g. the use of a computer, provided that this does not give an advantage over fellow pupils (e.g. through Internet access)).
    ii. Organisational level: e.g. extension of the processing time; additional breaks; exemption of the performance record in individual subjects or parts of a subject (e.g. in minor subjects); reduction of homework, due to the limited free time due to therapy and rest requirements
    iii. Structural level: e.g. replace written performance by oral performance; reduction of the number of tasks with the same level of difficulty; prefabricated handouts/scripts.
    iv. Physical relief: second set of school books in the school, so that no books have to be carried; special transport for pupils by school bus, if the sick person cannot manage

Table 4.4 Dealing with absenteeism (Hedderich & Tscheke, 2013)

Lessons in the clinic	– Entitlement from six weeks absence – Are taught by teachers in the clinic – Most of the time the teaching is done from the bedside or in small groups in a small furnished room. – The lessons are limited to the main subjects, as the patients are very busy with the side effects of the therapy and the many medical examinations and interventions during their stay in hospital.
Homeschooling	– Most states allow home schooling if the student will be ill for more than six weeks – Home schooling must be applied for at the responsible school supervisory authority and verified by a medical certificate.
Tutor	– Teacher of the home school is assigned
Contact between the sick pupil, fellow pupils and the teaching staff	– Contact through telephone calls, e-mails, new media, letters or regular visits – Contact between student and classmate allows the student to continue to be kept informed so that he or she still feels part of the class despite illness – Class teacher is responsible for informing the other teachers in most cases. – Through new media such as Skype, the sick student can participate in the lessons from his bedside.
Contact to the clinic	– It is very helpful to consult with the teacher of the hospital school about the structure of the lessons and the progress of the child/adolescent in order to avoid the emergence of large gaps in knowledge. – Exchanges between the clinic teacher, the home teacher, and the ill person can help to reduce anxiety about moving on to the next grade level
Return to school	– As a rule, the sick pupil can return to lessons immediately after inpatient therapy. – Depending on how physically limited the student is, it is recommended that the student initially attends school for only a few hours per day until they feel stronger both physically and mentally – In part, the affected persons are still very emotionally burdened and are afraid of a relapse. Therefore, the class climate should be kept in mind (avoidance of exclusion, isolation, bullying).

the way to school independently; organise sports lessons in such a way that the pupil is motivated to take part, but always has the possibility to take breaks or to stop if the state of illness does not allow it at that moment.

4.1.2.3 Dealing with Farewell and Preparation for Death

In the case of chronic illnesses, the big difference to sudden death is that a long illness process precedes death. For this reason, this book chapter has focused a great deal on the management of illness in the school context until death. However, mourning rituals and mourning reactions turn out to be similar to those in sudden death. The difference with sudden death, however, is that it is possible to support the grieving process through a variety of measures even before death occurs. If it becomes foreseeable that the illness has progressed to the point where it is clear that the person with the illness is going to die, the school can play an important role for the child or young person with the illness. By continuing to include the child, by continuing to offer that the child or young person can still come to lessons on an hourly basis or can continue to come to theatre performances, class parties or musical performances, pupils can continue to belong.

Organisations such as Make-A-Wish can also be supported by the school or the class community. Make-A-Wish is an international non-profit organization whose mission is to help seriously ill children and adolescents (ages 3–18) fulfill their heart's desire. Make-A-Wish sends the child a "Wish Box" that can be designed by the child and used to collect anything related to their heart's desire. Using the box, volunteers can work with the child or young person to identify what is important to them and talk about why different items, drawings, photos or similar are in the wish box. From these, the heart's desire that is right for the sick person is then selected. The organisation fulfils almost every wish and takes over the costs incurred (Make-A-Wish, 2020). Since the organization is financed by donations, it could be a nice gesture if a sick classmate is supported by a school-internal fundraising to fulfill the wish.

Considerations regarding the time after death begin even before the death. Especially questions and considerations regarding the participation of classmates in the funeral can be planned in advance in the case of chronic illnesses and discussed with the parents and the sick child or adolescent. It can be considered whether the classmates can say goodbye to the dying person at the deathbed or whether they may participate in the funeral (DHPV, 2017). If the classmates can participate in the funeral, it should also be discussed (in consultation with the parish and the family) whether the participation through speeches, the reading of intercessions, the singing of a song or a coffin gift is desired or not. In general, the decision and ideas of the family and the deceased are to be respected.

24 hours after being notified of the student's death, the teacher closest to the family of the deceased student should contact the bereaved family and offer condolences on behalf of the school (Bayerisches Staatsministerium für Bildung, Kultus, Wissenschaft und Kunst, 2015). Breaking the news to the teacher that the sick person has died will be very difficult and it is important that the teacher also takes time to perceive and accept their own grief. With regard to classmates, the grief reactions can be very different (see Chap. 3: Grief across the lifespan). Here it is very important that the different reactions are accepted. As a teacher, it is important to talk to students who want to talk, but to give space to others who do not. The topic should in no way be forced, as each child and young person processes grief individually. The organisation and participation of classmates in mourning

Table 4.5 Further measures to commemorate the deceased person. (Bayerisches Staatsministerium für Bildung, Kultus, Wissenschaft und Kunst, 2015)

Mourning table in the classroom	– The table of the deceased child or young person is decorated as a mourning table – The design is carried out by the classmates – Designed memorial materials can be given to the family of the deceased after the mourning period with the consent of the students. – Time frame for the bereavement table: taking into account the specific situation and the age of the student body: three to four weeks are recommended. – After dismantling the mourning table, the school table goes into table storage → This marks the beginning of a new era
Memorial in the assembly hall	– Place a picture of the deceased next to a candle at the memorial in the auditorium. – Classmates and teachers can design the memorial according to their own ideas (objects, handicrafts, etc.). – Depending on the religious affiliation of the deceased and the ideas of the group, the ritual is designed individually. – The items left behind can be given to the family of the deceased person – Other option permanent memorial: the photos, names and dates of the deceased are kept there until all students who knew the person have left the school.
More ideas	– Make small boats out of pieces of bark, load them with wishes for the deceased and place them in the river. – Plant a flower as a sign of new life – Craft a mourning candle – Shaping stones – Write a letter – Writing an article for the school newspaper – Write on or paint postcards with hopeful sayings for those who are grieving, collect helpful comforting items to fill a "comfort box" with. – Create a flower in memory of someone who has died: In the middle is the name of the deceased and in the seven petals the students write or paint their appearance, interests, characteristics, tasks, abilities and common memories.

ceremonies or funerals can help a lot in processing the loss. This allows classmates to say goodbye and realize that their reality has now changed. Especially for classmates who could no longer see the deceased due to a long absence from school, such a ritual is particularly meaningful in order to understand the situation more easily (Dachverband (DLFH) & Deutsche Krebsstiftung, 2014). If the family has expressed the wish in advance that the kindergarten group or school class should not attend the funeral, other measures (Table 4.5) can be taken to commemorate the deceased classmate, some of which can be determined together with the child or young person before the death.

After the death of their child, many families find it positive if those around them continue to remember the anniversary of the birth and death. Here, however, it is different

Table 4.6 Differences between normal coping with death and traumatic grief (Raphael et al., 2006)

	Normal coping with death	Traumatic grief
Cognitive	– Focus on the deceased person – Focus on images of the deceased person – Need to talk about the lost person – Comforting memories and dreams	– Focus on death/dying – Presentation of the events – Avoidance of talking about the loss – Search for motives, accuse – Imposing memories and nightmares
Emotional	– Yearning for the lost person – Protest – Grief – Separation/loss anxiety – Philosophy: "Life goes on"	– Need for security – Sense of menace – Anger/feeling of revenge – Irritability and loss of control – Depression – Numbness
Behavior	– Grief at memories of the lost person – Self-selected rituals for remembrance and appreciation of the person	– Hyperarousal with memories of the lost person – Compulsive behavior – Obsession with loss

for each family whether they are more pleased about a visit, a phone call or a card (DHPV, 2017). Especially with close people, such a gesture can be perceived as very appreciative.

4.1.3 Conclusion

With the diagnosis of a serious chronic disease, a difficult time full of ups and downs begins for the patients. The dynamic course of the disease leads to the fact that between phases of stability and "normality" they are repeatedly reminded of dying and death by crisis situations (Table 4.6). By educating the class community, teachers can make a significant contribution to ensuring that even in difficult moments, a piece of normality remains for the children and young people. Through the offers and materials of hospices and palliative care, the topics of "death and dying" can be communicated to children and adolescents in such a way that they can learn to understand how diverse mourning reactions can be, what cultural differences exist and that death is part of life. The special feature of mourning in chronically ill children and adolescents is that preparation can be made with regard to saying goodbye. Thus, among other things, it is possible to fulfil the last heartfelt wishes of the children and adolescents and to prepare mourning rituals together with them. Furthermore, together with the sick child or adolescent and his or her family, it can be ensured that his or her farewell takes place as he or she had imagined it.

4.2 Sudden Death

4.2.1 Suicide

Katharina Barcatta and Anna-Lynn Schlund

The holidays have just ended and school is starting again. Just before it's time to go to the classrooms, the students are frolicking in the schoolyard. But this year is not like every year. For Jasmin, Tobias and their classmates, the school year will never be the same. They know as soon as they enter the classroom, Matthias' empty chair and bench will stand out to them from everyone. Everyone caught on to what Matthias was doing at the bridge that summer night a few weeks before. No one really knows why, rumors circulate behind closed doors, everyone feels each other's depressed mood, but no one speaks of it.

4.2.1.1 Introduction

The suicide of schoolchildren is still often a taboo subject in schools, as it is rarely discussed and the topic is hardly ever addressed. Yet the figures from the Federal Statistical Office make it clear that "pupil suicide" is not a rare phenomenon. Suicide is the second most common cause of death among young people (Bründel, 2010). This is in contrast to children, where acts leading to suicide are rarely observed. However, this may be due to the fact that they do not yet have a developed concept of death as adolescents do (see Chap. 3, Sect. 3.1). This is because suicidal behaviour requires a fully developed concept of death (Fegert et al., 2011).

When a person commits suicide, be it a classmate, a parent of a student or a teacher, it leaves behind grief, shock and often incomprehension among those around them. This affects not only the family and acquaintances, but also the teachers and classmates at school. Because even if the act is not committed during the school year, but for example during the school holidays, the pupils and teachers, but also the staff in the whole school, are confronted with the absence of the respective person at the beginning of the school year. Be it an empty chair, an empty office, or an empty cubby; the person is no longer there. Each student and teacher also reacts differently to the sudden loss, so the situation forces teachers to cope with the shock and grief of the school system. However, at the same time, they must also try to deal with other teens who may now make similar self-destructive decisions and intervene when necessary (Stevenson, 1994). For due to such a self-imposed death of the close friend or acquaintance and the sudden occurrence of such news, individuals often exhibit complicated grief reactions that may lead to the development of a mental disorder or even their own future suicide (Cerel et al., 2008). This is because part of the grieving process for many individuals also involves searching for the answer to the question of why the classmate or friend committed the act. Consequently, young people may think they understand the reason for the suicide, identify with it or even think they are in the same situation as the friend or acquaintance, so that they think about their own suicide. Accordingly, in addition to the terms suicide and acute suicidal crisis, the following chapter discusses risk and protective factors in the context of school. The sudden suicide of a classmate, classmate or teacher, if certain factors are present, can lead children and adolescents to commit the same act as a grief reaction. Therefore, it is very important to pay attention to such factors, especially during the mourning period.

4.2.1.2 What Exactly Is Suicide?

Suicide describes the act of killing itself (Fegert et al., 2011). In the psychiatric definition, suicide also denotes a suicide attempt that leads to death (Bronisch, 2008). In addition to this definition, related terms such as suicidal behaviour are also important. Suicidal behaviour describes risk behaviours that are directed against one's own health and thus have a merging boundary with self-harming behaviours (Skegg, 2005). The latter are particularly noteworthy because they play a special role in adolescence. Contrary to the commonly held assumption that self-injurious behavior (e.g., cutting one's forearm) is merely a cry for attention or a failed suicide attempt, this type of behavior instead represents a paradoxical attempt at self-care. Originally unbearable tensions, such as urgent suicidal impulses or suicidal ideation, may be alleviated by the intentional performance of these behaviors. In addition to this so-called autoprotective character, self-injurious behaviour can nevertheless also be an important indicator of mental health problems and suicide risk (Cowie et al., 2004; Fegert et al., 2011). If you as a teacher recognise self-injurious behaviour, you can help affected pupils as described in the infobox.

Self-injurious behaviour

How teachers can help according to Cowie et al., 2004:

1. Recognize signs of distress and find a way to talk with the young person about how he or she is feeling;

2. Important: The young person must have the feeling that he or she is being listened to attentively;

3. Provide practical help in solving problems as appropriate;

4. Adopt a non-judgmental attitude, remain calm and constructive;

5. Make sure young people are aware of the risks of self-harm and that they know it is possible to stop with help;

6. Ask the young person if their parents and family will be able to give the necessary support. This can be difficult if there are many problems or arguments at home. Often, suicidal adolescents in particular find it difficult to communicate with and feel accepted by their parents. Ironically, however, effective communication with parents or another significant caregiver is of critical therapeutic value to the adolescent or teen. At least 80% of teens who commit suicide initially attempt to communicate their despair to others (Nelson, 1987);

7. Ensure that (if necessary) the young person gets the right kind of help as soon as possible. Referral to professionals may well be appropriate;

8. Generally encourage students to tell you if someone in the group is in trouble, seems upset, or is showing signs of self-harm. As young people are often afraid of betraying their trust with their friends, you may need to explain that self-harm can be life-threatening. For this reason it should not be kept secret (Royal College of Psychiatrists Fact Sheet, 1999 in Cowie et al., 2004). In addition, primary prevention is often in the hands of the young person themselves, as they usually seek help from a friend;

9. Self-harm can be seen as a habit. It is therefore helpful to encourage the young person to manage withdrawal symptoms and increase their readiness to change

Suicidal ideation is also an important aspect of understanding suicide. Suicidal thoughts can be said to occur when a person's thoughts are associated with dying wishes or death. These range from thinking about death in general to thoughts about one's own death to precise ideas about the possibilities of one's own suicidal actions (Bronisch, 2008; Warnke, 2008).

4.2.1.3 Acute Suicidal Crisis

Suicidality is usually not a persistent state, but often a state that becomes acute as a result of an escalating crisis. For example, acute suicidality may be triggered by current situations of loss or separation in which a person, in this case a student, has few resources and coping options available to deal with such experiences or other problems. Whether these problems are real or not is sometimes less important than the student's feeling of powerlessness and the unsolvability of a situation. Previously successful attempts at a solution can also prove to be useless. As a result, the student experiences an unbearable state of tension—an acute suicidal crisis. This can be characterised by a chaos of emotions but also by individual emotions such as fear, panic, anger, despair, feelings of alienation, confusion or massive helplessness. The risk of suicide can increase dramatically in such a state, especially for students with high pressure to act. Therefore, an important task is to buy time to prevent or delay a potential suicidal act (Althaus & Hegerl, 2004). Furthermore, in case of a presumption of an acute suicidal crisis, it is advisable to refer the affected student to professionals (i.e., clinical child and adolescent psychotherapists and psychiatrists) who can assess suicidality and a possible suicide risk. Of great importance here are above all suicide planning and acute suicidal thoughts for the assessment of suicidality (Fegert et al., 2011), as it has been proven that about one third of people with suicidal thoughts state a concrete suicide plan and from this in turn almost three quarters also make a suicide attempt (Kessler et al., 1999). However, the existence of suicide attempts in the past as well as access to potential suicide resources (e.g. razor blades) and other indicators (see information box for further indicators of increased suicide risk) must also be taken into account when assessing acute suicidality in order to identify an increased risk of suicide at an early stage (Fegert et al., 2011).

Indicators of increased suicide risk according to Althaus and Hegerl (2004):
1. pressing suicidal thoughts,
2. big hopelessness,
3. strong feelings of guilt,
4. strong pressure to act,
5. increasing social withdrawal,
6. saying goodbye to people,
7. giving away valuables,
8. arrangements for final matters (e.g., wills),
9. overt or covert announcement of suicide,

(continued)

Indicators of increased suicide risk according to Althaus and Hegerl (2004):

10. irritated or aggressive reactions of the person,
11. specific suicide plans or preparations,
12. - a failure to distance oneself from suicidal ideation after a prolonged conversation

4.2.1.4 Risk Factors in the School Context

Many components influence whether a child or adolescent will decide to commit suicide or whether a child or adolescent will be considered at risk for suicide. These so-called risk factors are conditions that increase the likelihood that suicide will be committed. Above all, mental disorders and psychosocial factors play a significant role in the school context and strongly influence the school setting. When the suicide of a best friend is added to this, the perceived shock, grief, emotional pain, lack of understanding, as well as the search for an explanation can exacerbate such conditions in the grieving phase. Therefore, these factors are described in more detail below in order to sensitize parents, guardians, teachers and educators in general to recognize suicidal students in the mourning phase at an early stage and to be able to intervene. In the following, different factors will also be repeated, as they have a direct effect on suicidal behaviour on the one hand, and on the other hand are often triggers for another risk factor, which in turn promotes suicidal behaviour.

4.2.1.4.1 Mental Disorders

Different mental illnesses, such as depression and anxiety disorders, can either be genetically inherited or developed through different environmental and contextual influences. These in turn often have an impact on the environment, but also on the person's own life. In the following, the three disorders depression, anxiety disorder and attention deficit hyperactivity disorder (ADHD) will be discussed.

▶ **Depression**

The WHO (2020) defines depression as

"a common mental disorder, characterized by sadness, loss of interes or pleasure, feelings of guilt or low self-worth, disturbed sleep or appatite, feelings of tiredness and poor concentration (and) … can be long lasting or recurrent, substantially impairing a person's ability to function at work or school, or cope with daily life."Among adolescents, depression as a mental illness is a leading cause of decision to take one's own life worldwide (WHO, 2019), such that adolescents with major depression are at the highest risk of committing suicide (Xu et al., 2018). One of the characteristics of depression is the recurrence of suicidal thoughts (Dilling & Freyberger, 2016). One study was also able to show that a high level of depression is also related to suicide attempts, meaning that the more depressed adolescents are, the more often they try to take their own lives (Chou et al., 2016). However, adolescents who have only mild depression, as opposed to those with major depression, are also at increased risk. In relation to peers who do not suffer from depression, adolescents with mild depression are three times more likely to have suicidal thoughts, while adolescents with major depression are even nine times more likely to worry about ending their lives (Balázs et al., 2013). This means that if, for example, an adolescent who does not suffer from depression thinks about committing suicide once in a day, an adolescent with mild depression thinks about it three times a day, while an adolescent with severe depression thinks about taking his or her own life a full nine times a day. Therefore, as a parent, teacher, or general caregiver, you should pay attention to whether a child or adolescent appears to be suffering from or developing depression. Characteristics that may be present in children and adolescents with depression and by which depression can be recognised are listed in the information box. If several of these characteristics are observed in a child or adolescent, they should first be discussed with the child or adolescent and it may then be suggested that he or she consult a specialist.

Characteristics of depression (Dilling & Freyberger, 2016):
1. Loss of interest or pleasure in activities that were usually enjoyable;
2. Decreased drive or increased fatigability;
3. Loss of self-confidence or self-esteem;
4. Unfounded self-blame or pronounced, inappropriate guilt;
5. Recurrent thoughts of death or suicide or suicidal behavior;
6. Complaints of or evidence of decreased ability to think or concentrate, indecision or indecisiveness;
7. Psychomotor agitation or inhibition (subjective or objective);
8. Sleep disorders of any kind;
9. Loss of appetite or increased appetite with corresponding change in weight;

Anxiety disorder The term anxiety disorder mainly represents a group of disorders in which anxiety is caused by situations that are actually hazard-free and objectively hazard-free (Dilling & Freyberger, 2016). If an anxiety disorder is present in adolescents, whether mild or severe, the risk of suicidal ideation is increased in contrast to adolescents who do not exhibit excessive anxiety (Balázs et al., 2013). Adolescents with a mild anxiety disorder are two times more likely to have suicidal thoughts than those without an anxiety disorder, while those with a severe anxiety disorder are two and a half times more likely to have suicidal thoughts (Balázs et al., 2013). While these are not the same high risks as depression, it should be noted that anxiety disorders and depression are very common together (Hill et al., 2018). Accordingly, a child or adolescent may suffer from both depression and excessive anxiety at the same time. This, in turn, can lead to a higher risk of committing suicide, as both risk factors promote suicidal ideation.

ADHD (Attention Deficit Hyperactivity Disorder) A long-term study was able to show that ADHD in adolescents, regardless of whether other disorders are also present, is both a risk factor for suicide attempts and for repeated suicide attempts (Huang et al., 2018). This means that adolescents diagnosed with ADHD are at an increased risk of wanting to commit suicide or will attempt it again if they have already tried once. Nevertheless, children and adolescents with ADHD also have comorbidities, such as depression and anxiety disorders (Balázs et al., 2014), so these children and adolescents also suffer from depression and anxiety disorders. As described above, they are also at increased risk of suicide.

4.2.1.4.2 Psychosocial Factors

In contrast to the general population, suicidal children and adolescents more frequently exhibit psychosocial stresses, such as family stresses (Warnke & Hemminger, 1999). Experiences of abuse in particular appear to have a particularly high influence on later suicidality (Fegert et al., 2011). A long-term study showed that repeated sexual abuse and sexual abuse by a family member in particular were associated with a higher risk of suicide attempts (Brezo et al., 2008). However, in addition to these traumatic experiences, factors that appear far less severe also contribute to an increased risk of suicide, such as family, friends and school as a setting itself, which will be discussed in more detail below.

Family For children and adolescents to grow up, the family or other caregivers are of particular importance. The first years of life are decisive in determining whether a person develops a basic trust or basic mistrust in the course of his or her life. Disputes and conflicts, which are part of daily life in every family, can, if unresolved and accumulated over time, be among the most influential factors in this regard (Bründel, 2010). Family influencing factors that lead to increased suicide risk include family abuse and family conflict, as well as family crisis events such as the loss of a parent, a parent's mental illness, or a parent's separation/divorce, and a family history of suicidal behavior, a difficult parent-child relationship, or severely restrictive parenting behaviors (Cash & Bridge, 2009; Bründel, 2004). It is important to note, however, that it is not the individual events as such that are suicide-promoting, but rather a long-lasting history of problems, usually beginning in childhood, that contributes to the breaking down of the will to live in adolescence and can lead to suicidal behaviour (Bründel, 2010).

Friends In addition to the family, relationships with friends are particularly important in childhood and adolescence. Especially during puberty, adolescents have to face many demands and developmental tasks. Not only do they have to cope with strong hormonal and other physiological changes, but also with changes in relationships with peers (whether male or female). The newfound emotional independence from parents allows adolescents to grow closer to their friends during this time (Bründel, 2004). These so-called peer relationships (Fegert et al., 2011) offer the exchange of feelings as well as freedom for new activities, which parents usually do not always tolerate. They also provide security and orientation. However, the opposite can also be the case, as some adolescents are sidelined, excluded or have regular conflicts within their circle of friends (Bründel, 2010). Public exposure or humiliation by peers, rejection of a longed-for romantic partner, or general negative experiences among peers have in the past often acted as direct triggers for completed suicide or indirectly increased the risk of suicidal ideation, which in turn potentially increases the risk of suicide as such (Feigelman & Gorman, 2008; Giletta et al., 2015). In addition, the breakup of a friendship or romantic relationship in particular can cause suicidality, especially if there is no other viable or familial support outside of close ties to friends (Warnke & Hemminger, 1999). The impact on adolescents' suicidal behavior is particularly big when such events have occurred in the recent past. In addition to these factors, the suicide of a friend is still worth mentioning as an important influencing factor. The death of a friend by suicide can have a direct reinforcing influence on depression, suicide attempts or suicidal thoughts in those adolescents who have experienced the traumatic event (Feigelman & Gorman, 2008).

School School plays an important role in childhood and adolescence, not only because students spend the majority of their day there, but also because many of the peer relationships are cultivated at school (Bründel, 2004; Fegert et al., 2011). With its structure, its susceptibility to clashes with teaching staff and classmates, and its often high performance expectations, the school setting often represents a place prone to crisis. While school is not usually a direct causal factor, experienced stress at school can be an indirect trigger for events that have been planned or imagined for some time. This is because school problems usually exacerbate already existing stresses, such as family or psychological problems, and thus contribute to these being perceived as subjectively unbearable. Since teachers spend a relatively large amount of time with students, they have the opportunity to notice changes and keep an eye on them. This is because 90% of suicidal students make comments about not feeling well or thinking about taking their own lives.

Mobbing In addition to poor grades or high performance requirements, school problems can also be caused by misbehaviour of classmates or teaching staff. A phenomenon that plays an important role in this context is bullying (Bründel, 2010). Bullying is a specific form of negative, hostile social behavior among children and adolescents (Fekkes et al., 2005; Winter, 2014). In situations where students are bullied, they are "exposed, repeatedly and over time, to negative actions on the part of one or more other persons" (Olweus, 1994, p. 98). Characteristic of bullying is often the power imbalance between the victim and the perpetrator, which severely limits the victim's ability to fight back (Winter, 2014). As described in the information box, other factors besides the power imbalance also increase the risk of becoming a victim of bullying perpetrators. Typically, bullying is either physical (e.g., hitting, pushing, or kicking) or verbal (e.g., name-calling, threatening, or slandering), but also includes other behaviors such as social exclusion or grimacing (Fekkes et al., 2005). In addition, digital media can be used as a means for bullying-type activities or acted out through them. This form of bullying is called cyberbullying and constitutes a separate form of bullying (Back, 2020). Unlike physical bullying, it is difficult to exclude cyberbullying from the school context, as children and young people nowadays have 24/7 access to digital media. Due to this local independence, cyberbullying can take place within as well as outside the school context.

In addition to the distinction between bullying and cyberbullying, it is also important to distinguish between the bullying activities of boys and girls, as they usually bully in different ways. In general, boys bully more actively than girls and in a more direct way. Girls, on the other hand, tend to bully in a more indirect way, for example, they exclude other students or spread rumours. Furthermore, bullying can be seen as a group phenomenon, where not only the victim and the perpetrator are involved, but also other children and young people. In most cases, however, the bystanders do not try to stop the bullying, which can be interpreted by the perpetrators as confirmation, so that the bullying does not stop but continues (Fekkes et al., 2005). By idealizing the perpetrator, classmates encourage the bullying relationship between the perpetrator and the victim. Further, exacerbating bullying is the fact that the victim is usually merely a single student. If bullying goes undamped, this can lead to serious psychological consequences, especially if the victim feels powerless (Winter, 2014). Involvement in bullying alone is associated with an increased risk of suicide for young people (Kim et al., 2009). However, a consistent association between bullying and suicidal ideation has also been found in youth (Kim & Leventhal, 2008). Compared to young people who are not involved in bullying, both perpetrators and victims of bullying are at higher risk of developing depression, having suicidal thoughts or even attempting suicide (Klomek et al., 2007; Mills et al., 2004; Van der Wal et al., 2003a, b). Thus, bullying should be seen as a significant risk factor in the school setting and should not be overlooked. Often teaching staff tend to leave it to their students to resolve disputes themselves, this is helpful in some cases but makes it difficult for victims to get support from teachers. Therefore, it is important to encourage teachers as well as students to intervene and stop bullying of any kind in school (Bründel, 2010).

Risk factors of becoming a victim of bullying according to Winter (2014):
1. Small body size
2. Overweight
3. Physical disability and/or illness
4. Motor development disorder
5. Low self-esteem
6. Social withdrawal
7. Depression
8. Fear
9. ADHD
10. Autism

The risk factors described above have the greatest influence on committing suicide in the context of school, when pupils are already grieving and feeling emotional pain due to the suicide of a fellow pupil. Other risk factors, however, which can also have an influence on suicidality among adolescents and thus in turn have an increased influence on adolescents committing suicide themselves as a grief reaction, are listed in the information box.

> Other risk factors for suicidality according to Porter et al. (2019):
> 1. Conduct disorders
> 2. Psychological and emotional child abuse
> 3. Previous suicidal ideation
> 4. Suicidal thoughts and behaviors in the family history
> 5. Media suspension
> 6. Substance abuse and use
> 7. Self-injurious behaviour
> 8. Aggressive behaviour
> 9. Low self-esteem
> 10. Sleep disturbances
> 11. Neurotic personality

4.2.1.5 Protective Factors in the School Context

Protective factors are components, conditions and characteristics that balance the influence of risk factors and thus protect students from the negative influences of risk factors. Often, even the opposite expression of a risk factor is a protective factor. For example, family and friends can also be a protective factor and have a positive influence (Porter et al., 2019) in that children and young people feel connected, accepted and have a good relationship with their parents or friends. This also makes children and young people feel that they are important and that family and friends are always there for them and support them. This is especially important during the mourning period for a best friend. But school can also be a protective factor. If teachers show an honest interest in the students' well-being and also behave respectfully towards them, this protects considerably against suicidal thoughts as well as suicide attempts among adolescents (Eisenberg et al., 2007). In addition, students would be more likely to turn to teachers with their feelings during their grieving period and seek help from them. However, academic success and interest in school also have a positive effect (Taliaferro & Muehlenkamp, 2014). Thus, students who have good grades in school and also enjoy going to school and enjoy learning, in turn, show a lower risk of harboring suicidal thoughts and committing suicide than students who do not enjoy going to school and also do not achieve good grades. Another very important factor is high self-esteem. When children and adolescents value themselves, among other things, this also has a decreasing effect on depression symptoms, so it follows that children and adolescents have a lower risk of exhibiting suicidal thoughts (Huang & Wang, 2019). In addition, being able to determine one's emotions well, regulate them, and thus effectively manage stress may also lead children and adolescents to be less influenced by their friends' and peers' risk behaviors, such as drug use (Wang et al., 2010). For example, if an adolescent has good emotion regulation skills and is asked by friends to use drugs as well, they are more likely not to be tempted to do so. However, the development of different coping strategies, focusing on addressing and solving the problem, also condition adolescents to be at lower risk for suicide attempts (Roberts et al., 2010). All protective factors in the context of school are listed again in the infobox. On the whole, protective factors can vary from person to person, so that it is important to recognise the most important factors of each person in the grieving process at school and to work on them so that the grief and shock can be dealt with appropriately.

> Protective factors in the context of school:
> 1. Family
> 2. Friends
> 3. School
> 4. Academic success and enjoyment of school
> 5. High self-esteem
> 6. Emotion regulation capacity
> 7. Problem-focused coping strategies

4.2.1.6 Conclusion

Children and adolescents spend a lot of time at school, where they have built up a social network with their classmates and friends, in whose structure everyone takes their place. If a pupil, a teacher or, for example, a parent of a pupil decides to take his or her own life, the school is also affected. Usually no one is prepared for this, which means that the shock is very big and far-reaching, and support is needed in grieving and processing this event. Additionally, each person also deals with the situation differently on an individual basis. Some students are at increased risk of a complicated grief response, putting them at risk of developing a mental health disorder or even committing suicide themselves as a reaction (Cerel et al., 2008). This is because the sudden onset of grief, the lack of understanding, the search for an explanation, and the feeling of not being able to cope with the situation can overwhelm a person. In addition, these feelings, in combination with the risk factors described in this chapter, can lead children and young people to imitate the act of the fellow pupil, classmate or teacher. Accordingly, it is very important to identify risk factors during the mourning phase at school and to pay special attention to children and adolescents who exhibit risk factors so that they are not also at risk of committing suicide. In addition, protective factors can also be used to give children and young people support at school so that they can cope with this difficult time (Taliaferro & Muehlenkamp, 2014) and overcome their grief.

Whether self-injurious behaviour (see infobox above), suicide attempts or cautious attempts to talk about the suicide attempts, all these are warning signals to be taken seriously, which can be understood as an opportunity. As an opportunity for teachers and classmates to help potentially suicidal classmates to cope appropriately with the mourning phase together.

4.2.2 Accidents

Lena Schwind and Vera Hilger

4 Causes of Grief

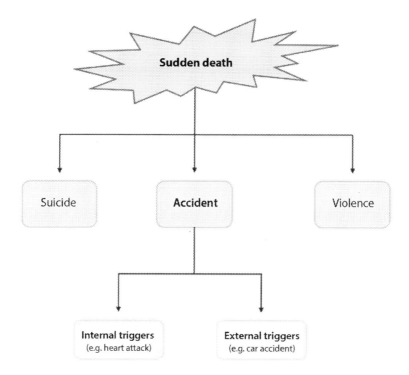

Fig. 4.1 Different causes of sudden death

Death—like many other stages of life—is part of life, but in view of its finality and the resulting future physical absence of a loved one, it is not easy to accept. Death continues to be one of the taboo subjects in today's society. Nonetheless, it is a topic that should be talked about, as people around the world encounter death and grief on a daily basis. In some cases, we may be prepared for it to some extent because the sad event was preceded by a serious illness, for example. In other cases, however, it hits us completely unexpectedly and unpredictably. Reasons for this may include suicide, death by violence or accidents. Figure 4.1 provides an overview of these different causes of sudden death.

This chapter will focus specifically on accidental deaths that occur in the school context. The main focus will be on the deaths of pupils and teaching staff.

Of course, stresses and grief caused by deaths in the private environment of the individual often have an impact on school events. Examples of this are the death of siblings, parents, grandparents or even pets. In the context of this chapter, we will limit ourselves to the death of those persons who have a direct connection to the actual events at school. These are primarily pupils and teachers. In addition to an explanation of various terms and distinctions, the prevalence of different causes of accidents is discussed, along with a few examples for illustration. In addition, advice is given on how to behave adequately immediately after such an event. Finally, possible interventions are briefly mentioned, which are explained in more detail in Sect. 4.2.4 of this book.

4.2.2.1 Sudden Death

"Death is not a misfortune for him who dies, but for him who survives." This quote by Karl Marx (Marx & Engels, 1973, p. 460) comes into play a lot especially after a fatal accident or in general in case of sudden death. When a known or close person dies suddenly, specifically the aspect of unpredictability plays an important role, which is often difficult for the bereaved to understand and usually causes a different grief reaction than when the process is longer term and predictable (Worden, 1999). Due to the lack of warning, deaths of this nature are also referred to as traumatic deaths (Wagner, 2013). In this context, those affected often report an inability to perceive what has happened as real and to accept it as such, with there often being a sense of "numbness" following a sudden death of someone close (Wagner, 2013). In addition, the possibility of saying goodbye in the case of an unforeseeable death is different from when the death is already foreseeable, for example, due to a serious illness.

> Death is a constant companion of life—sometimes we can prepare for its occurrence, and sometimes it comes upon us completely unexpectedly. An example of this are those sudden deaths caused by accidents.

For this reason, relatives are often specifically advised to say goodbye to the corpse after a sudden death. This can help to better relate what has happened to reality and possibly reduce the psychological stress afterwards (Wagner, 2013). However, in the context of school, for example when a whole school class is affected, this is difficult to implement. Therefore, it is even more important here to use interventions adapted for the target group after a sudden death of a student or teacher, which differ from intervention approaches after a predictable death, for example due to a chronic illness. In addition to suicide and violence, accidents resulting in death in particular fall into the category of unpredictable and sudden deaths.

4.2.2.2 Sudden Death Due to Accidents

Nowadays, one encounters the terms "sudden death" and "accident" with an almost frightening frequency, for example in the news or in the newspaper. But what exactly is meant by the term accident? The term "accident" is defined in the Duden as "an incident suddenly interrupting the normal course of something, unintentional event in which people are injured or killed or property damage occurs" (Bibliographisches Institut GmbH Duden 2019). This explanation of the term once again emphasizes the unpredictability of the event. In this context, however, it seems significant to make a further distinction—that between internal and external triggers of an accident. Internal triggers include medical incidents that have a potentially fatal outcome. Examples include heart attacks, strokes, and sudden cardiac death. Such conditions that can trigger sudden death are described in more detail in a subsequent section. External triggers, on the other hand, include influences that are not directly attributable to internal, physical processes. Examples include traffic accidents involving various road users (drivers and passengers of motor vehicles, cyclists and pedestrians), as well as sports, household and work accidents.

In 2018, a total of 3275 traffic fatalities were recorded in Germany (Statista, 2020) and in 2017, 39,872 people died in Germany due to various external causes, such as injuries or poisoning (Statista, 2020). The number of accidents caused by internal causes is even greater. The number of deaths due to cardiovascular diseases alone—the most common cause of death—amounted to 344,530 in 2017. A total of 48,669 people died due to a heart attack, which is the most common of the cardiovascular diseases. Diseases of the respiratory system, which can be classified in third place, cost the lives of 57,408 people—also in 2017 (Statista, 2020). These facts and figures illustrate the high relevance of sudden deaths caused by various types of accidents. Regarding the total number of deaths, without taking into account the cause, but differentiated by age, the Statistisches Bundesamt (2020) provided the following data for 2018: 964 children and adolescents aged 6 to 19 died and 94,107 adults aged 24 to 65 died. The age ranges chosen are intended to represent those children and adolescents who, based on their respective ages, could potentially be students and those adults who, based on their respective ages, could potentially be teachers, respectively, given the topic of this book. Further information regarding the causes of death of children can be found in Crumb and Griffith Taylor (2010). The authors state that accidents and homicides are the leading causes of death among children in well-developed and high-income countries. Globally, traffic accidents, drowning, burns, falls, and poisonings represent the most common types of accidents or types of "unintentional injuries" in childhood Crumb & Griffith Taylor, 2010. Given these figures, it seems neither surprising nor unlikely that some of these events have already occurred or are recurring in the school context. In a later section, three examples with initial intervention steps are described for illustrative purposes.

> **Accidents** are defined primarily by their **suddenness and unpredictability** and by their possible **consequences.** A further distinction can be made in terms of their triggers or causes. Thus, there are **external** (e.g. traffic accidents with fatal outcomes) **and internal triggers** (e.g. cardiovascular diseases leading to sudden and unexpected death) of accidents. Statistics regarding the **number of deaths** with the aforementioned triggers underline the **relevance of this issue.**

4.2.2.3 Sudden Death Caused by External Triggers

As mentioned in Sect. 4.2.2.2, accidents caused by external triggers are the most common type of accident, especially among children. For this reason, the following section focuses on this group of people. Crumb and Griffith Taylor (2010) list road traffic accidents and drowning as the two most common types of accidents in childhood worldwide, which according to Ellsäßer (2006) are among the most common causes of fatal accidents, especially at school age. In road traffic accidents with a fatal outcome for children, they are most often involved in traffic as pedestrians or as cyclists Crumb & Griffith Taylor,

2010. For this reason, the *United Nations Children's Fund* (UNICEF) recommends, among other things, the development of teaching programs on safe traffic behavior for children as a starting point for prevention measures. In drowning accidents, which mostly occur in domestic swimming pools or open water, children under the age of five are particularly at risk worldwide Crumb & Griffith Taylor, 2010. However, it is not only in the case of drowning accidents that age plays a decisive role. In general, age—along with gender, accident location and time, and psychosocial factors—is one of the main risk factors for the occurrence of (potentially fatal) accidents (Spitzer et al., 2007). Although the risk of accidents is particularly high in young children, aspects such as emotional imbalance or testing one's own limits through risky behaviour can increase the probability of accidents in adolescence, for example. In terms of gender, boys appear to be statistically at increased risk of accidents compared to girls (Spitzer et al., 2007). Another risk factor is the location of the accident, which in the case of schoolchildren between the ages of five and fourteen is primarily in road traffic and schools, as well as in home and leisure settings (Ellsäßer, 2006). With regard to the timing of accidents, the highest rates are shown in the afternoon after school and during the journey to school (Spitzer et al., 2007). With regard to psychosocial risk factors, the enormous importance of the role model function of parents and other caregivers with regard to the behaviour of children and adolescents is evident in the context of accidents—as in many other areas (Spitzer et al., 2007). In summary, the risk factors mentioned reflect school age as a vulnerable phase for a wide variety of accidents. In Germany, for example, it is estimated that around 49,000 children and adolescents of school age are specifically injured in a school context every year (Schürch, 2016). Even if fatal accidents, for example in school sports, are rather rare (Schürch, 2016), they should nevertheless receive attention—among other things because of their large radius of involvement.

> The most common **causes of fatal accidents** among school-age children and adolescents worldwide are **traffic accidents** and **drowning**. Whether an accident occurs depends on a variety of **risk factors**. These include age, gender, accident location and time, and psychosocial factors.

4.2.2.4 Sudden Death Caused by Internal Triggers

Heart Attack As already mentioned, death from cardiovascular diseases is the most common cause of death in Germany. A very well-known example of a serious consequence of such a disease is the heart attack (or *myocardial infarction*). In the case of a heart attack, a blood vessel within the heart (known as a *coronary vessel*) is blocked by a blood clot. As a result, blood can no longer flow to the affected part of the heart muscle, which means that the oxygen transported with the blood can no longer supply the heart properly (Gehring & Klein, 2015). If this process continues for an extended period of time, irreversible damage can occur, which in the worst case scenario can result in cardiac arrest and death (Vögele, 2009). The cause of a heart attack is often a previous and sometimes even undetected *coronary artery disease,* which is caused by calcification of the coronary vessels *(arteriosclerosis)* (Baer & Rosenkranz, 2011; Gehring & Klein, 2015). Every year, around 270,000 people in Germany die of a heart attack—around half of them in the first two hours after the incident, before an emergency doctor arrives (Gehring & Klein, 2015).

Sudden Cardiac Death Another serious complication in the field of cardiovascular diseases is sudden cardiac death. According to Baer and Rosenkranz (2011), this is a form of natural death originating in the heart muscle, which is accompanied by an immediate loss of consciousness, a few minutes after the onset of symptoms of discomfort. Sudden cardiac death can be the cause of different and possibly still unrecognized clinical pictures, which relate either to structural or functional deficits in the cardiovascular system. However, as in the case of myocardial infarction, sudden cardiac death is often caused by a life-threatening advanced form of coronary artery disease. Every year, around 150,000 people in Germany succumb to sudden cardiac death (Baer & Rosenkranz, 2011).

Stroke: Cerebral Infarction and Cerebral Haemorrhage In addition to the consequences of cardiovascular diseases, complications in the area of the brain are also frequently the cause of sudden deaths. The best-known example of this is probably strokes, which are the third most common cause of death in industrialized nations (Schubert & Lalouschek, 2011). In general, a stroke corresponds to the sudden onset of neurological deficits caused by pathological processes in blood vessels of the brain. However, not every stroke has the same cause and course. The most common form of stroke is a cerebral infarction (or *ischemic stroke*), which occurs in about 80% of cases. Due to damage to a blood vessel in the brain, similar to a heart attack, the corresponding part of the brain cannot be supplied with blood properly and thus can no longer be supplied with oxygen. As a result, the affected region can no longer function properly and, in the worst case, can suffer irreversible damage that can be fatal (Schubert & Lalouschek, 2011). In the remaining 20% of cases, cerebral haemorrhage occurs either inside the brain (*intracerebral haemorrhage,* in around 15% of cases) or in the space between the skull bones and the brain (*subarachnoid haemorrhage,* in around 5% of cases). In the case of intracerebral haemorrhage, damage occurs in the neighbouring regions of the brain after a blood vessel bursts. In the case of a subarachnoid haemorrhage, an already existing weakness, a so-called aneurysm (bulge) of a blood vessel in the subarachnoid space (space between the skull bones and the brain) bursts. Although this form of stroke is the rarest, it is nevertheless a type that is often the cause of strokes in young people (Schubert & Lalouschek, 2011).

> Specific and **common internal triggers** for sudden death are heart attacks, sudden cardiac death and strokes. In a **heart attack,** a coronary artery becomes blocked, which can cause cardiac arrest in the worst case scenario. **Sudden cardiac death** is a natural form of death that involves an immediate loss of consciousness. **Strokes** are caused by **cerebral infarcts in** 80% of cases and by cerebral **hemorrhages** inside the brain or in the area between the skull bones and the brain in 20% of cases.

4.2.2.5 Case Studies with Initial Intervention Steps

4.2.2.5.1 Death of a Pupil

It is a normal weekday evening when Ms. T—the teacher of a 12th grade—is relaxed and on her way to dinner with friends. On the way, she gets a Facebook notification—a text posted by a student at her school. The content is shocking. A classmate, Maja, is reported to have died. Ms. T is overwhelmed by her feelings and stunned. Still on the way home the question pops into her head: "How should I behave? To the class, to the parents of the deceased child?" After a restless night, the teacher goes to school the next day and seeks out the principal before going to her class. The latter is equally shaken and contacts the school psychological service as well as the pastoral care. He also cannot tell Ms. T how to deal with her class for the next minutes, hours and even days and weeks. So Ms. T trusts her instincts, and with tissues in her backpack, seeks out the classroom. As expected, there is a chaos of emotions there—some students still do not seem to know exactly what happened the day before, while others are crying and hugging each other because they have already heard about the sad and upsetting incident. Mrs. T greets the class and explains briefly and succinctly that her classmate Maja had been involved in a tragic traffic accident the day before and had suffered a fatal accident. Her voice trembles and her eyes are filled with tears. She informs the classmates that staff from the school psychological service will be arriving later today to take care of them. She offers to take the students for a walk together. The whole class goes along and everyone finds a different way to deal with the situation. Some remain silent, others cry quietly, and some share memories of their classmate. But one thing is clear: the pain is great and this misfortune will be present for a long time and never forgotten.

Reports like this make you think, shake you up. On one day, everything is still normal: a young woman who is well integrated into her class community is actively participating in class and chatting with her friends. Everything on this day is so self-evident and delightfully banal. In the afternoon she goes home and suddenly everything is different: she will never come to school again. Her parents, her siblings, her classmates and friends, her teachers—all are affected in different ways and all have to find a way to deal with this situation. But how does something like this work? How does one know how to behave, what to do and not to do? Nobody is prepared for such a situation and often there is a great sense of being overwhelmed. This makes it all the more important that there are ways to prepare school staff for such incidents and that information is provided on how a school community can get through something like this with appropriate consideration for those closest to them.

Background Information
The example described is based on two true events. The respective contributions are available at: https://www.sueddeutsche.de/bildung/lehrer-blog-in-der-schule-rechnen-wir-nicht-mit-dem-tod-1.1927445

https://www.spiegel.de/lebssenundlernen/schule/tod-eines-schuelers-wie-lehrer-und-klasse-damit-umgingen-a-1009082.html (Last access: January 27, 2020).

4.2.2.5.2 Death of a Teacher

It is a day like any other when the eighth grade students of a high school enter the chemistry room of their school. Their teacher, Mr. A, is already there, preparing the blackboard. Class begins and, as usual, Mr. A jokes around and tries to generate a little more enthusiasm for the subject in his class. He is just about to write down a formula when he suddenly slumps down. Some students are frozen, but the three students in the front row luckily react immediately and run to him. He does not react, but is still breathing shallowly. Other students run to the secretary's office and call for help. Panic slowly spreads in the classroom. Mr. A stops breathing and no one knows what to do. Then other teachers arrive and try to resuscitate Mr. A—in vain. The emergency doctor arrives and can only testify the death of Mr. A. Later examinations reveal that the sixty-year-old succumbed to a brain haemorrhage as a result of a ruptured aneurysm. So it could have happened at any time. The class is taken to a common room by some teachers who try to catch the initial reactions. However, they themselves are also shocked and somewhat overwhelmed by the situation. Some students are crying bitterly, others are just staring into space. The headmaster arrives, expresses his shock and thanks the young students for their helpful behaviour and quick action. Since the school does not have a permanently employed school psychologist and is also not informed about the services offered by the responsible school psychology service, there is a lack of clarity about how to proceed. So first of all the parents of the children involved are contacted and informed about what has happened. In the course of the week, the children and their parents are offered an appointment with a child psychologist arranged through the school. Almost no one takes up this offer.

Here, too, it becomes clear how important professional support is in such situations. If schools do not have in-house school psychologists, then it should be ensured that they are informed about the tasks of the nearby school psychology service. It would also be useful to train school staff in crisis intervention, for example. Witnessing such tragedies is terrible for anyone, but especially the children who were directly involved should receive appropriate support immediately afterwards.

4.2.2.5.3 Death of a Group in a School Context

A Monday in April last year—what was a normal day for many people was one of the most exciting days in a long time for the fifth graders of the local comprehensive school, as they went on a class trip. The bus, filled with 26 children and two young teachers, set off early in the morning to a youth hostel to spend the next three days. The children were excited, especially when their teachers announced over the microphone more information regarding the planning for the day ahead. However, after just a few minutes, tragedy struck. The bus went off the roadway and plunged many feet down a slope. For all occupants, any help came too late. Investigations revealed that the experienced and conscientious bus driver suffered a heart attack during the journey, which led to cardiac arrest. In this case, this accident caused by an internal trigger, which already took the life of one person suddenly, immediately led to another accident, which had a fatal outcome for 28 more people. The families and friends of 29 people lost a loved one that day, and the school faced its greatest challenge ever. The school administration and the family of the bus driver were immediately informed of the accident by the police. Along with the guidance counselors, the principal informed the families of both teachers as well as the students. But how do you inform 28 people about the death of a loved one when you yourself are completely shaken and overwhelmed with emotion and cannot believe what has just happened? How do you deal with the silence on the other end of the phone line and the questions that follow? How do you explain something to someone else that you cannot believe yourself? The school staff kept asking themselves: If the pain is so great for us as teachers, how must the parents and siblings or partners of the deceased feel at this moment? They wanted so much to help, but did not know how.

Strokes of fate like these shake numerous families and the school community at the same time. The number of those directly affected is usually very large. But how can a school help to provide some support for those who are grieving? One prerequisite is that the school is aware of the support services available in the acute situations themselves and afterwards. What these options are will be described in more detail in a later section on interventions.

4.2.2.6 Conclusion

The occurrence of sudden deaths in the school context caused by accidents should not be underestimated, especially because of the high prevalence rates and the potentially far-reaching consequences for the school environment. Whether the triggers of the accident are external or internal, such an event affects a large number of people. A particular challenge in the school context is the heterogeneity of the group of people affected. Often this group consists of adults (teaching staff) as well as children and adolescents of different age groups (pupils). In order to be able to provide adequate support to all those affected in such a situation, it is essential that schools not only inform themselves about possible courses of action, but also have a concrete plan of action and are practically prepared for such an event.

> Sudden deaths like these occur more frequently than expected. It is therefore all the more important **that a school is as well prepared as possible** to be able to provide **the necessary support to all those involved and their relatives in** the event of an emergency.

4.2.3 Violence

Jan Hamborg and Charlotte Ries

4.2.3.1 Introduction

In addition to the occurrence of sudden death in schools due to suicide and accidents, the third aspect is death due to violence. Violent deaths at schools entail a complex, serious mourning process, which is often accompanied by incomprehension, anger and mental health consequences for those affected and those left behind. Violent deaths are characterized by human intentions or negligence and must therefore be treated separately from sudden accidents and classic suicides in the school context.

Serious violence at schools includes targeted, planned acts of violence against specific individuals or against all people within the school (e.g. school shootings), but also acts committed by rival groups, for example from the drug scene. In addition, thefts, escalating jealousy dramas, fights and bullying between students, students and teachers, as well as parents, and extended suicide (see Infobox 1) can also be triggers for violent deaths in schools. This paper looks in depth at school shootings as well as bullying and cyberbullying. Bullying and cyberbullying can be lethal in that they can lead to suicide or the execution of school shootings.

▶ **Infobox 1: Extended suicide**
Contrary to classical suicide, "aggression is not (exclusively) directed against one's own self" (Schmidbauer, 2009), but also, intentionally or unintentionally, before or simultaneously against other people.

Common to all forms of lethal violence in schools is that the act is very difficult for survivors to comprehend and accept. The perpetrators are often still minors (Holland et al., 2019) and were usually part of the normal school routine until the act. An act of violence resulting in death abruptly uproots the school, school community, family and friends from everyday life and can have serious psychological consequences, such as the development of depression, persistent grief disorder, anxiety disorders or post-traumatic stress disorder (PTSD). Deaths caused by violence in schools also attract a comparatively large amount of media attention and, shortly after the crime, can trigger discussions about a wide range of grievances in schools and about possible prevention and intervention measures, as well as fuelling copycat crimes and hindering bereaved families in the process of coming to terms with their grief.

In the following sections, after a brief introduction to the general state of knowledge on violence in schools, the different forms of violence school shootings, bullying and cyberbullying in schools, including their consequences, will be dealt with in more detail, before these are brought into a context with the accompanying mourning process in the case of a death due to violence in schools.

4.2.3.2 Violence in Schools

Until the end of the 1980s, the topic of violence in schools was largely taboo in Germany and has only been increasingly discussed by researchers, schools, police and youth welfare services since the 1990s. In the 1990s, in particular, the worldwide reputation of rampage killings significantly increased the discussion about acts of violence in schools and the necessary crisis management (Storath & Engelbrecht, 2004). Over the years, it has become increasingly clear that crises and acts of violence are also omnipresent in the school context. A study conducted by the Federal Criminal Police Office at the Ruhr-Universität in Bonn (Feltes, 2003) shows that about 6% of schoolchildren in Germany have been threatened or injured with a weapon at some time. In addition, almost one in three reported having witnessed a fight with injuries at least once a month. A representative student survey in Bavaria showed a general slight decrease in violence at schools between 1994 and 2004 (Fuchs et al., 2009). However, in 2004, 10% of all students surveyed reported having brought a weapon to school and 14.9% reported having threatened to use one (Fuchs et al., 2009). Forms of verbal violence are at the same time considered the most frequent and usually less serious form of violence, and more serious acts of violence are usually perpetrated by a small core of pupils, which is around 2–3% (Fuchs et al., 2009). However, if a more serious act occurs, this is serious for the pupils concerned, the school, community and relatives.

A tragic case in Lünen from 2018, for example, shows the arbitrariness of some homicides at schools. There, a 15-year-old pupil, who had left school a few months earlier and had come to the school that day for a talk with a social worker and mother, stabbed to death a 14-year-old pupil because the latter would have looked provocatively at the perpetrator's mother (Wette, 2018; "Murder warrant issued against fellow pupil in Lünen" 2018). The school, teachers and students, parents and the whole city of Lünen were in shock after the crime. Why could the student bring a knife to school? Could the crime have been prevented? And how could it have come to this in the first place?

As in the case of Lünen, psychological and physical violence in schools is now a regular topic of public discussion (almost ten million hits on Google alone with the keyword "violence in schools in Germany", as of January 31, 2020). However, many reports from the media on the occurrence of acts of violence at schools are ambiguous and very unclear, as such reports are often written and published before the facts of the case have been conclusively clarified. This is problematic above all because it hinders the formation of a realistic assessment of the issue, and false or inaccurate reporting in no way does justice to victims and perpetrators. Unfortunately, it is usually impossible to answer the question of a clear trigger for a serious act of violence. The multitude of possible situations triggering violence also makes it difficult to determine a reliable number of these serious violent incidents. Data from the Centers for Disease Control and Prevention's (CDC; Holland et al., 2019) "School Associated Violent Death Surveillance System" nonetheless shed light on the characteristics of homicides in schools in the United States of America between 1994 and 2018. School-associated homicides collectively account for less than two percent of all juvenile homicides in the United States. In doing so, the report includes 393 single-victim cases between July 1994 and June 2016 and 28 multiple-victim cases resulting in 121 homicides between July 1994 and June 2018, with the number of cases with more than one fatality increasing over the time period studied, while single-victim homicides remained at the same level. Single homicide crimes in schools mostly involved male victims (77.4%) between the ages of eight and fifteen (77.9%), most of whom belonged to an ethnic minority. In addition, the results showed that an urban environment was a risk factor for school violence and the most common motives for such acts were disputes between hostile gangs (34.1%) or interpersonal disputes (29.3%). Violent acts in schools that involved more than one victim showed no gender difference in the number of victims. The perpetrators were mostly people unknown to the victims (36.2%) or schoolmates (36.2%). It is also striking that the majority of homicides involving both single and multiple victims were carried out by firearm (95% for multiple victims; 62.8% for single victims) and the perpetrators were mostly male. This picture corresponds to the low proportion of female prisoners of 5.2% in Germany (Robertz & Wickenhäuser, 2010, p. 20). Compared to the German female population share of 51%, only a small proportion of girls and women are registered as suspects in Germany at 23.7% (Robertz & Wickenhäuser, 2010). These differences are even more noticeable with regard to suspicion for homicide. In the age group between eight and 14 years, female suspects for homicides account for 0.24%, among 14 to 18 year-olds it is 4.87%, among 18 to 21 year-olds it is 9.82%, and at the age of 21 to 25 it is 8.70% (Robertz & Wickenhäuser, 2010).

As mentioned earlier, homicides in the school context, regardless of the number of victims, are devastating to families, schools, and communities left behind. Different forms of school violence and their consequences are discussed in more detail below.

4.2.3.2.1 School Shootings

The general homicide rate among children and adolescents has been declining for many years, not only in Germany but also in the USA. For example, a report on the development of violence in Germany shows that the number of homicides by juveniles decreased by 22.7% between 2003 and 2013 (Pfeiffer et al., 2018). Unfortunately, an opposite picture can be observed for school shootings (Robertz & Wickenhäuser, 2010). It is worth mentioning that statements about the frequency of school shootings and perpetrator/victim characteristics are thereby mostly based on information painstakingly collected from public media reports and, if available, police reports and court records, which are counter-researched and verified against scientific studies and publications (Robertz & Wickenhäuser, 2010).

After the first school shooting on December 30, 1974 in Olean, New York, nine more incidents took place in the following ten years. Between the years 1999 and 2010, 71 school shootings have been recorded. This increase can also be attributed, at least in part, to copycat acts, particularly in the wake of the globally sensational act at Columbine High School on April 20, 1999. Since 2002, the number of school shootings, which is very high in the USA compared to other countries, has decreased slightly. Germany has the second highest incidence of school shootings in the world (Robertz & Wickenhäuser, 2010). By 2012, twelve school shootings had occurred there, resulting in 33 fatalities and approximately 68 injuries. Eleven of these school shootings were committed by male perpetrators, five of whom committed suicide following their crime. On average, the perpetrators were 17.5 years old (Bondü, 2012) and the general tendency of single perpetrators and the use of firearms can be observed (Robertz & Wickenhäuser, 2010).

School shootings are accompanied by great public interest and a sensational media hype. First, a number of media outlets report on the events as quickly and extensively as possible and provide a multitude of pictures and video footage of the suffering that has occurred. What is disregarded is that such "media hype" could potentially limit important space for emergency responders. Afterwards, politicians usually turn their attention to the events and emphasize that they will do everything to prevent such incidents in the future. By then, however, the actual causes of the acts have usually not been determined. Therefore, games or music that contain violence or glorify violence quickly move to the forefront of discussions as supposed triggers. This gives the impression that one is supposedly critically dealing with the possible triggers of serious acts of violence and that the problem can be solved quickly and easily. Internet sites, online communities, etc. that provide access to otherwise inaccessible information (e.g., bomb-making instructions) and materials (e.g., access to weapons) are in conversation to promote violent behavior. It appears that youth who actively seek out violent content are at greater risk in this regard than youth who come across such content by chance (Robertz & Wickenhäuser, 2010). In the same way, active engagement in killer games is also seen as highly problematic. Violent games, in contrast to non-violent games, lead to more arousal, increase of aggressive thoughts but also positive feelings, happiness or relaxation (Robertz & Wickenhäuser, 2010). They do not, as often assumed in the media, lead to an increase in hostile feelings (Robertz & Wickenhäuser, 2010) and studies consistently show that violent video games only slightly (Vossekuil et al., 2002; Willoughby et al., 2012) to not at all change the violent behaviour of adolescents (Ybarra et al., 2008; Ferguson et al., 2012). Isolated studies even show that violence in video games leads to a reduction of aggression in real life (Shibuya et al., 2008). The attempt to make violent media the sole trigger of school shootings cannot therefore be upheld.

Furthermore, the media are often held responsible for supporting the copycat effect of school shootings (Meindl & Ivy, 2016; Towers et al., 2015). The often dramatizing reporting publishes and discusses a lot of information about the perpetrator, the crime, the motives, preparations and presumed character traits of the perpetrator(s), which, however, is often done hastily and, in the worst case, leads to erroneous reporting (Murray, 2017). The notoriety of the perpetrator(s) encourages other potential perpetrators, who get new ideas about their own plans or fuel fantasies of carrying out an act of similar or perhaps even greater magnitude (Hickey, 2010; Towers et al., 2015). Towers et al. (2015) report that mass murders by firearm use, which include school shootings, are significantly inspired by similar incidents. Within the first thirteen days of the incident, the risk of a copycat crime is highest in this regard (Bunch, 2012; Towers et al., 2015). Despite the risk that coverage of school shootings may appeal to potential perpetrators who may be encouraged in their fantasies, ideas and justifications, it is important not to blame any media exposure as the sole cause of a school shooting. There are many different reasons underlying such an extreme act, such as acute crises, problems in processing difficult experiences, the belief that the act of violence is an act to be justified, access to weapons, etc., which interact and lead to the implementation of a school shooting in an escalating process (Robertz & Wickenhäuser, 2010). Within the process leading up to the crime, violent fantasies on the part of the perpetrator also usually emerge (Meloy et al., 2001). These may be present before or at the beginning of the planning of the crime, but they become increasingly real and more likely to be embedded in reality (Robertz & Wickenhäuser, 2010). Destructive fantasies and their incorporation into reality can be reinforced by a lack of social relationships, and in many cases the intense fantasy activity leads to fantasy and reality becoming mixed at the time of the crime (Robertz & Wickenhäuser, 2010). Most offenders exhibit increased risk-taking behaviors shortly before the crime, display characteristics such as despair, fantasies of grandeur, and grievability, and typically leak information about crime planning and existing violent fantasies. This phenomenon is also referred to as "leaking" (see Infobox 2).

▶ **Infobox 2: Leaking**
Leaking refers to "utterances, signs, thoughts, fantasies of a person that suggest a possible violent act. These may be expressed verbally or non-verbally in threats, diaries, videos, drawings, essays, tattoos, and the like." (O'Toole, 1999)

Apart from that, the perpetrators usually do not show any serious mental disorders, but usually depressive symptoms (see Infobox 3). Moreover, in the known cases, perpetrators were often described as introverted loners who committed their crime due to social insecurities and low self-esteem (Baumeister et al., 2000). However, more recent considerations point to the possibility that a high number of perpetrators have narcissistic personalities (see Infobox 4) or at least narcissistic tendencies and commit the act primarily to highlight their ego (Bushman, 2017; Hoffmann et al., 2009; Langman, 2009). Bondü and Scheithauer (2011) list narcissistic personality traits, rejection by classmates (e.g. through bullying), experiences of loss and a negative school climate among the most important risk factors for amok acts at schools.

▶ **Infobox 3: Depressive symptoms**
Symptoms of depression include, but are not limited to, persistent sadness, hopelessness, discouragement, or dejection in those affected. Also, the general loss of interest as well as the loss of pleasure in activities are among other common symptoms in people with depression. Children and adolescents with depressive symptoms often seem irritable rather than sad. In addition, changes in appetite, weight, sleep, and psychomotor activity may occur. People with depression often feel worthless or guilty, have difficulty concentrating, and experience recurring thoughts of death, up to and including suicidal intentions, plans, and attempts. (American Psychiatric Association 2015)

Infobox 4: Narcissistic personality disorder
Characteristics of narcissistic personality disorder include a profound pattern of grandiosity (in fantasy or behavior), an increased need for admiration from outsiders, and a lack of empathy. People with narcissistic tendencies often overestimate their abilities, appear boastful about accomplishments, and are usually consumed with fantasies of success and power. In addition, their self-worth is often quickly fragile, as they react very sensitively to devaluations and injuries. Thus, people with narcissistic tendencies often experience pronounced feelings of worthlessness and humiliation after personal criticism and react with contempt and anger (APA 2015).

These psychosocial factors, together with individual personality traits (e.g. depressive tendencies or a narcissistic personality structure) and structural preconditions (e.g. access to information thanks to the Internet), form part of a developmental process that ultimately leads to a rampage. Figure 4.2 depicts this development schematically and illustrates the interplay of various factors in the development of a school shooting.

4.2.3.2.2 Bullying

Bullying is a special form of violence (Alsaker, 2012; Haller et al., 2018) that extends over a longer period of time and aims to exclude others from a social community (Kampwerth, 2009, p. 7). The term "mobbing", which became widespread mainly under the influence of Scandinavian research (Olweus, 2002), is now often used synonymously with the international term "bullying". In this chapter, the term "bullying" is used to describe systematic physical or psychological violence in a school context.

Bullying *"means that a pupil or a group of pupils is systematically, repeatedly and over a long period of time exposed to the negative actions of another pupil (or group of pupils) (...)"*. (see Spröber et al., 2008a, p. 6). A single aggressive action of one student towards another student, or a fight between opponents of equal strength, is therefore not to be understood as bullying, but as aggression (Scheithauer et al., 2003). Bullying is further characterized by an asymmetrical relationship between perpetrator and victim, so that the victim subjectively and/or objectively does not have the strength to extricate himself from the situation on his own and stop the repeated harassment (Spröber et al., 2008a, p. 6). The intention to harm, the systematic and repetitive aspect of the harmful behaviour, the power

4 Causes of Grief

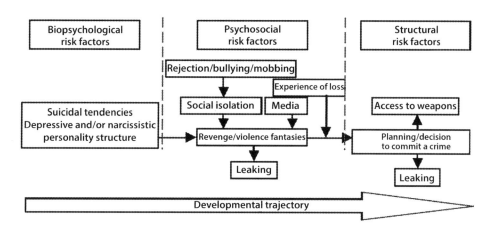

Fig. 4.2 Explanatory/developmental model for school shootings

imbalance between perpetrator and victim and the resulting helplessness can therefore be understood as the main criteria of mobbing. Furthermore, bullying occurs in different forms. First, a distinction can be made between bullying of a physical (e.g. kicking, hitting, forcibly taking property, etc.) and verbal (e.g. name-calling, verbal threats, being mean, making fun) nature, both of which belong to direct bullying (Haller et al., 2018). Physical bullying is less prevalent in schools than verbal bullying (Alsaker & Brunner, 1999; Boulton & Underwood, 1992). Thus, name-calling has been found to be the most common type of bullying across cultures in studies of eight to twelve year olds (Baldry, 1998; Bentley & Li, 1995; Genta et al., 1996; O'Moore et al., 1997; Vettenburg, 1999; Whitney & Smith, 1993). Only in Portugal has an increased prevalence for physical violence been reported (Pereira et al., 1996). Relational bullying (e.g., spreading rumors, deliberately kicking people out of a group, ignoring them), an indirect form of bullying (Haller et al., 2018), is more inconspicuous than direct forms and is often not perceived as bullying by outsiders (Politi, 2020, p. 7). Direct bullying is typically carried out by male perpetrators, whereas indirect bullying is more likely to be carried out by female perpetrators (Crick & Grotpeter, 1995; Genta et al., 1996; Wolke et al., 2001). Another specific form of bullying is cyberbullying, which is discussed in Sect. 4.2.3.

In addition, the number of people involved in bullying varies. Individuals or groups can bully individuals or groups. However, in any case, bullying lives through a group dynamic in which students can take on different roles (see Infobox 5; Haller et al., 2018) (Salmivalli et al., 1996). Typically, peers support perpetrators rather than stop the behavior (Sutton & Smith, 1999). The bystander group includes more female than male students who demonstrate highly developed achievement status and healthy self-esteem (Melzer et al., 2004). Perpetrators, on the other hand, are more often male than female (e.g., Spröber et al., 2008b; Wolke et al., 2001; Whitney & Smith, 1993) and often show below-average school performance (Melzer et al., 2004). Victims of bullying tend to experience social isolation, anxiety, and lower self-esteem (Olweus, 1997). Interestingly, a considerable proportion of victims or perpetrators can be classified as "perpetrator-victims" (see Infobox 5). However, the prevalence of this group is unclear and varies from 4.4% (Boulton & Smith, 1994) to 35.3% (Borg, 1999). The roles of perpetrators, victims, mixed types and bystanders are not fixed and may change over time (Melzer et al., 2004). As age increases, the group of bystanders increases, physical bullying tends to decrease and indirect bullying tends to increase. In general, there is a decrease in bullying behavior and an increase in prosocial behavior with age (Melzer et al., 2004; Rigby, 1997).

In general, prevalences of bullying in schools vary widely by culture and due to methodological differences between studies (e.g. survey method, sample, etc.). Studies in different countries report prevalence between 4% and 60.5% for bullying victims and prevalences between 6% and 48.9% for perpetrators (Alsaker & Valkanover, 2001; Boulton & Underwood, 1992; Genta et al., 1996; Borg, 1999; Nansel et al., 2001; Spröber et al., 2008b; Whitney & Smith, 1993; Wolke et al., 2001). Data from the Global School-based Student Health Survey (Koyanagi et al., 2019) from 48 countries showed an overall prevalence of bullying of 30.4%. Nevertheless, the international Health Behaviour in School-aged Children (HBSC; Kolip et al., 2013) survey, commissioned by the World Health Organization (WHO) and conducted every four years since 1983 among students aged eleven to fifteen, reports a steady decrease in bullying prevalence and an increase in students without bullying experience from 63.4% in 2002 to 76.9% in 2014. The number of students who "never" became a perpetrator also grew from 54.6% to 73.2% in the perpetrator self-report during this period. Perpetrator prevalence decreased from 13% to 8%, perpetrator victim prevalence decreased from 4% to 1%, and victim prevalence decreased to 8% during this time. The bystander group, on the other hand, shows a constant increase from 9% in 2002 to 83% in 2014. A decline in bullying prevalence has been recorded in most countries in Western Europe, Scandinavia, Eastern Europe, and the United States since the 1990s (Molcho et al., 2009). In contrast, a slight increase in bullying prevalence has been recorded in England and Canada (Molcho et al., 2009). However, the international trend seems to be towards a general decrease in the prevalence of bullying.

> **Infobox 5: Roles in the group dynamics of a bullying situation** (Haller et al., 2018)*Perpetrator*: He/she takes the initiative to bully and feeds their self-esteem through the recognition they receive from their actions.
> *Victims*: Are the target of harassment by the perpetrator(s). The victim(s) do not know how to help themselves out of the situation because of an asymmetrical power relationship with the perpetrator(s).
> *Assistants*: They orient themselves to the offenders and actively help to shape the situation.
> *Reinforcers*: They laugh along and cheer on the perpetrators and assistants, which is reinforcing.
> *Defenders*: They side with the victim(s) and try to do something about the bullying.

Outsiders: They passively experience the situation, but stay out of the bullying as much as possible.

Perpetrators/victims: Are perpetrators who are victims in other situations or victims who are perpetrators in other situations.

4.2.3.2.3 Cyberbullying

Cyberbullying as a separate form of psychological violence, which often occurs in a school context, is a relatively new phenomenon and was first described in 2003 (Bauman & Bellmore, 2015). Among other things, cyberbullying can be defined as repetitive online behaviours such as name-calling, threatening, making derogatory comments, defaming, exposing, humiliating or spreading rumours towards a person (Price & Dalgleish, 2010; Weitzmann, 2017). However, there is no single definition of this phenomenon in the literature. For example, Peter and Petermann (2018), identified twenty-four different interpretations between 2009 and 2014. All of the definitions included in this study contained the following attributes: "information and communication technologies", "repetition", "intentionality", "harm" and "a person". Derived from this, Peter and Petermann (2018), define cyberbullying as the use of information and communication technologies (ICTs) to repeatedly and *intentionally harm*, harass, inflict pain, *harass* and/or *embarrass* a target (*"using information and communication technologies (ICT) to repeatedly and intentionally harm, harass, hurt and/or embarrass a target"*; p. 359). Other definitional approaches refer to the use of the medium (e.g. bullying through text messages; pictures or videos; chat; websites; etc.; Smith et al., 2008), or to the distinction between direct (private communication, e.g. as text messages) and indirect (communication in the public domain, e.g. in social networks) cyberbullying (Langos, 2012).

Many definitions refer to so-called traditional "offline" bullying and interpret cyberbullying as a transfer of traditional bullying into the digital world (Schenk, 2020). However, this seems to be too short-sighted, as cyberbullying, apart from some similarities with traditional bullying, has very specific characteristics that should be considered separately in order to do justice to this phenomenon in its complexity. For this reason, Pieschl et al. (2015), among others, advocate recognizing cyberbullying as a separate phenomenon. A detailed explanation and comparison of the similarities and differences between traditional and cyberbullying can be found in Schenk (2020), as an elaboration exceeds the capacity of this chapter.

The disagreement regarding a uniform definition of cyberbullying, in addition to different samples and measurement methods used, is problematic in the research of the phenomenon as it complicates the generalization of the results. In this context, prevalence rates of cyberbullying victims range from 1.5% (Ortega et al., 2008) to 72% (Juvonen & Gross, 2008). The prevalence rates of cyberbullying perpetrators show an even wider range between 0% (Didden et al., 2009) and 60.4% (Xiao & Wong, 2013). One of the consequences of these wide ranges is that the seriousness of cyberbullying is assessed very differently, even among experts. For example, Morgan (2012) writes that experiencing cyberbullying is ubiquitous for adolescents and is almost a taken-for-granted experience, which threatens to spiral out of control. Olweus (2012), on the other hand, describes cyberbullying as a phenomenon that is often misunderstood and decreasing in frequency (Betts, 2016). Regarding prevalence figures in Germany, 34% of children and adolescents between the ages of 12 and 19 in the Youth, Information, Media (YIM) study conducted by the Medienpädagogischer Forschungsverbund Südwest (mpfs) (2018), stated that they had already witnessed cyberbullying among their acquaintances (39% of female and 30% of male respondents). This proportion was highest between 16 and 17 year olds (40%, 12–13 years 28%, 14–15 years 32%, 18–19 years 35%). There was no significant difference in the survey results between the different types of school (33% of grammar school pupils, 35% of secondary modern school pupils). Whether they themselves had ever been a victim of cyberbullying was answered in the affirmative by 9% of the female respondents and 6% of the male respondents. In this context, Hauptschule and Realschule students were affected more frequently (10%) than Gymnasium students (6%).

4.2.3.3 Consequences of Violence in Schools

After the presentation of different forms of violence in the school context (school shootings, bullying, cyberbullying) in Sect. 4.2 "Violence in schools", Sect. 4.3 deals with the consequences of school shootings, bullying and cyberbullying.

4.2.3.3.1 Consequences of School Shootings

Although school shootings receive a great deal of media attention and carry a high risk of trauma, there are comparatively few research findings that address the consequences for people who have witnessed these horrific acts. The few studies that are available usually point to serious consequences for many of those involved. Traumatization is often associated with feelings of life threat, helplessness, powerlessness, and loss of control and security (Flatten, Bär, et al., 2011a). Students' learning and performance may deteriorate (Cornell & Mayer, 2010), and the risk for developing mental illness increases, for example, post-traumatic stress disorder (PTSD), depression, anxiety and sleep disorders, somatoform disorders, self-harming behaviors, and substance abuse (Robertz & Wickenhäuser, 2010). Suicide attempts by family members and classmates are also repeatedly reported, such as in the case of the Colombine School Shooting, in which the mother of one victim, as well as a surviving classmate, committed suicide the following year (Robertz & Wickenhäuser, 2010). In addition to the potential secondary disorders of victims and their families, a school shooting also has consequences for the school. For example, a decrease in enrollment and a decline in student achievement has been observed (Beland & Kim, 2016; Saltzman et al., 2001).

Kirsch et al. (2010) report that almost all affected individuals exhibit acute stress reactions in the first phase after a school shooting, which include, for example, a change in the experience of the self, reality, and time, memories and thoughts of the traumatic experience, or somatoform symptoms (Flatten, Bär, et al., 2011a; Höhn, 2019). In this context, affected children more often than adults report having perceived the shooting as an extreme stressor (Schwarz & Kowalski, 1991). In most cases, however, a spontaneous remission of stress symptoms occurs after a short period of usually a few weeks and can therefore be understood as a normal reaction in the adaptation process regarding traumatic experiences (Kirsch et al., 2010). If this is not the case and the symptoms persist for longer than one month, they can manifest themselves in post-traumatic stress disorder (PTSD) (see Infobox 6). One of the strongest risk factors for the development of PTSD is the experience of dissociations (see Infobox 7) in the context of a traumatic experience (Ozer et al., 2003). Different degrees of severity in the aftermath of school shootings could be due to different coping styles, among other factors (Lowe & Galea, 2015). Active, process-oriented, and accepting coping styles appear to be helpful with regard to symptom expression, whereas ruminative and avoidant coping styles are not (Lowe & Galea, 2015). Guilt, insecurity, and anxiety sensitivity are associated with negative health outcomes following school shootings, whereas self-efficacy, spirituality, and perceived benevolence of others, are protective factors (Lowe & Galea, 2015). Low socioeconomic status, low educational attainment, and prior trauma are also associated with poorer processing of school shootings (Lowe & Galea, 2015). Additionally, a close personal relationship with the victim (s) negatively influences the level of trauma experienced by affected children and adolescents (Elklit & Kurdahl, 2013). Social support from family and friends in the aftermath of a traumatic event also has a strong influence on the ability of victims to cope (Brewin, Andrews, & Valentine, 2000), with a negative impact of the social environment having a stronger effect on the severity of traumatisation than a positive impact preventing it (Brewin & Holmes, 2003).

▶ **Infobox 6: Post-traumatic stress disorder (PTSD; APA 2015)**
Post-traumatic stress disorder (PTSD) can occur when one or more traumas have been experienced and not sufficiently processed. The symptoms of PTSD vary greatly depending on the person affected, with the extent of the disorder being determined by the timing, duration and severity of the underlying trauma.

A Review of Symptoms Includes

A. A confrontation with an event involving death, danger of death, serious injury, or threat to physical integrity, to which one responds with intense fear, helplessness, and/or horror.
B. A persistent re-experiencing of the event either through distressing memories, recurrent dreams, actions or feelings as if the traumatic event is recurring or, when confronted with cue stimuli, psychological distress and physical reactions.
C. The avoidance of key stimuli in at least three of the following symptoms: (1) avoidance of thoughts, feelings, conversations of activities, places, or people; (2) inability to recall important aspects of the trauma; (3) decreased interest, decreased participation in activities; (4) feeling detached and alienated; (5) restricted affect; (6) feeling of a restricted future.

D. A persistent, increased arousal with at least two of the following symptoms: (1) difficulty falling asleep or staying asleep through the night; (2) irritability or angry outbursts; (3) difficulty concentrating; (4) excessive vigilance; (5) exaggerated startle reactions.
E. The disturbance must exist for more than one month.
F. It is a clinically significant condition with impairments in social, occupational, and other important areas of functioning.

In general, there is an overall prevalence of PTSD after experiencing a violent crime of about 25% (Flatten, Gast, et al., 2011b). Prevalence rates of PTSD related to school shootings range from 17% to 27% (Kirsch et al., 2010). Lowe and Galea (2015) report prevalences of a minimum of 3% for parents of children who were victims of a school shooting six to 14 months prior, and a maximum prevalence of 91% for affected children. However, the wide range of these prevalences can be attributed to the aforementioned remission of the symptoms of posttraumatic stress that were usually present initially. The same is true for the prevalences listed by Lowe and Galea (2015) for depression, which is the second most commonly recorded disorder related to school shootings. The authors report a prevalence with a low of 4.9% one year after a school shooting and a high of 71% two weeks after a school shooting. Thus, the timing of PTSD or depression should not be ignored when interpreting study results. In addition, comparison between studies is complicated by differences in sample characteristics and the use of different measurement instruments and diagnostic manuals, and not all studies include the possibility of the presence of mental health complaints even before the crime (Lowe & Galea, 2015). In addition to PTSD and depression, prevalences have been reported for the development of generalized anxiety disorder (0.0–0.9%), acute stress disorder (33%), alcohol-related problems (0–9%), substance abuse problems (0–0.7%), panic disorder (1–2.4%), adjustment disorder (9.1%), social phobias (3%), and antisocial personality disorder (0–0.8%) (Lowe & Galea, 2015).

▶ **Infobox 7: Dissociation**
Dissociation is the detachment or splitting off of mental processes such as perception, identity and motor function. (APA 1994). Peritraumatic dissociations describe dissociations that occur during or immediately after a traumatic experience.

For outsiders, school shootings are quickly forgotten. But what remains, besides the relatives and others involved, is a school community whose members have to deal with and live with the aftermath of the experience. People who come into contact with this form of violence in schools will most likely not forget the experience for the rest of their lives. The feeling that school is a place of safety is ripped away from students and their families, faculty and other staff, and what is left behind is a sense of insecurity and fear. The grieving process after such a traumatic experience is explored in more detail in chapter four.

4.2.3.3.2 Consequences of Bullying

Bullying, apart from possible physical consequences of direct physical bullying, also has consequences for psychosocial development and mental health development in childhood, adolescence and young and middle adulthood (Isaacs et al., 2008; Takizawa et al., 2014). First and foremost, bullying attacks self-worth, which is extremely important for psychological stability and health across the lifespan. Especially at a young age, negative experiences can be crucial for psychosocial development and psychological stability in life (Alsaker, 2004; Dittmann, 2011). It is important to note that bullying not only negatively impacts bullying victims, but also perpetrators, the entire class community, and especially perpetrator-victims (Alsaker, 2004). For example, perpetrator-victims also show reduced self-esteem (Alsaker, 2004) and are comparatively the most affected by psychological disorders (Nordhagen et al., 2005). For example, perpetrators, unlike victims, are characterized by a higher prevalence for substance abuse (Forero et al., 1999; Nansel et al., 2001). One difference is that bullying victims tend to show internalizing problems (anxiety, depressive symptoms, self-esteem problems), whereas perpetrators tend to show externalizing problems (impulsivity, hyperactivity, aggressiveness, norm violation, social behavior disorders). Furthermore, bullying leads to behavioural problems and psychosomatic distress as a result of bullying experiences, such as hyperactivity, increased tension and sleep problems in victims, perpetrators and perpetrator-victims, increased dizziness and behavioural problems in victims and perpetrator-victims, and problems with classmates in victims of bullying (Gini, 2008) Especially in social terms, bullying experiences have far-reaching consequences and lead, for example, to lower peer group involvement and lower levels of peer recognition (Rothon et al., 2011; Wachs, 2012). This often leads to perceived social isolation, which can also negatively affect school performance (Nakamoto & Schwartz, 2009; Rothon et al., 2011), as social isolation exacerbates a general decline in cognitive performance and problems with concentration and attention (Politi, 2020). In addition, motivation and enjoyment of learning also decline (Boulton & Underwood, 1992) and school avoidance often occurs to avoid bullying. Perpetrators also show poorer school performance than uninvolved students and drops in performance can also be referred to within the whole class community (Dittmann, 2011). Bullying victims show increased risks for depression (Alsaker, 2006; Hawker & Boulton, 2000), anxiety disorders (Alsaker, 2004; Bond 2001; Hawker & Boulton, 2000), and psychotic symptoms (Arseneault et al., 2011; Schreier et al., 2009), increased rates of self-harm (Fisher et al., 2012; Lereya et al., 2013), and increased risk for suicidal ideation and suicide attempts. Koyanagi et al. (2019) report a threefold increased risk for bullying victims to commit a suicide attempt for 47 out of 48 countries. In this context, the frequency of bullying experiences also appears to increase the risk (Koyanagi et al., 2019). Brunstein-Klomek et al. (2007) also reports a six-fold higher risk of suicidal ideation for frequently bullied students. The association between bullying and suicidal ideation has also been shown to be stronger for indirect than direct bullying (Van der Wal et al., 2003a, b; Weitzel, 2019).

However, the consequences of bullying are not only evident after direct exposure to bullying in childhood and adolescence, but have been shown to extend into middle adulthood. Takizawa et al. (2014), analyzed data from the British national child development study, a cohort study conducted in 1958 that included children aged seven and eleven. 7771 participants in the study reported having bullying experiences, with 28% of children reporting being bullied occasionally and 15% reporting being bullied frequently. Follow-up measures at ages 23 and 50 years at both measurement time points showed increased psychological distress for participants who experienced bullying in childhood as opposed to participants without bullying experience. Frequent bullying was still associated with increased risk for depression and anxiety disorders at age 45, and occasional bullying was associated with increased risk for depression. Bullying experiences were also associated with low general health at ages 23 and 50 and with decreased cognitive function at age 50. In addition, childhood bullying negatively affected educational attainment, economic status, social relationships, general well-being, and life satisfaction (Takizawa et al., 2014).

4.2.3.3.3 Consequences of Cyberbullying

Cyberbullying has a similar impact as classic bullying and has negative consequences not only for victims but also for perpetrators. Campbell et al. (2013), among others, have shown that cyberbullying perpetrators have poorer mental health than people who do not engage in cyberbullying. This relates to comparatively higher levels of depression (Selkie et al., 2015), anxiety (Lam et al., 2013) and reduced self-esteem (Patchin & Hinduja, 2006). The negative consequences of cyberbullying on victims are well documented and manifold (see, for example, Patchin & Hinduja, 2006). With regard to negative psychosocial adjustment as a direct consequence of cyberbullying experiences, the main focus is on massive psychological stress (Kubiszewski et al., 2015). As it progresses, mental health deterioration occurs (Imamura et al., 2009). Thus, cyberbullying victimization is associated with depression (Kowalski & Fedina, 2011; Landoll et al., 2015), anxiety disorders (Betts, 2016), psychosomatic symptoms such as headaches, abdominal pain, and insomnia (Sourander et al., 2010), self-injurious behavior (Lam et al., 2013), and suicidal ideation (Hinduja & Patchin, 2010). Furthermore, Sinclair et al. (2012) report that young people with cyberbullying experiences are approximately four times more likely to attempt suicide compared to young people without such experiences, and suicidal behaviours can extend into adulthood (Copeland et al., 2013). Victims of cyberbullying report significantly lower self-worth (Fernandes et al., 2015) and more social anxiety (Dempsey et al., 2009; Landoll et al., 2015) than those without cyberbullying experiences and are viewed as less popular by those around them (Festl et al., 2013). The accompanying negative impact on the development and maintenance of social relationships leads victims of social relationships to turn away and have problems trusting other people (Crosslin & Crosslin, 2014).

Particularly problematic here is that trust plays an important role in the development of satisfying relationships (Rotenberg, 1994).

Other consequences include lower engagement in the school day and a decline in academic performance among those with cyberbullying experiences (Patchin & Hinduja, 2006). School is also often no longer perceived as a safe place (Varjas et al., 2009). Additionally, excessive alcohol and cannabis use are also associated with cyberbullying victimization (Goebert et al., 2011).

4.2.3.4 Grief in the Context of Violence

The loss of fellow human beings through exposure to violence leaves the bereaved and survivors in shock, and the accompanying grief can be understood as "grief like no other" (Turunen & Punamäki, 2016). Different aspects play an important role in this process. Stevenson (2008), describes the following characteristics of violent loss that may specifically affect the subsequent grieving process. *The loss of people to violence usually happens suddenly and unexpectedly.* Thus, bereaved individuals cannot prepare for the loss and say goodbye. Additionally, the traumatic experience is compounded by the fact that in some cases, bereaved families and survivors have to wait for official confirmation of death or do not have the opportunity to revisit the body of the deceased due to the cause of death (Turunen & Punamäki, 2016). *Losing people to violence can increase the impact of other stressors.* Confrontation with severe physical violence and the accompanying stress response complicates the grieving process, which in the context of pre-existing problems can further complicate coping. *Feelings of guilt can complicate the grieving process.* Experiencing feelings of guilt and self-blame is a common reaction to sudden, violent loss (Lehman et al., 1987). For example, survivors may develop feelings of not having done enough to help victims or feel guilt that they themselves survived (Weisæth, 1989). *Survivors and survivors experience a loss of control.* Common emotional reactions to sudden, violent loss have been described as extreme experiences of anger, irritability and sadness, which can alternate unpredictably and trigger either insensitivity or overwhelming, uncontrollable bouts of grief in survivors (Turunen & Punamäki, 2016). *The media and other public reactions can hinder the grieving process.* For example, school shootings are accompanied by a great deal of media attention in which the background, family histories, police investigations and judicial proceedings are extensively reported and explored. Thus, victims are continually reminded of the events and deaths, preventing the grieving process from coming to a natural end (Murphy et al., 2003).

In the context of natural loss, bereaved people usually overcome the grieving process without long-term problems and professional help, with the help of their family and friends (Kristensen et al., 2012). However, unexpected and violent loss differs from natural loss, mainly because the death was caused by human intention or negligence (Turunen et al., 2014). This loss is understood as a traumatizing experience and one of the most common causes of post-traumatic stress disorder (PTSD) has been described (Van Ameringen et al., 2008). Table 4.1 lists differences between normal coping with death and traumatic grief at the cognitive, emotional and behavioural levels. According to this, the unexpected, violent loss of a family member, classmate or teacher is followed by repeated recollections of the traumatising events and the search for the usually inexplicable reasons for the loss. The "ground is pulled out from under the feet" of the bereaved and they are also confronted with their own vulnerability.

A large number of studies have shown that the unexpected, violent loss of a fellow human being entails a more complicated, more severe grieving process than natural loss (Kristensen et al., 2012). In particular, prolonged grief disorder, major depression and post-traumatic stress disorder (PTSD), as well as anxiety and mood swings, are frequently observed as a result of sudden, violent loss (Turunen & Punamäki, 2016). In this context, the violence used appears to be a stronger predictor of persistent grief disorders (Currier et al., 2006) and PTSD (Kaltman & Bonanno, 2003) than the suddenness of the death. The recovery process for survivors of victims of violence also appears slower than for survivors of natural causes of death (Kristensen et al., 2012). For example, it was observed that depressive symptoms lasted longer in survivors of violent deaths than in survivors of natural deaths (Kaltman & Bonanno, 2003). In addition, the cause of death also influences the bereavement process and the mental health of the bereaved. For example, survivors of suicide victims are more likely to describe grief-specific symptoms such as rejection, shame, stigma, and blame, and are more likely to conceal the deceased person's cause of death (Sveen & Walby, 2008). Survivors of violent crimes, unlike survivors of suicide and accident victims, experience more frequent persistent grief disorders and PTSD (Currier et al., 2006).

There are different constructs to describe the grieving process after traumatic loss. Commonly cited in the literature are traumatic loss (Green et al., 2001), traumatic death (Rando, 1996), traumatic bereavement (Raphael & Martinek, 2004) or traumatic grief (Prigerson et al., 1999), and complicated grief (Horowitz et al., 1997). For example, Raphael et al. (2006) use the concept of traumatic bereavement to describe the complex relationships between traumatic stress and the loss of others. Complicated grief was initially defined as a grief reaction that did not meet the criteria of normal "uncomplicated" grief (Turunen et al., 2014). This term is often used in the context of death from severe physical violence in children and subsequent psychological problems in the parents (Kristensen et al., 2012). In this context, complicated grief has been used since the early 1990s to describe primarily grief processes characterized by separation distress and traumatic symptoms that resulted from the loss of important relationships (Prigerson et al., 1997). However, often the above constructs are used interchangeably in the grief and trauma literature (Kristensen et al., 2012). In ICD-11, prolonged grief disorder is included as a disorder for the first time in a diagnostic manual and is at least conceptually aligned with complicated grief (see Infobox 7; Killikelly & Maercker, 2018). In the DSM-5, persistent complex bereavement disorder is listed as a compromise between persistent grief disorder and complicated grief in the area of disorders requiring further research (Killikelly & Maercker, 2018; Reynolds et al., 2017).

> **Infobox 8: Diagnostic criteria for prolonged grief disorder (ICD-11) by** Killikelly and Maercker (2018)

A: At least one of the following:

1. persistent and pervasive longing for the deceased
2. persistent and pervasive preoccupation with the deceased

B: Examples of intense emotional pain.
Accompanied by intense emotional pain e.g. sadness, guilt, anger, denial, blame;
Difficulty accepting the death;
Feeling one has lost a part of one's self;
An inability to experience positive mood.
Emotional numbness.
Difficulty in engaging participating with social or other activities.
C: Time and impairment criterion.
Persisted for an abnormally long period of time (more than 6 months at a minimum): following the loss, clearly exceeding expected social, cultural or religious norms for the individual's culture and context. Grief reactions that have persisted for longer periods that are within a normative period of grieving given the person's cultural and religious context are viewed as normal beravement responses and are not assigned a diagnosis.

The disturbance causes significant impairment in personal, family, social, educational, occupational or other important areas of functioning.

In relation to school shootings, suicide and other forms of serious physical violence resulting in death, severely traumatised victims may not be able to participate in a mourning process organised by the school, e.g. by performing rituals. Some bereaved persons may use systematic avoidance strategies or do not want to be able to deal with what they have experienced. These must be respected. Also, too early confrontation with what has happened, e.g. through participation in rituals, could have a negative effect on them by triggering dissociations (see: PTSD) or intensifying other symptoms (anxiety and panic states, re-experiencing what has happened, etc.). In this context, Green et al. (1985), point out that grief can and should only be dealt with following the treatment of trauma. The special nature of grief after sudden, violent loss compared to other causes of loss must be observed in the context of grief counselling in schools in order to be able to do justice to all those affected and their individual reactions and needs.

4.2.3.5 Conclusion

Psychological and physical violence in schools is ubiquitous. Fortunately, however, the causes of death in schools as a result of physical violence or preceding psychological violence (bullying/cyber-bullying) are very low compared to other causes of death in this context. However, media coverage sometimes creates a contrary picture. Events such as school shootings gain an incredible media presence, which can negatively influence the organisation of support as well as the grieving process of the victims and distort the public image of such cruel acts and their triggers. While reporting cannot be identified as the sole factor in copycat crimes, it does seem to appeal to potential perpetrators to some extent. Therefore, careful consideration should be given to what information is released to the public and when. Grief after sudden, violent loss is closely interwoven with the traumatisation of bereaved families and trauma-relevant mental health disorders. Accordingly, the increased risk of trauma as well as the degree of trauma caused by deaths after violence in schools must be taken into account when accompanying the mourning processes within the circle of the school. This is the only way to minimise the risk of a possible negative influence of these projects for dealing with trauma on those affected and the bereaved.

References

4.1 Chronic Diseases

Adler, R., Hermann, K., Köhle, K., Langewitz, W., Schonecke, O., von Uexküll, et al. (2003). *Psychosomatische Medizin*. Urban & Fischer Verlag.

Bayerisches Staatsministerium für Bildung und Kultus, Wissenschaft und Kunst. (2015). *Hospiz und Schule–Abschied, Sterben, Tod und Trauer als Thema für Schule und Unterricht*. Appel und Klinger.

Deutscher Hospiz- und PalliativVerband e. V. (DHPV). (2017). *Abschied nehmende Kinder- Eine Handreichung des DHPV*. Springer.

DKHV–Deutscher Kinderhospizverein e. V. (2015). *Immer wieder neu... Geduld, Staunen, Zuversicht. Schriftenreihe des Deutschen Kinderhospizvereins e. V. (Band 5)*. der Hospizverlag.

Droste, E., & Hartekopf, M. (2013). Nähe gestalten, Teilhabe ermöglichen, Trauer begleiten. In Deutscher Kinderhospizverein e. V (Ed.), *Nähe gestalten, Teilhabe ermöglichen, Trauer begleiten. Die Vielfalt der Kinderhospizarbeit. Schriftenreihe des Deutschen Kinderhospizvereins e. V* (pp. 13–19). Ludwigsburg.

Etschenberg, K., Kösters, W., & Raimund, S. (n.d.). Chronische Erkrankungen als Problem und Thema in Schule und Unterricht. *Köln: BZgA*.

Etschenberg, K. (n.d.). Chronische Erkrankungen im Kindesalter–ein gemeinsames Thema von Elternhaus. *Kindertagesstätte und Schule. Villingen-Schwenningen: BZgA*.

Haslbeck, J., Klein, M., Bischofberger, I., & Sottas, B. (2015). *Leben mit chronischer Krankheit- Die Perspektive von Patientinnen, Patienten und Angehörigen (Obsan Dossier 46)*. Schweizerisches Gesundheitsobservatorium.

Hedderich, I., & Tscheke, J. (2013). Auswirkungen chronischer körperlicher Erkrankungen auf Schule und Unterricht. In M. Pinquart (Ed.), *Wenn Kinder und Jugendliche körperlich chronisch krank sind- Psychische und soziale Entwicklung, Prävention, Intervention*. Springer.

Hospizverein Bamberg e.v. (2020). Accessed Mar 8, 2020, from https://hospizverein-bamberg.de/angebote/sterbebegleitung/

Hoß, K., & Maier, R. (2013). Medizinische Grundlagen. In M. Pinquart (Ed.), *Wenn Kinder und Jugendliche körperlich chronisch krank sind- Psychische und soziale Entwicklung, Prävention, Intervention*. Springer.

Jennessen, S., Bungenstock, A., & Schwarzenberg, E. (2011). *Kinderhospizarbeit. Konzepte, Erkenntnisse, Perspektiven.* Kohlhammer.

Jurack, U. (2009). *Krankheitsbewältigung bei chronischen Erkrankungen im Kindes- und Jugenalter.* Accessed Mar 9, 2020, from https://www.dsai.de/fileadmin/user_upload/Vortraege/Jurack__Krankheitsbewaeltigung.pdf

Make-A-Wish. (2020). https://www.make-a-wish.at/ueber-make-a-wish/

Mehmke, H. (2016). *Leben mit einer chronischen Erkrankung.* Accessed Mar 9, 2020, from https://www.initiative-sma.de/download/leben-mit-einer-chronischen-krankheit-heike-mehmke/

Sitte, T., & Stöbener, A. (2017). *Am Start das Ziel im Blick haben- Unterrichtsmaterial- Leben und Sterben gehören zusammen.* Rindt-Druck.

Schristenreihe der Deutschen Leukämie-Forschungshilfe Aktion für krebskranke Kinder e. V.-Dachverband (DLFH) und deutsche Kinderkrebsstiftung. (2014). *Ein Leitfaden für Lehrer- Wenn ein Schüler Krebs hat.* Universitätsklinikum.

Schönekerl. (2009). *Chronisch kranke Schüler im Schulalltag- Empfehlungen zur Unterstützung und Förderung.* Union Druckerei Dresden.

Sticker, E., & Grosser, M. (2016). *Wir in der Schule: Chronische Erkrankungen und Behinderungen im Schulalltag- Informationen aus der Selbsthilfe.* Düsseldorf: Bundesarbeitsgemeinschaft Selbsthilfe von Menschen mit Behinderung und chronische Erkrankung und ihre Angehörigen e. V. (BAG Selbsthilfe).

Zernikow, B., Craig, F., & Nauck, F. (2013). Todeskonzepte und individuelle Bedürfnisse von sterbenden Kindern und Jugendlichen. In B. Zernikow (Ed.), *Palliativversorgung von Kindern, Jugendlichen und jungen Erwachsenen.* Springer.

4.2.1 Suicide

Althaus, D., & Hegerl, U. (2004). Ursachen, Diagnose und Therapie von Suizidalität. *Nervenarzt, 75*(11), 1123–1135. https://doi.org/10.1007/s00115-004-1824-2

Back, S. N. (2020). Exkurs: Mediale Inszenierung von Mobbing–Zusammenhänge zwischen jugendlichem Medienkonsum, Mobbing und Suizid. In M. Böhmer & G. Steffgen (Eds.), *Mobbing an Schulen* (pp. 57–77). Springer VS.

Balázs, J., Miklósi, M., Keresztény, Á., Dallos, G., & Gádoros, J. (2014). Attention-deficit hyperactivity disorder and suicidality in a treatment naïve sample of children and adolescents. *Journal of Affective Disorders, 152–154,* 282–287. https://doi.org/10.1016/j.jad.2013.09.026

Balázs, J., Miklósi, M., Keresztény, Á., Hoven, C. W., Carli, V., Wasserman, C., et al. (2013). Adolescent subthreshold-depression and anxiety: Psychopathology, functional impairment and increased suicide risk. *Journal of Child Psychology and Psychiatry, 54*(6), 670–677. https://doi.org/10.1111/jcpp.12016

Bronisch, T. (2008). Suizidalität. In H. J. Möller, G. Laux, & H. P. Kapfhammer (Eds.), *Psychiatrie und Psychotherapie* (pp. 1281–1306). Springer.

Brezo, J., Paris, J., Vitaro, F., Hebert, M., Tremblay, R. E., & Turecki, G. (2008). Predicting suicide attempts in young adults with histories of childhood abuse. *The British Journal of Psychiatry, 193*(2), 134–139. https://doi.org/10.1192/bjp.bp.107.037994

Bründel, H. (2004). *Jugendsuizidalität und Salutogenese. Hilfe und Unterstützung für suizidgefährdete Jugendliche.* Kohlhammer.

Bründel, H. (2010). *Schülersuizid–Was Lehrerinnen und Lehrer wissen sollten.* Accessed Apr 2, 2020, from https://schulpsychologie.nrw.de/cms/upload/Dokumente/Artikel/schuelersuizid_praevention.pdf

Cash, S. J., & Bridge, J. A. (2009). Epidemiology of youth suicide and suicidal behavior. *Current Opinion in Pediatrics, 21*(5), 613–619. https://doi.org/10.1097/MOP.0b013e32833063e1

Cerel, J., Jordan, J. R., & Duberstein, P. R. (2008). The impact of suicide on the family. *Crisis, 29*, 38–44. https://doi.org/10.1027/0227-5910.29.1.38

Chou, W.-J., Liu, T.-L., Hu, H.-F., & Yen, C.-F. (2016). Suicidality and its relationships with individual, family, peer, and psychopathology factors among adolescents with attention-deficit/hyperactivity disorder. *Research in Developmental Disabilities, 53–54*, 86–94. https://doi.org/10.1016/j.ridd.2016.02.001

Cowie, H., Boardman, C., Dawkins, J., & Jennifer, D. (2004). *Emotional health and Well-being: A practical guide for schools.* Sage.

Dilling, H., & Freyberger, H. J. (Eds.). (2016). *Taschenführer zur ICD-10-Klassifikation psychischer Störungen.* Hogrefe.

Eisenberg, M. E., Ackard, D. M., & Resnick, M. D. (2007). Protective factors and suicide risk in adolescents with a history of sexual abuse. *The Journal of Pediatrics, 151*, 482–487. https://doi.org/10.1016/j.jpeds.2007.04.033

Fegert, J. M., Eggers, C., & Resch, F. (Eds.). (2011). *Psychiatrie und Psychotherapie des Kindes- und Jugendalters.* Springer VS.

Feigelman, W., & Gorman, B. S. (2008). Assessing the effects of peer suicide on youth suicide. *Suicide and Life-threatening Behavior, 38*(2), 181–194.

Fekkes, M., Pijpers, F. I., & Verloove-Vanhorick, S. P. (2005). Bullying: Who does what, when and where? Involvement of children, teachers and parents in bullying behavior. *Health Education Research, 20*(1), 81–91.

Giletta, M., Prinstein, M. J., Abela, J. R., Gibb, B. E., Barrocas, A. L., & Hankin, B. L. (2015). Trajectories of suicide ideation and nonsuicidal self-injury among adolescents in mainland China: Peer predictors, joint development, and risk for suicide attempts. *Journal of Consulting and Clinical Psychology, 83*(2), 265.

Hill, R. M., del Busto, C. T., Buitron, V., & Pettit, J. W. (2018). Depressive symptoms and perceived burdensomeness mediate the association between anxiety and suicidal ideation in adolescents. *Archives of Suicide Research, 22*, 555–568. https://doi.org/10.1080/13811118.2018.1427163

Huang, H.-W., & Wang, R.-H. (2019). Roles of protective factors and risk factors in suicidal ideation among adolescents in Taiwan. *Public Health Nursing, 36*, 155–163. https://doi.org/10.1111/phn.12584

Huang, K.-L., Wei, H.-T., Hsu, J.-W., Bai, Y.-M., Su, T.-P., Li, C.-T., . . . Chen, M.-H. (2018). Risk of suicide attempts in adolescents and young adults with attention-deficit hyperactivity disorder: A nationwide longitudinal study. *The British Journal of Psychiatry, 212*, 234–238. https://doi.org/10.1192/bjp.2018.8

Kessler, R. C., Borges, G., & Walters, E. E. (1999). Prevalence of and risk factors for lifetime suicide attempts in the National Comorbidity Survey. *Archives of General Psychiatry, 56*(7), 617–626.

Kim, Y. S., & Leventhal, B. (2008). Bullying and suicide: A review. *International Journal of Adolescent Medicine & Health, 20*, 133–154. https://doi.org/10.1515/IJAMH.2008.20.2.133

Kim, Y. S., Leventhal, B. L., Koh, Y.-J., & Boyce, W. T. (2009). Bullying increased suicide risk: Prospective study of Korean adolescents. *Archives of Suicide Research, 13*(1), 15–30. https://doi.org/10.1080/13811110802572098

Klomek, A. B., Marrocco, F., Kleinman, M., Schonfeld, I. S., & Gould, M. S. (2007). Bullying, depression, and suicidality in adolescents. *Journal of the American Academy of Child & Adolescent Psychiatry, 46*, 40–49. https://doi.org/10.1097/01.chi.0000242237.84925.18

Mills, C., Guerin, S., Lynch, F., Daly, I., & Fitzpatrick, C. (2004). The relationship between bullying, depression and suicidal thoughts/behavior in Irish adolescents. *Irish Journal of Psychological Medicine, 21*, 112–116.

Nelson, F. L. (1987). Evaluation of a youth suicide prevention school program. *Adolescence, 22*(88), 813–825.

Olweus, D. (1994). Bullying at school. In L. R. Huesmann (Ed.), *Aggressive behaviour* (pp. 97–130). Springer.

Porter, A. C., Kearns, J. C., Esposito, E. C., & Glenn, C. R. (2019). Risk and protective factors for suicidal thoughts and behaviors and adolescents. In M. Berk (Ed.), *Evidence-based treatment approaches for suicidal adolescents: Translating science into practice* (pp. 21–62). American Psychiatric Association Publishing.

Roberts, R. E., Ramsey Roberts, C., & Xing, Y. (2010). One-year incidence of suicide attempts and associates risk and protective factors among adolescents. *Archives of Suicide Research, 14*, 66–78. https://doi.org/10.1080/13811110903479078

Royal College of Psychiatrists. (1999). *Fact sheet: Deliberate self harm in young people*. Royal College of Psychiatrists.

Skegg, K. (2005). Self-harm. *Lancet, 366*(9495), 1471–1483. https://doi.org/10.1016/S0140-6736(05)67600-3

Stevenson, R. G. (Ed.). (1994). *What will we do? Preparing a school community to cope with crises*. Baywood.

Taliaferro, L. A., & Muehlenkamp, J. (2014). Risk and protective factors that distinguish adolescents who attempt suicide from those who only consider suicide in the past year. *Suicide and Life-threatening Behavior, 44*, 6–22. https://doi.org/10.1111/sltb.12046

Van der Wal, M. F., de Wit, C. A. M., & Hirasing, R. A. (2003a). Psychosocial health among young victims and offenders of direct and indirect bullying. *Pediatrics, 111*, 1312–1317. https://doi.org/10.1542/peds.111.6.1312

Wang, R.-H., Hsu, H.-Y., Lin, S.-Y., Cheng, C.-P., & Lee, S.-L. (2010). Risk behaviors among early adolescents: Risk and protective factors. *Journal of Advanced Nursing, 66*(2), 313–323. https://doi.org/10.1111/j.1365-2648.2009.05159.x

Warnke, A. (2008). Suizid und Suizidversuch–Suizidalität. In B. Herpertz-Dahlmann, F. Resch, M. Schulte-Markwort, & A. Warnke (Eds.), *Entwicklungspsychiatrie: Biopsychologische Grundlagen und die Entwicklung psychischer Störungen* (pp. 1006–1023). Schattauer Verlag.

Warnke, A., & Hemminger, U. (1999). Der Umgang mit suizidalen Kindern und Jugendlichen. *Psychotherapie in Psychiatrie, Psychotherapeutischer Medizin und Klinischer Psychologie, 4*(2), 164–171.

Winter, S. (2014). Schikaniert bis zum Suizid. *MMW-Fortschritte der Medizin, 156*(14), 45–49.

World Health Organization (WHO). (2019). *Depression, fact sheets*. Accessed Jan 24, 2020, from https://www.who.int/news-room/fact-sheets/detail/depression

Xu, Y., Wang, C., & Shi, M. (2018). Identifying Chinese adolescents with a high suicide attempt risk. *Psychiatry Research, 269*, 474–480. https://doi.org/10.1016/j.psychres.2018.08.085

4.2.2 Accidents

Baer, F. M., & Rosenkranz, S. (2011). Koronare Herzkrankheit und akutes Koronarsyndrom. In E. Erdmann (Ed.), *Klinische Kardiologie* (pp. 13–72). Springer.

Ellsäßer, G. (2006). Epidemiologische Analyse von Unfällen bei Kindern unter 15 Jahren in Deutschland-Ausgangspunkt für die Unfallprävention. *Das Gesundheitswesen, 68*(7), 421–428.

Crumb, E., & Griffith Taylor, A. (2010). Children, unintentional injuries, and homicide. In C. A. Corr & D. E. Balk (Eds.), *Children's encounters with death, bereavement, and coping* (pp. 109–129). Springer.

Gehring, J., & Klein, G. (2015). Der akute Herzinfarkt. In J. Gehring & G. Klein (Eds.), *Leben mit der koronaren Herzkrankheit* (pp. 20–32). Urban und Vogel.

Marx, K., & Engels, F. (1973 [1881–1883]). *Marx-Engels-Werke MEW Band 35*. Berlin: Dietz.

Schubert, F., & Lalouschek, W. (2011). Schlaganfall. In J. Lehmer, E. Fertl, I. Kryspin-Exner, G. Pusswald, & W. Strubreither (Eds.), *Klinische Neuropsychologie* (pp. 345–356). Springer.

Schürch, B. (2016). *Unfallprävention an Schulen*. Information und Anleitung für Schulleitungen, Gesundheitsverantwortliche und Behördenmitglieder. Accessed Jan 25, 2020, from https://www.bfu.ch/media/dbqjezeg/2016_anleitung_information_fuer_schulen_de.pdf

Spitzer, P., Kurz, R., & Höllwarth, M. E. (2007). Unfälle. In M. J. Lentze, F. J. Schulte, J. Schaub, & J. Spranger (Eds.), *Pädiatrie* (pp. 168–175). Springer.

Statista. (2020). *Anzahl der Todesfälle in Deutschland nach häufigsten Todesursachen und Geschlecht im Jahr 2017*. Accessed Jan 26, 2020, from https://de.statista.com/statistik/daten/studie/215791/umfrage/todesfaelle-in-deutschland-nach-todesursachen-und-geschlecht/

Statistisches Bundesamt. (2020). *Gestorbene: Deutschland*, Jahre, Geschlecht, Altersjahre. Accessed Jan 26, 2020, from https://www-genesis.destatis.de/genesis/online/data?operation=abruftabelleBearbeiten&levelindex=1&levelid=1580320415133&auswahloperation=abruftabelleAuspraegungAuswaehlen&auswahlverzeichnis=ordnungsstruktur&auswahlziel=werteabruf&code=12613-0003&auswahltext=&werteabruf=Werteabruf

Vögele, C. (2009). *Klinische Psychologie: Körperliche Erkrankungen*. Weinheim.

Wagner, B. (2013). Spezifische Todesumstände und Trauergruppen. In B. Wagner (Ed.), *Komplizierte Trauer* (pp. 33–86). Springer.

Worden, J. W. (1999). *Beratung und Therapie in Trauerfällen*. Huber.

4.2.3 Violence

Alsaker, F. D. (2004). *Quälgeister und ihre Opfer: Mobbing unter Kindern-und wie man damit umgeht*. Huber.

Alsaker, F. D. (2006). Psychische Folgen von Mobbing. In H.-C. Steinhausen (Ed.), *Schule und psychische Störungen* (pp. 35–47). Kohlhammer.

Alsaker, F. D. (2012). *Mutig gegen Mobbing in Kindergarten und Schule*. Huber.

Alsaker, F. D., & Brunner, A. (1999). Switzerland. In R. Catalano, J. Junger-Tas, Y. Morita, D. Olweus, P. Slee, & P. K. Smith (Eds.), *The nature of school bullying: A cross-national perspective* (pp. 250–263). Routledge.

Alsaker, F. D., & Valkanover, S. (2001). Early diagnosis and prevention of victimization in kindergarten. In J. Juvonen & S. Graham (Eds.), *Peer harassment in school: The plight of the vulnerable and victimized* (pp. 175–195). Guilford.

American Psychiatric Association (APA). (1994). *Diagnostic and statistical manual of mental disorder* (4th ed.). American Psychiatric Association.

American Psychiatric Association (APA). (2015). *Diagnostisches und statistisches Manual psychischer Störungen DSM-5*. Hogrefe.

Arseneault, L., Cannon, M., Fisher, H. L., Polanczyk, G., Moffitt, T. E., & Caspi, A. (2011). Childhood trauma and children's emerging psychotic symptoms: A genetically sensitive longitudinal cohort study. *American Journal of Psychiatry, 168*, 65–72.

Baldry, A. C. (1998). Bullying among Italian middle school students. *School Psychology International, 19*, 361–374. https://doi.org/10.1177/0143034398194007

Bauman, S., & Bellmore, A. (2015). New directions in cyberbullying research. *Journal of School Violence, 14*, 1–10. https://doi.org/10.1080/15388220.2014.968281

Baumeister, R. F., Bushman, B., & Campbell, K. (2000). Self-esteem, narcissism, and aggression: Does violence result from low self-esteem or from threatened egotism? *Current Directions in Psychological Science, 9*, 26–29. https://doi.org/10.1111/1467-8721.00053

Beland, L. P., & Kim, D. (2016). The effect of high school shootings on schools and student performance. *Educational Evaluation and Policy Analysis, 38*(1), 113–126. https://doi.org/10.3102/0162373715590683

Bentley, K. M., & Li, A. K. F. (1995). Bully and victim problems in elementary schools and student's beliefs about aggression. *Canadian Journal of School Psychology, 11*(2), 153–165. https://doi.org/10.1177/082957359601100220

Betts, L. R. (2016). *Cyberbullying: Approaches, consequences and interventions.* Springer.

Borg, M. G. (1999). The extent and nature of bullying among primary and secondary school children. *Educational Research, 41*, 137–153. https://doi.org/10.1080/0013188990410202

Boulton, M. J., & Smith, P. K. (1994). Bully/victim problems in middle-school children: Stability, self-perceived competence, peer perceptions and peer acceptance. *British Journal of Developmental Psychology, 12*, 315–329. https://doi.org/10.1111/j.2044-835X.1994.tb00637.x

Boulton, M. J., & Underwood, K. (1992). Bully/victim problems among middle school children. *British Journal of Educational Psychology, 62*(1), 73–87. https://doi.org/10.1111/j.2044-8279.1992.tb01000.x

Brewin, C. R., Andrews, B., & Valentine, J. D. (2000). Meta-analysis of risk factors for posttraumatic stress disorder in trauma exposed adults. *Journal of Consulting and Clinical Psychology, 68*(5), 748–766. https://doi.org/10.1037//0022-006x.68.5.748

Brewin, C. R., & Holmes, E. A. (2003). Psychological theories of posttraumatic stress disorder, clinical psychology review. *Special Issue: Post Traumatic Stress Disorder, 23*(3), 339–376. https://doi.org/10.1016/s0272-7358(03)00033-3

Brunstein-Klomek, A. B., Marrocco, F., Kleinman, M., Schonfeld, I., & Gould, M. (2007). Bullying, depression and suicidality in adolescents. *Journal of the American Academy of Child and Adolescent Psychiatry, 46*(1), 40–49. https://doi.org/10.1097/01.chi.0000242237.84925.18

Bushman, B. J. (2017). Narcisissm, fame seeking and mass shootings. *The American Behavioral Scientist, 00*, 1–13. https://doi.org/10.1177/0002764217739660

Bunch, J. G. (2012, July 26). Colorado copycats seek attention and payback, experts say. *Denver Post*. Accessed Apr 15, 2020, from https://www.denverpost.com/2012/07/26/colorado-copycats-seek-attention-and-payback-experts-say/

Bondü, R. (2012). *School Shootings in Deutschland: Internationaler Vergleich, Warnsignale, Risikofaktoren, Entwicklungsverläufe.* Inagurationsdissertation zur Erlangung eines Doktors der Philosophie an der Freien Universität Berlin.

Bondü, R., & Scheithauer, H. (2011). Explaining and preventing school shootings: Chances and difficulties of control. In W. Heitmeyer, H.-G. Haupt, S. Malthaner, & A. Kirschner (Eds.), *Control of violence: Historical and international perspectives on violence in modern societies* (S. 295–314). Springer.

Campbell, M. A., Slee, P. T., Spears, B., Butle, S., & Kift, S. (2013). Do cyberbullies suffer too? Cyberbullies' perceptions of the harm they cause to others and their own mental health. *School Psychology International, 34*, 613–629. https://doi.org/10.1177/0143034313479698

Copeland, W. E., Wolke, D., Angold, A. A., & Costello, E. J. (2013). Adult psychiatric outcomes of bullying and being bullied by peers in childhood and adolescence. *JAMA Psychiatry, 70*(4), 419–426. https://doi.org/10.1177/1541204016650004

Cornell, D. G., & Mayer, M. J. (2010). Why do school order and safety matter? *Educational Researcher, 39*, 7–15.

Crick, N. R., & Grotpeter, J. K. (1995). Relational aggression, gender, and social-psychological adjustment. *Child Development, 66,* 710–722.

Crosslin, K., & Crosslin, M. (2014). Cyberbullying at a Texas University–A mixed methods approach to examining online aggression. *Texas Public Health Journal, 66,* 26–31. 7 Accessed Mar 23, 2020, from https://www.researchgate.net/publication/266142241_Cyberbullying_at_a_Texas_Unversity_-_A_Mixed_Methods_Approach_to_Examining_Online_Aggression

Currier, J. M., Holland, J. M., & Neimeyer, R. A. (2006). Sense-making, grief and the experience of violent loss: Toward a mediational model. *Death Studies, 30,* 403–428. https://doi.org/10.1080/07481180600614351

Dempsey, A. G., Sulkowski, M. L., Nichols, R., & Storch, E. A. (2009). Differences between peer victimization in cyber and physical settings and associated psychosocial adjustment in early adolescence. *Psychology in the Schools, 46,* 962–972. https://doi.org/10.1002/pits.20437

Didden, R., Scholte, R. H. J., Korzilius, H. D., Moor, J. M. H., Vermeulen, A., O'Reilly, M., Lang, R., & Lancioni, G. E. (2009). Cyberbullying among students with intellectual and developmental disability in special education settings. *Developmental Neurorehabilitation, 12*(3), 146–151. https://doi.org/10.1080/17518420902971356

Dittmann, C. (2011). *Mobbing und Schulleistung-der Wechsel zur Förderschule und seine sozialen Auswirkungen.* Pädagogische Hochschule Ludwigsburg, Fakultät für Sonderpädagogik Reutlingen. Hochschulbibliothek Reutlingen.

Elklit, A., & Kurdahl, S. (2013). The psychological reactions after witnessing a killing in public in a Danish high school. *European Journal of Psychotraumatology, 4*(1), 19826. https://doi.org/10.3402/ejpt.v4i0.19826

Feltes, T. (2003, 02 July). *Pressegespräch zur BKA-Studie zu Gewalt an Schulen: Aggression und Delinquenz unter Jugendlichen–Untersuchungen von kognitiven und sozialen Bedingungen.* BKA.. https://www.bka.de/SharedDocs/Downloads/DE/UnsereAufgaben/Ermittlungsunterstuetzung/Forschung/AggressionJugendliche/bkaStudiezuGewaltanSchulenAggressionundDelinquenzunterJugendlichen.pdf%3F__blob%3DpublicationFile%26v%3D1 .

Ferguson, C. J., SanMiguel, C., Garza, A., & Jerabeck, J. (2012). A longitudinal test of video game violence effects on dating violence, aggression and bullying: A 3-year lon- gitudinal study of adolescents. *Journal of Psychiatric Research, 46,* 141–146. https://doi.org/10.1016/j.jpsychires.2011.10.014

Fernandes, T., Sanyal, N., & Chada, S. (2015). Self-esteem and social interaction anxiety in cyberbullied adolescents. *Indian Journal of Health and Wellbeing, 6*(7), 648–655.

Festl, R., Scharkow, M., & Quandt, T. (2013). Peer influence, internet use and cyberbullying: A comparison of different context effects among German adolescents. *Journal of Children and Media, 7*(4), 446–462. https://doi.org/10.1080/17482798.2013.781514

Fisher, H. L., Moffitt, T. E., Houts, R. M., Belsky, D. W., Arseneault, L., & Caspi, A. (2012). Bullying victimization and risk of self-harm in early adolescence: Longitudinal cohort study. *BMJ.* https://doi.org/10.1136/bmj.e2683

Flatten, G., Bär, O., Becker, K., Bengel, J., Frommberger, U., Hofmann, A., et al. (2011a). S2–Diagnostik und Behandlung von akuten Folgen psychischer Traumatisierung. *Trauma & Gewalt, 3,* 214–221.

Flatten, G., Gast, U., Hofmann, A., Knaevelsrud, C., Lampe, A., Liebermann, P., et al. (2011b). S3–Leitlinie Posttraumatische Belastungsstörung. *Trauma & Gewalt, 3,* 202–210.

Forero, R., McLellan, L., Rissel, C., & Bauman, A. (1999). Bullying behaviour and psychosocial health among school students in New South Wales, Australia: Cross sectional survey. *BMJ, 319,* 344–348. https://doi.org/10.1136/bmj.319.7206.344

Fuchs, M., Lamnek, S., Luedtke, J., & Baur, N. (2009). *Gewalt an Schulen: 1994–1999–2004. (2. überarbeitete und aktualisierte Aufl.)*. VS Verlag.

Genta, M. L., Menesini, E., Fonzi, A., & Costabile, A. (1996). Bullies and victims in schools in central and southern Italy. *European Journal of Psychology of Education, 11*, 97–110. https://doi.org/10.1007/BF03172938

Gini, G. (2008). Associations between bullying behaviour, psychosomatic complaints, emotional and behavioural problems. *Journal of Paediatrics and Child Health, 44*(9), 492–497. https://doi.org/10.1111/j.1440-1754.2007.01155.x

Goebert, D., Else, I., Matsu, C., Chung-Do, J., & Chang, J. Y. (2011). The impact of cyberbullying on substance use and mental health in a multiethnic sample. *Maternal and Child Health Journal, 15*, 1282–1286. https://doi.org/10.1007/s10995-010-0672-x

Green, B. L., Grace, M. C., & Gleser, G. L. (1985). Identifying survivors at risk: Long-term impairment following the Beverley Hills supper Club fire. *Journal of Consulting and Clinical Psychology., 53*, 672–678. https://doi.org/10.1037//0022-006x.53.5.672

Green, B. L., Krupnick, J. L., Stockton, P., Goodman, L., Corcoran, C., & Petty, C. (2001). Psychological outcomes associated with traumatic loss in a sample of young women. *American Behavioral Scientist, 44*, 817–837. https://doi.org/10.1177/00027640121956511

Haller, B., Gümüs, Z., Schuschnig, U., Jäger, J., Buchegger, B., Prochazka, E., et al. (2018). *Mobbing an Schulen: Ein Leitfaden für die Schulgemeinschaft im Umgang mit Mobbing*. Bundesministerium für Bildung, Wissenschaft und Forschung Abteilung Schulpsychologie-Bildungsberatung.

Hawker, D. S., & Boulton, M. J. (2000). Twenty years' research on peer victimization and psychosocial maladjustment: A meta-analytic review of cross-sectional studies. *The Journal of Child Psychology and Psychiatry and Allied Disciplines, 41*(4), 441–455. https://doi.org/10.1111/1469-7610.00629

Hickey, E. W. (2010). *Serial murderers and their victims* (5th ed.). Cengage Learning.

Hinduja, S., & Patchin, J. W. (2010). Bullying, cyberbullying, and suicide. *Archives of Suicide Research, 14*, 206–221. https://doi.org/10.1080/13811118.2010.494133

Hoffmann, J., Roshdi, K, & Robertz, F. (2009). Zielgerichtete schwere Gewalt und Amok an Schulen: Eine empirische Studie zur Prävention schwerer Gewalttaten. *Kriminalistik, 4*. Institut für Psychologie und Bedrohungsmanagement.

Holland, K. M., Hall, J. E., Wang, J., Gaylor, E. M., Johnson, L. L., Shelby, D., & Simon, T. R. (2019). Characteristics of school-associated youth homicides: United States 1994–2018. *Morbidity and Mortality Weekly Report (MMWR), 68*(3), 53–60.

Horowitz, M., Siegel, B., Holen, A., Bonanno, G., Milbrath, C., & Stinson, C. (1997). Diagnostic criteria for complicated grief disorder. *American Journal of Psychiatry, 154*(7), 904–910. https://doi.org/10.1176/ajp.154.7.904

Höhn, L. (2019). Nachsorge. In M. Böhmer (Ed.), *Amok an Schulen: Prävention, intervention und Nachsorge bei school shootings* (pp. 205–240). Springer.

Imamura, A., Nishida, A., Nakazawa, N., Shimodera, S., & T anaka, G., Kinoshita, H., & Okazaki, Y. (2009). Effects of cellular phone email use on the mental health of junior high school students in Japan. *Psychiatry and Clinical Neurosciences, 63*, 703.

Isaacs, J., Hodges, E., & Salmivalli, C. (2008). Long-term consequences of victimization: A follow-up from adolescence to young adulthood. *European Journal of Developmental Science, 2*, 387–397.

Juvonen, J., & Gross, E. F. (2008). Extending the school grounds? Bullying experiences in cyberspace. *Journal of School Health, 78*(9), 496–505. https://doi.org/10.1111/j.17461561.2008.00335.x

Kaltman, S., & Bonanno, G. A. (2003). Trau- ma and bereavement: Examining the impact of sudden and violent deaths. *Journal of Anxiety Disorders, 17*, 131–147. https://doi.org/10.1016/s0887-6185(02)00184-6

Kampwerth, K. (2009). *Alles easy. Prima Klima in der Klasse*. Thienemann Verlag.

Killikelly, C., & Maercker, A. (2018). Prolonged grief disorder for ICD-11: The primacy of clinical utility and international applicability. *European Journal of Psychotraumatology, 8*(6). https://doi.org/10.1080/20008198.2018.1476441

Kirsch, V., Fegert, M., & Goldbeck, L. (2010). Psychische Folgen von Schulamokläufen für Überlebende. *Nervenheilkunde, 29*(7–8), 456–459.

Kolip, P., Klocke, A., Melzer, W., & Ravens-Sieberer, U. (Eds.). (2013). *Gesundheit und Gesundheitsverhalten im Geschlechtervergleich. Ergebnisse des WHO-Jugendgesundheitssurvey Health Behaviour in School-aged Children*. Weinheim.

Kowalski, R. M., & Fedina, C. (2011). Cyber bullying ADHD and Asperger syndrome populations. *Research in Autism Spectrum Disorders, 5*(3), 1201–1208. https://doi.org/10.1016/j.rasd.2011.01.007

Koyanagi, A., Oh, H., Carvalho, A. F., Smith, L., Haro, J. M., Vancampfort, D., Stubbs, B., & DeVylder, J. (2019). Bullying victimization and suicide attempt among aolescents aged 12–15 years from 48 countries. *Journal of the American Academy of Child and Adolescent Psychiatry, 58*(9), 907–918. https://doi.org/10.1016/j.jaac.2018.10.018

Kristensen, P., Weisaeth, L., & Heir, T. (2012). Bereavement and mental health after sudden and violent losses: A review. *Psychiatry, 75*, 76–97. https://doi.org/10.1521/psyc.2012.75.1.76

Kubiszewski, V., Fontaine, R., Potard, C., & Auzoult, L. (2015). Does cyberbullying overlap with school bullying when taking modality of involvement into account? *Computers in Human Behavior, 43*, 49–57. https://doi.org/10.1016/j.chb.2014.10.049

Lam, L. T., Cheng, Z., & Liu, X. (2013). Violent online games exposure and cyberbullying/victimization among adolescents. *Cyberpsychology, Behavior and Social Networking, 16*, 159–164. https://doi.org/10.1089/cyber.2012.0087

Landoll, R. R., La Greca, A. M., Lai, B. S., Chan, S. F., & Herge, W. M. (2015). Cyber victimization by peers: Prospective associations with adolescent social anxiety and depressive symptoms. *Journal of Adole- scence, 42*, 77–86. https://doi.org/10.1016/j.adolescence.2015.04.002

Langman, P. (2009). Rampage school shooters: A typology. *Aggression and Violent Behavior, 14*, 79–86. https://doi.org/10.1016/j.avb.2008.10.003

Langos, C. (2012). Cyberbullying: The challenge to define. *Cyberpsychology, Behavior and Social Networking, 15*, 285–289. https://doi.org/10.1089/cyber.2011.0588

Lehman, D. R., Wortman, C. B., & Williams, A. F. (1987). Long-term effects of losing a spouse or child in a motor vehicle crash. *Journal of Personality and Social Psychology, 52*, 218–231. https://doi.org/10.1037/0022-3514.52.1.218

Lereya, S. T., Winsper, C., Heron, J., Lewis, G., Gunnell, D., Fisher, H. L., & Wolke, D. (2013). Being bullied during childhood and the prospective pathways to self-harm in late adolescence. *Journal of the American Academy of Child and Adolescent Psychiatry, 52*, 608–618. https://doi.org/10.1016/j.jaac.2013.03.012

Lowe, S. R., & Galea, S. (2015). The mental health consequences of mass shootings. *Trauma, Violence & Abuse*, 1–21. https://doi.org/10.1177/1524838015591572

Meindl, J.N., & Ivy, J.W. (2016). Mass shootings: The role of the media in promoting generalized imitation. *Published online ahead of print, e1–e3*. https://doi.org/10.2105/AJPH.2016.303611.

Meloy, J. R., Hempel, A. G., Mohandie, K., Shiva, A. A., & Gray, B. T. (2001). Offender and offense characteristics of a nonrandom sample of adolescent mass murderers. *Journal of the American Academy of Child and Adolescent Psychiatry, 40*(6), 719–728. https://doi.org/10.1097/00004583-200106000-00018

Melzer, W., Schubarth, W., & Ehninger, F. (2004). *Gewaltprävention und Schulentwicklung. Analysen und Handlungskonzepte.* Klinkhardt.

Molcho, M., Craig, W., Due, P., Pickett, W., Harel-Fisch, Y., & Overpeck, M. (2009). Cross-national time trends in bullying behaviour 1994–2006: Findings from Europe and North America. *International Journal of Public Health, 54*(17), 225–234. https://doi.org/10.1007/s00038-009-5414-8

Morgan, H. (2012). What teachers and schools can do to control the growing problem of school bullying. *The Clearing House, 85,* 174–178. https://doi.org/10.1080/00098655.2012.677075

Murphy, S. A., Johnson, L. C., Chung, I. J., & Beaton, R. D. (2003). The prevalence of PTSD following the violent death of a child and predictors of change 5 years later. *Journal of Traumatic Stress, 16,* 17–26. https://doi.org/10.1023/A:1022003126168

Murray, J. L. (2017). Mass media reporting and enabling of mass shootings. *Cultural Studies Critical Methodologies, 17*(2), 114–124. https://doi.org/10.1177/1532708616679144

Nansel, T. R., Overpeck, M., Pilla, R. S., Ruan, W. J., Simons-Morton, B., & Scheidt, P. (2001). Bullying behaviors among US youth: Prevalence and association with psychosocial adjustment. *Journal of the American Medical Association, 285,* 2094–2100.

Nakamoto, J., & Schwartz, D. (2009). Is peer victimization associated with academic achievement? A meta- analytic review. *Developmental Psychology, 19,* 221–242. https://doi.org/10.1111/j.1467-9507.2009.00539.x

Nordhagen, R., Nielsen, A., Stigum, H., & Köhler, L. (2005). Parental reported bullying among nordic children: A population-based study. *Child: Care, Health and Development, 31*(6), 693–701. https://doi.org/10.1111/j.1365-2214.2005.00559.x

Olweus, D. (1997). Bully/victim problems in school: Facts and intervention. *European Journal of Psychology of Education, 2,* 495–510. https://doi.org/10.1007/BF03172807

Olweus, D. (2002). *Gewalt in der Schule: Was Lehrer und Eltern wissen sollten–und tun können.* Huber Verlag.

Olweus, D. (2012). Cyberbullying: An over-rated phenomenon? *European Journal of Developmental Psychology, 9,* 520–538. https://doi.org/10.1080/17405629.2012.682358

O'Moore, A. M., Kirkham, C., & Smith, M. (1997). Bullying behaviour in Irish schools: A nationwide study. *The Irish Journal of Psychology, 18*(2), 141–169. https://doi.org/10.1080/03033910.1997.10558137

Ortega, R., Calmaestra, J., & Mora-Merchan, J. (2008) Cyberbullying. *International Journal of Psychology and Psychological Therapy, 8,* 183–192. Accessed Mar 23, 2020, from https://www.ijpsy.com/volumen8/num2/194/cyberbullying-ES.pdf

O'Toole, M. E. (1999). *The school shooter: A threat assessment perspective.* Accessed Apr, 2020, from https://www.fbi.gov/file-repository/stats-services-publications-school-shooter-schoolshooter/

Ozer, E. J., Best, S. R., Lipsey, T. L., & Weiss, D. S. (2003). Predictors of posttraumatic stress disorder and symptoms in adults: A meta-analysis. *Psychological Bulletin, 129*(1), 52–73. https://doi.org/10.1037/0033-2909.129.1.52

Patchin, J. W., & Hinduja, S. (2006). Bullies move beyond the schoolyard. A preliminary look at cyberbullying. *Youth Violence and Juvenile Justice, 4*(2), 148–169. https://doi.org/10.1177/1541204006286288

Pereira, B., Mendonca, D., Netto, C., Almeida, A., Valentre, L., & Smith, P.K. (1996). Facts and figures of the first survey on bullying in Portuguese schools. *Paper presented at theEuropean Conference on Educational Research*, Seville. Accessed Apr 3, 2020, from https://repositorio.iscte-iul.pt/bitstream/10071/14359/1/Violence%20in%20Portuguese%20schools.pdf

Peter, I. K., & Petermann, F. (2018). Cyberbullying: A concept analysis of defining attributes and additional influencing factors. *Computers in Human Behavior, 86*(350), 366. https://doi.org/10.1016/j.chb.2018.05.013

Pfeiffer, C., Baier, D., & Kliem, S. (2018). *Zur Entwicklung der Gewalt in Deutschland: Schwerpunkte Jugendliche und Flüchtlinge als Täter und Opfer*. Soziale Arbeit. Accessed Dec 10, 2019, from https://www.zhaw.ch/storage/shared/sozialearbeit/News/gutachten-entwicklung-gewalt-deutschland.pdf

Pieschl, S., Kuhlmann, C., & Prosch, T. (2015). Beware of publicity! Perceived distress of negative cyber incidents and implications for defining cyberbullying. *Journal of School Violence, 14*, 111–132. https://doi.org/10.1080/15388220.2014.971363

Politi, S. (2020). Was ist Mobbing und wie kann man es erkennen? In M. Böhmer & G. Steffgen (Eds.), *Mobbing an Schulen: Maßnahmen zur Prävention, Intervention und Nachsorge* (pp. 1–19). Springer.

Price, M., & Dalgleish, J. (2010). Cyberbullying: Experiences, impacts and coping strategies as described by Australian young people. *Youth Studies Australia, 29*(2), 51–59. https://doi.org/10.1080/15388220.2014.971363

Prigerson, H. G., Bierhals, A. J., Kasl, S. V., Reynolds, C. F., Shear, K., Day, N., et al. (1997). Traumatic grief as a risk factor for mental and physical morbidity. *American Journal of Psychiatry, 154*, 616–623. https://doi.org/10.1176/ajp.154.5.616

Prigerson, H. G., Shear, M. K., Jacobs, S. C., Reynolds, C. F., Maciejewski, P. D., Davidson, J. R. T., Rosenheck, R., Pilkonis, P. A., Wortman, C. B., Williams, J. B. W., Widiger, T. A., Frank, E., Kupfer, D. J., & Zistook, S. (1999). Consensus criteria for traumatic grief. *British Journal of Psychiatry, 174*, 67–73. https://doi.org/10.2190/FKM2-YJTY-F9VV-9XWY

Rando, T. A. (1996). Complications in mourn-ing traumatic death. In K. J. Doka (Ed.), *Living with grief after sudden loss (S. 139–160)*. Taylor & Francis.

Raphael, B., & Martinek, N. (2004). Assess- ing traumatic bereavement and posttraumatic stress disorder. In J. Wilson & T. Keane (Eds.), *Assessing psychological trauma and PTSD* (pp. 492–510). Guilford.

Raphael, B., Stevens, G., & Dunsmore, J. (2006). Clinical theories of loss and grief. In E. K. Rynearson (Ed.), *Violent death. Resilience and intervention beyond the crisis* (pp. 3–29). Taylor and Francis Group.

Reynolds, C. F., Cozza, S. J., & Shear, K. (2017). Clinically relevant diagnostic criteria for a persistent impairing grief disorder putting patients first. *JAMA Psychiatry, 74*(5), 433–437. https://doi.org/10.1001/jamapsychiatry.2017.0290

Rigby, K. (1997). What children tell us about bullying in schools. *Children Australia, 22*(2), 28–34. https://doi.org/10.1017/S1035077200008178

Robertz, F. J., & Wickenhäuser, R. (2010). *Der Riss in der Tafel: Amoklauf und schwere Gewalt in der Schule* (2nd ed.). Springer.

Rothon, C., Head, J., Klineberg, E., & Stansfeld, S. (2011). Can social support protect bullied adolescents from adverse outcomes? A prospective study on the effects of bullying on the educational achievement and mental health of adolescents at secondary schools in East London. *Journal of Adolescence, 34*(3), 579–588. https://doi.org/10.1016/j.adolescence.2010.02.007

Rotenberg, K. J. (1994). Loneliness and interpersonal trust. *Journal of Social and Clinical Psychology, 13*, 152–173. https://doi.org/10.1521/jscp.1994.13.2.152

Salmivalli, C., Lagerspetz, K. M. J., Bjorkvist, K., Ostermann, K., & Kaukiainen, A. (1996). Bullying as a group process: Participant roles and their relations to social status within the group. *Aggressive Behavior, 22*, 1–15. https://doi.org/10.1002/(SICI)1098-2337

Saltzman, W. R., Layne, C. M., Pynoos, R. S., Steinberg, A. M., & Aisenberg, E. (2001). Trauma- and grief-focused intervention for adolescents exposed to community violence: Results of a school-based screening and group treatment protocol. *Group Dynamics: Theory, Research, and Practice, 5*(4), 291–303. https://doi.org/10.1037//1089-2699.5.4.291

Scheithauer, H., Hayer, T., & Petermann, F. (2003). *Bullying unter Schülern: Erscheinungsformen, Risikobedingungen und Interventionskonzepte.* Hogrefe.

Schenk, L. (2020). Was ist Cybermobbing. In M. Böhmer & G. Steffgen (Eds.), *Mobbing an Schulen: Maßnahmen zur Prävention und Nachsorge.* Springer.

Schmidbauer, W. (2009). *Psychologie des Terrors: Warum junge Männer zu Attentätern werden.* Gütersloher Verlagshaus.

Schreier, A., Wolke, D., Thomas, K., Horwood, J., Hollis, C., Gunnell, D., Lewis, G., Thompson, A., Zammit, S., Duffy, L., Salvi, G., & Harrison, G. (2009). Prospective study of peer victimization in childhood and psychotic symptoms in a nonclinical population at age 12 years. *Archives of General Psychiatry, 66*, 527–536. https://doi.org/10.1001/archgenpsychiatry.2009.23

Schwarz, E. D., & Kowalski, J. M. (1991). Malignant memories: PTSD in children and adults after a school shooting. *Journal of American Academic Children and Adolescence Psychiatry, 30*(6). https://doi.org/10.1097/00004583-199111000-00011

Selkie, E. M., Kota, R., Chan, Y. F., & Moreno, M. (2015). Cyberbullying, depression, and problem alcohol use in female college students. A multisite study. *Cyberpsychology, Behavior and Social Networking, 18*, 79–86. https://doi.org/10.1089/cyber.2014.0371

Shibuya, A., Sakamoto, A., Ihori, N., & Yukawa, S. (2008). The effects of the presence and contexts of video game violence on children: A longitudinal study in Japan. *Simulation & Gaming, 39*(4), 528–539. https://doi.org/10.1177/1046878107306670

Sinclair, K. O., Bauman, S., Poteat, P., Boenig, B., & Russell, S. T. (2012). Cyber and bias based harassment: Associations with academic, substance use, and mental health problems. *Journal of Adolescent Health, 50*, 521–523.

Smith, P. K., Mahdavi, J., Carvalho, M., Fisher, S., Russell, S., & Tippett, N. (2008). Cyberbullying: Its nature and impact in secondary school pupils. *Journal of Child Psychology and Psychiatry, 49*, 376–385. https://doi.org/10.1111/j.14697610.2007.01846.x

Sourander, A., Klomek, A. B., Ikonen, M., Lindroos, J., Luntamo, T., Koskelainen, M., Ristkari, T., & Helenius, H. (2010). Psychological risk factors associated with cyberbullying among adolescents: A popula- tion-based study. *Archives of General Psychiatry, 67*(7), 720–728. https://doi.org/10.1001/archgen-psychiatry.2010.79

Spröber, N., Schlottke, P. F., & Hautzinger, M. (2008a). *Bullying in der Schule. Das Präventions- und Interventionsprogramm ProACT+E.* Beltz Verlag.

Spröber, N., Schlottke, P. F., & Hautzinger, M. (2008b). *Bullying in der Schule.* Weinheim.

Stevenson, R. G. (2008). Good violence/bad violence: Its impact on children and suggested responses. In R. G. Stevenson & G. R. Cox (Eds.), *Perspectives on violence and violent death.* Baywood Publishing Co.

Storath, R., & Engelbrecht, A. (2004). *Krisensituationen, Gewalt und Tod in der Schule: Schulpsychologie als Unterstützungssystem bei außerordentlichen Ereignissen.* Krisen in Schule Schulverwaltung Spezial, 1.

Sutton, J., & Smith, P. K. (1999). Bullying as a group process: An adaptation of the participant role approach. *Aggressive Behavior, 25*, 97–111. https://doi.org/10.1002/(SICI)1098-2337(1999)25:2%3c97::AID-AB3%3e3.0.CO;2-7

Sveen, C. A., & Walby, F. A. (2008). Suicide survivors' mental health and grief reactions: A systematic review of controlled studies. *Suicide and Life-threatening Behavior, 38*, 13–29. https://doi.org/10.1521/suli.2008.38.1.13

Takizawa, R., Maughan, B., & Arseneault, L. (2014). Adult health outcomes of childhood bullying victimization: Evidence from a five-decade longitudinal British birth cohort. *American Journal of Psychiatry, 171*(7), 777–784. https://doi.org/10.1176/appi.ajp.2014.13101401

Towers, S., Gomez-Lievano, A., Khan, K., Mubayi, A., & Castillo-Chavez, C. (2015, July 2). Contagion in mass killings and school shootings. *PLoS One, 10*(7). https://doi.org/10.1371/journal.pone.0117259

Turunen, T., Haravuori, H., Punamäki, R., Suomalainen, L., & Marttunen, M. (2014). The role of attachment in recovery after a school-shooting trauma. *European Journal of Psychotraumatology, 5*(1), 22728. https://doi.org/10.3402/ejpt.v5.22728

Turunen, T., & Punamäki, R.-L. (2016). Professionally led peer support group process after the school shooting in Finland: Organization, group work, and recovery phases accepted for publication in omega. *Journal of Death and Dying, 73*(1), 42–69. https://doi.org/10.1177/0030222815575700

Van Ameringen, M., Mancini, C., Patterson, B., & Boyle, M. H. (2008). Post-traumatic stress disorder in Canada. *CNS Neuroscience & Therapeutics, 14*, 171–181. https://doi.org/10.1111/j.1755-5949.2008.00049.x

Van der Wal, M. F., de Wit, C. A., & Hirasing, R. A. (2003b). Psychological health among young victims and offenders of direct and indirect bullying. *Paediatrics, 111*, 1312–1317. https://doi.org/10.1542/peds.111.6.1312

Varjas, K., Henrich, C. C., & Meyers, J. (2009). Urban middle school student's perceptions of bullying, cyberbullying and school safety. *Journal of School Violence, 8*, 159–176. https://doi.org/10.1080/15388220802074165

Vettenburg, N. (1999). Belgium. In P. K. Smith, Y. Morita, J. Junger-Tas, D. Olweus, R. Catalano, & P. Slee (Eds.), *The nature of school bullying: A cross-national perspective* (pp. 187–204). Routledge.

Vossekuil, B., Fein, R., Reddy, M., Borum, R., & Modzeleski, W. (2002). *The Final Report and Findings of the Safe School Initiative: Implications for the Prevention of School Attacks in the United State*s. Accessed Apr 3, 2020, from https://www.secretservice.gov/ntac/ssi_final_report.pdf

Wachs, S. (2012). Moral disengagement and emotional and social difficulties in bullying and cyberbullying: Differences by participant role. *Emotional and Behavioural Difficulties, 17*(3–4), 347–360. https://doi.org/10.1080/13632752.2012.704318

Weisæth, L. (1989). The stressors and the post-traumatic stress syndrome after an industrial disaster. *Acta Psychiatrica Scandinavica, 355*, 25–37. https://doi.org/10.1111/j.1600-0447.1989.tb05251.x

Weitzel, L. (2019). *Bullying involvement, suicidal ideation, and the role of perceived social support*. University of Luxembourg.

Weitzmann, J. H. (2017). *Cyber-Mobbing und was man dagegen tun kann (I): Erscheinungsformen, Gründe und Auslöser*. Accessed Mar 25, 2020, from https://irights.info/artikel/cyber-mobbingcyberbullying-und-was-man-da-gegen-tun-kann-2/6919

Wette, S. (2018, 14. Juni). Bluttat in Gesamtschule: 16-jähriger wegen Mordes vor Gericht. *Westfälische Rundschau*. Accessed Dec 14, 2020, from https://www.wr.de/panorama/gericht/bluttat-in-gesamtschule-16-jaehriger-wegen-mordes-vor-gericht-id214575923.html

Willoughby, T., Adachi, P. C., & Good, M. (2012). A longitudinal study of the association between violent video game play and aggression among adolescents. *Developmental Psychology, 48*(4), 1044–1057. https://doi.org/10.1037/a0026046

Whitney, I., & Smith, P. K. (1993). A survey of the nature and extent of bullying in junior/middle and secondary schools. *Educational Research, 35*, 3–25. https://doi.org/10.1080/0013188930350101

Wolke, D., Woods, S., Stanford, K., & Schulz, H. (2001). Bullying and victimization of primary school children in England and Germany: Prevalence and school factors. *British Journal of Psychology, 92*, 673–696. https://doi.org/10.1348/000712601162419

Xiao, B. S., & Wong, Y. M. (2013). Cyberbullying among university students: An empirical investigation from the social cognitive perspective. International Journal of Business and Information, 8, 34–69. Accessed Apr 3, 2020, from https://pdfs.semanticscholar.org/4c23/3fc6080735e7b5869b3125bbed0198138b55.pdf

Ybarra, M., Diener-West, M., Markow, D., Leaf, P., Hamburger, M., & Boxer, P. (2008). Linkages between internet and other media violence with seriously violent behavior by youth. *Pediatrics, 122*(5), 929–937. https://doi.org/10.1542/peds.2007-3377

Interventions

Iris Cranfield and Maria Kohl

5.1 Guide to the Delivery of the Message

In the event of an unforeseen death within the school or class community or in the personal environment of the students, many teachers are faced with the question of how they can step in front of the class and competently and sensitively break the death news to the students. In the following, different aspects are pointed out which have to be considered by the school staff.

In the best case, the message should be delivered as quickly as possible and not alone (Becker et al., 2008). The class teacher breaking the news should seek the support of an external person, for example the head teacher, a religion or ethics teacher or a liaison teacher, in order to be able to hand over the reins of the conversation to this person in the event that he or she is strongly affected. In order to prevent the development and spread of rumours about the death, the news should be conveyed as quickly as possible and on the basis of reliable information, which the teacher should obtain in advance (Becker et al., 2008).

To deliver the message, it is advisable to change the usual seating arrangement of the class, for example by creating a circle of chairs. In this way, and through verbal communication, it should be made clear to the class that no lessons are taking place. It is important to create a protected space, as talking about death and one's own feelings is a very sensitive topic. This can be done, for example, by making an agreement that (emotional) expressions remain within the class and are not carried outside (Becker et al., 2008).

I. Cranfield (✉) · M. Kohl
Department of Behavioural and Cognitive Sciences, University of Luxemburg, Esch-sur-Alzette, Luxembourg
e-mail: iris.jandach.001@student.uni.lu

When breaking the news of the death, start by explaining to the students, based on the established facts, how the death occurred. The circumstances of the death should not be glossed over or concealed, but explained in brief, understandable terms. This also applies to the transmission of a suicide, not least in order to prevent the development of rumours and the passing on of partial truths, which can lead to anxiety and thus to further stress, especially among children and young people. After informing the pupils, time should be left for reactions (including silence), which should be taken up by the teacher in the discussion. In the following conversation it can be discussed, among other things, what the death means to the students, how they can deal with the situation, what thoughts they are brought to by the death or what their relationship to the deceased person was like. Subsequently, the further procedure, for example questions about the funeral or how to deal with personal things of the deceased in the school, should be clarified. The exact content of the conversations should be adapted to the respective age group of the children and adolescents (Becker et al., 2008).

After a break, which should be spent within the class community, initial mourning rituals (e.g. writing a farewell letter, chair circle with a candle for the deceased in the middle, minute of remembrance, prayer) or relieving elements such as a joint walk can be carried out (Becker et al., 2008).

For the first few days after the event, a place of mourning should also be set up within the school where students are given the opportunity to grieve undisturbed (Becker et al., 2008).

After the message has been delivered, class time should not be shortened, as it cannot be guaranteed that people will be available to talk to the students when they return home after class. It is also advisable to send a short information letter from the school office to the parents of the affected class, in which the event and the school routine for the coming days should be briefly described. If necessary, a parents' evening can also be offered (Becker et al., 2008).

In the aftermath of a sudden death within the school or class community or in the environment of one or more pupils, there are also a number of points to bear in mind when dealing with those affected. It is important that teachers take the grief of children and young people seriously and acknowledge that they cannot empathise with their feelings. Even irritating or inappropriate behaviour should be accepted and not judged, as each person can show an individual way of dealing with grief (Becker et al., 2008).

Especially when a student in a class has experienced a loss, classmates should be prepared by the teacher to deal with the fellow student, for example by expressing their sympathy to the fellow student (Naierman, 1997). In addition, sharing with caregivers such as the parents of the grieving child can be useful by providing feedback on the child's development within the school context after a death. The teacher should behave as normally as possible towards the child, but at the same time monitor closely for any symptoms of stress or changes in behaviour, particularly depressive or suicidal reactions (Naierman, 1997; Lawhon, 2004). Lawhon (2004) recommends offering the affected child a daily one-on-one conversation, but accepting if the child does not want to talk about the death. Teachers should also be aware that anxiety, stress and sadness associated with the grief response may impact on pupils' ability to concentrate. In this case, there may be short-term flexibility in adjusting the services to be provided. Support in the case of impaired concentration can also be provided by writing down homework, appointments and important information for the child rather than just communicating it verbally. In addition, grieving students may be given extra time during performance reviews or a learning partner may be sought within the class to assist the child with academic tasks. In addition, it can be discussed with the student what place of retreat he can go to within the school when he needs time for himself (Lawhon, 2004).

The lesson plan can also include a lesson on death as a part of life. This can be done using the cycle of the seasons to make students aware of the different cycles in life (Naierman, 1997). Students should be taught that all living things die, that grieving is a normal process of saying goodbye to a loved one, and that it takes time to get over the loss. In this way, students can be made aware that their feelings are normal and that things will turn around (Lawhon, 2004).

As teachers spend a great deal of time with their students and thus often notice the changes in behaviour following bereavement, it may be necessary to make some of the adjustments described above within the school context in order to provide support to grieving students. In addition, a variety of interventions can be implemented within the school. The following sections present individual and group interventions that teachers can use to help their students process loss.

5.2 Individual and Group Interventions

What does the death of a close person mean for a child or young person? Initially, grief will be the predominant feeling in most cases. Far less realised by many is that the death of a loved one can continue to affect a young person into adulthood if the death is not given sufficient attention and the child or young person is not offered support to cope with or express their grief and pain (Slyter, 2012). Often those left behind do not manage to help each other as they struggle with their own pain and grief, which can lead to the student wanting to express their grief in school when they are unable to receive any or sufficient support in their home environment (Eppler, 2008). For this reason, it is important to learn about possible interventions for the school context. So what can be done and what should be considered in such offers of help?

First of all, it has to be decided whether an individual or group intervention should be carried out. An individual intervention is appropriate if only one pupil is affected, e.g. because a family member who has no direct connection to the school has died. In this case it is not necessary to conduct interventions with the whole class or school. On the other hand, group interventions are suitable in cases where, for example, a pupil or a teacher has died and the whole class or even several classes are affected. Group interventions are particularly suitable when a violent crime has taken place within the school, such as a school shooting.

In both cases, it is important for teachers to note that they should not only allow students to talk about their feelings and thoughts in the classroom, but even encourage students to do so (Winter, 2000). Clark (1997) also mentions that listening is the greatest help adults can provide to children or adolescents who have lost a loved one. At the same time, if students feel very uncomfortable talking about their personal feelings, they should not be forced to do so (Winter, 2000).

5.2.1 Individual Interventions

Once it has been decided that a one-to-one intervention is useful, the question arises as to what this should look like and what needs to be taken into account. Noppe and Noppe (2004) mention several aspects that should be considered by a teacher or (school) psychologist who wants to carry out the intervention: the relationship of the deceased to the mourner, the circumstances of how the person died, but also the personality of the bereaved. It is important that on the one hand the student is given information about the grieving process, as well as ways to deal with grief. On the other hand, it is important that the student is involved in discussions about dying and ideas about possible rituals to commemorate the deceased. Also, it is important to emphasize that the griever is not alone, but that others are grieving as well, such as family members, friends of the deceased, etc. (Christ et al., 2002).

But what specifically is done in these interventions?

A single intervention that has been scientifically studied is grief expression through multiple varieties of art and creative activities. This type of intervention has been shown in scientific research to be helpful and healing for the full spectrum of adolescents who keep their feelings to themselves to adolescents who actively voice and express their feelings (Slyter, 2012). Art is often experienced as less threatening or intimidating than words and thus allows for a safe, alternative method of expressing grief (Hayes, 2009).

Musical Interventions Two established interventions are "Musical Chronology" by Duffey (2005) and the program by Dalton and Krout (2006) called "Grief Songwriting Process."

Duffey's intervention consists of several steps. First, the young person is to select pieces of music that have high personal meaning. Finally, a CD is to be created from these, which is used to trigger memories, feelings and thoughts about the deceased (Duffey, 2005). Attention can also be paid to similarities and differences between the griever's current situation and the situation described in the songs. This is useful so that the bereaved person recognises that, on the one hand, their situation is unique, but on the other hand, there are some experiences in their own grieving process that others also experience (Gladding et al.,

2008). Lastly, a song is chosen that expresses for the young person their personal hopes and goals for a future without the deceased (Duffey, 2005).

The "Grief Songwriting Process" according to Dalton and Krout (2006) involves creating one's own musical pieces, as well as writing original lyrics to songs that deal with five different aspects of grief: Understanding, feeling, remembering, integrating, and evolving. While lyrics on the theme of "Understanding" often revolve around understanding the cause of the deceased's death as well as understanding one's own reaction, lyrics on the theme of "Feeling" give students the opportunity to express the emotions they themselves have experienced. Texts on the topic of "Remembering" can include events experienced together or special features of the deceased, whereas "Integrating" primarily addresses how one's own life can and will continue after the death of the close person. Last but not least, texts on the theme of "Evolving" are useful to give the young person the opportunity to find meaning or personal growth and development through the death of the loved one.

However, there are not only musical interventions, but also interventions for expressing and coping with grief through artistic works such as painting or crafts.

Artistic Works An artistic-creative intervention presented by Kahn (1999) consists of three phases: Entry phase, exploration phase and implementation phase. Each phase consists of specific questions and tasks. In the entry phase, the student is asked to introduce himself through his art. For example, the student may be asked to create a collage that introduces him or herself as a person. In the exploration phase, the main goal is to reveal feelings of the student that the student may be evaluating as difficult or inappropriate and therefore avoiding to deal with these feelings. This is attempted through a focus on self-representation, for example, with the task of painting a picture that represents the student and his or her feelings about the loss. Finally, the last stage is to work with the student to identify what goals they would like to set for themselves in the future in relation to how they deal with the loss and what behaviours of the student need to change in order to achieve these goals. A specific task at this stage might be to draw a bridge to represent where the student is currently and how he will be when the intervention is successfully completed. In doing so, the student should also consider the obstacles that may lie along the way and what needs to be done to overcome those hurdles (Kahn, 1999).

Further Interventions Not all pupils find the idea of becoming artistically active themselves appealing. For these students other interventions are more suitable. One intervention presented by Sharp et al. (2002) is called "Cinematherapy". This gives the teacher or educational psychologist the opportunity to engage in conversation with the student by first watching a video or film together, which is then discussed. The footage should be relevant, meaning the person or situation depicted should roughly match the student's characteristics and situation (Slyter, 2012). Furthermore, the footage should have a positive message and reflect the values of the student in the video/film. This is especially important if the student belongs to a religious group or faith community that has particular rituals or attitudes towards death and dying. In this case, it is crucial that the teacher or educational psychologist selects footage that represents these values and attitudes, otherwise the student may not feel addressed or, in the worst case, may even feel personally attacked (Slyter, 2012).

The method of "Cinematherapy" has proven to be particularly helpful in this respect, as the viewers (in this case the grieving student) become aware of their emotions and recognize what possible changes can look like. Films are often more suitable than other forms of communication because they appeal particularly to young people, in that films are fun, entertaining and do not require much time or effort (Sheperis et al., 2003).

When implementing each intervention, always make sure that the student can identify with and benefit from the intervention. It is also possible to combine several interventions (Slyter, 2012).

Apart from interventions using art and art expression, there have been few scientifically studied successful individual interventions, so more research is needed in this area (Brown et al., 2007).

5.2.2 Group Interventions

So far, only individual interventions that make sense for a student who has lost a loved one outside of school have been highlighted. But what about when a classmate or teacher dies and the whole class or several classes are affected?

Some of the artistic interventions described can also be applied as group interventions.

An interesting group intervention that also involves students' own creative making of art was described by Morganett (1990). The main aim of this intervention is to give students the opportunity to produce a lasting piece of work that expresses feelings to and about the deceased. Whether this is through painting a picture, writing a story, song or poem, or making an object is left up to the students. However, it should be noted that each student should create an individual piece of work that expresses what the student is feeling.

> **Infobox**
> Very different aspects can be included in this task:
>
> 1. Characteristics of the deceased (age, place of origin, appearance, etc.)
> 2. the relationship of the deceased to the pupils
> 3. particular life events of the deceased
> 4. Hobbies of the deceased
> 5. Favorite food, color, number, etc.
> 6. Commonalities/shared experiences with the deceased

5 Interventions

This is only a selection of aspects, but many more can be included that seem significant to the students.

In the event that some students have difficulty coming up with an idea, it may be helpful for the teacher to bring and present their memorial artwork (Morganett, 1990). While students work on their artwork on their own at the beginning of the intervention, it is important to allow enough time for the discussion that follows, in which students are asked to present their personal memory artwork of the deceased. If students do not engage in discussion on their own, the teacher or school psychologist can stimulate discussion by asking the following exemplary questions (Morganett, 1990):

- What feelings did you have while working on the personal memory artwork?
- How did you feel about presenting your personal memory artwork in front of the class?
- How do you think the memorial artwork will help you remember the person who has passed away?

Another intervention option for a group of grieving students is psychodrama. Psychodrama, in contrast to pure communication methods, represents an action method (Weber, 2020) with the aim of activating and integrating spontaneity and creativity (Moreno, 1959). The person should find a new, appropriate reaction to a new or an already known situation (Moreno, 1959).

This intervention can be effective in that students (re)gain control over their lives in addition to learning about new life roles (Gladding, 2005). The intervention is divided into three sections: Warm-up, action phase, and integration (Blatner, 1997). In the first intervention phase, the warm-up, students are emotionally and practically prepared for the psychodrama by setting up the stage or set and engaging students in affective activities (Moreno, 1999). This is followed by the action phase in which the psychodrama is performed. In this, one student assumes the role of the main character, who assigns roles to the other students. These roles are supposed to represent significant people or things (objects, emotions, as well as personal values) in the life of the main character. The exact process of the psychodrama may vary depending on the needs of the participants. The actors may be given the task of describing their own perception of the situation in the form of monologues while the situation is being acted out. In some cases, it is also useful to have the students switch roles after a while so that they can gain insight into each other's perspectives. In the last phase, the integration phase, the teacher or school psychologist helps the students to process emotionally and intellectually the content that happened during the psychodrama. Particular emphasis should be placed on understanding and integration (Gladding, 2003).

In the setting of a school class, the psychodrama should be performed several times, so that each student takes on the role of the main character once, choosing their own significant roles.

The psychodrama method gives grieving students the opportunity to work on internal conflicts, as well as group conflicts that may arise during the grieving process (Slyter, 2012).

Again, it should be noted that there is little scientific evidence on which group interventions are effective, so further research in this area is needed (Brown et al., 2007).

> **Infobox**
> In summary, individual and group interventions are helpful and healing for students in the grieving process. It is important to consider which intervention is most appropriate for the situation at hand. The main concern is that students are given opportunities to talk about their own feelings and thoughts, as this is how adults can provide the most support. In general, some interventions related to art are well known and scientifically evaluated. Apart from that, there is still a strong need for research on other possible interventions.

5.3 Training of Teachers in Dealing with Grieving Pupils

As teachers spend a great deal of time with their students and are therefore often an important caregiver in their lives, it is important that teachers adequately address the needs of their students, especially during periods of grief. The relevance of the topic is made clear by studies showing that teachers' own attitudes regarding death and grief influence the emotional support they are able to pass on to their grieving students (Cullinan, 1990). However, teachers are usually inadequately prepared, or not prepared at all, as part of their training to deal with death and bereavement within schools - a gap that can be filled by qualified in-service training. Although there are still few training offers, some private institutes and associations in the German-speaking countries offer lectures, seminars, consultations, advanced trainings and workshops on dealing with mourners. These are usually not aimed exclusively at teachers, but more generally at professional groups that may be confronted with grieving people, such as medical professionals, police officers, teachers and educators (Dellanima, n.d.). Within the training courses, concrete teaching options and materials on the topic of death and mourning are provided in part, but on the other hand also options for dealing with grieving students (Schroeter-Rupieper, 2018).

> **Infobox**
> Selection of training providers in Germany
>
> 1. Deutscher Hospiz- und PalliativVerband e. V./www.dhpv.de
> 2. Deutscher Kinderhospizverein e. V./www.deutscher-kinderhospizverein.de
> 3. Institut Dellanima/www.dellanima.de
> 4. M.I.T. Münchner Institut für Trauerpädagogik/www.mit-institut.de
> 5. Further information is available from the Bundesverband Trauerbegleitung e. V.: www.bv-trauerbegleitung.de.

In addition to these offers, however, one searches in vain in German-speaking countries for adequately evaluated, scientifically-based training programs for teachers on how to deal with grieving students. In order to counteract this problem and to ensure the protection of grieving people, the Bundesverband Trauerbegleitung (BVT) e. V. (Federal Association for Bereavement Support) has developed standards for bereavement support qualification programmes to ensure quality in bereavement support (BVT e. V., n.d.). The aim of the qualifications should be an extended competence to act, which should be achieved by training professional competence, self-competence, methodological competence as well as social competence. In the area of professional competence, the distinction between grief counselling and end-of-life counselling should be taught, and the participants should receive basic knowledge about grief processes and grief symptoms as well as knowledge about transference and counter-transference in the grief process. In addition, the systemic effect of grief should be conveyed. In the area of methodological competence, conversation skills, creative methods and grief rituals should be passed on to the participants. They should also be given crisis intervention skills and insights into the design possibilities of a grief counselling process. In the area of self-competence, BVT recommends that trainees learn to have respect for the griever's ability to make decisions and to reflect on their own attitudes and values about different religious backgrounds, different types of loss, and their own worldview. Within the training, participants should be provided with opportunities for role and self-reflection, as this is an ongoing process even after the training has ended. In addition, the teaching of self-care (mental hygiene) is an important component in the training of self-competence. In addition, training in social skills should take place through learning within a group, encountering one's own and others' grief, experiencing different reactions and ways of coping, perceiving one's own feelings and dealing with them. Interdisciplinary competences to be taught are competences in leading conversations and shaping processes, shaping contracts and conclusions as well as dealing with the resources of the accompanied and the accompanying persons (BVT e. V., n.d.). According to BVT, these competences should be taught by means of case discussions, role plays, simulations and other creative methods in order to achieve a practical transfer and to support the participants' own experience. In order to ensure a high quality of the training courses, an academic education, didactic qualifications, practical experience in grief counselling and therapeutic training are desirable on the part of the instructors (BVT e. V., n.d.).

Based on these quality standards, BVT e. V. certifies the courses of external providers of further training and qualifications in grief counselling for different target groups and thus of different scope. There is a choice between three different courses certified by BVT. The "Large Basic Qualification" is aimed at employees of psychosocial, pastoral and health care professions and comparable occupational groups. Within at least 200 teaching units, the course participants are taught skills for the independent accompaniment of grieving people in individual conversations and group settings as well as for the implementation of bereavement support projects in various professional contexts. The course is divided into the basic course, which prepares participants to accompany grieving adults, and an advanced course, which teaches skills for dealing with grieving children and adolescents (BVT e. V., n.d.).

The "Small Basic Qualification" with a scope of 80 teaching units is aimed at volunteers and enables the course participants to accompany grieving adults in the context of individual conversations or within an institution. In addition, the BVT certifies profession-specific additional qualifications, for example for psychotherapists (BVT e. V., n.d.).

One possibility of training in dealing with grieving pupils is offered by the Münchner Institut für Trauerpädagogik (M.I.T.), which is certified by the BVT. The M.I.T. offers further training to become a grief counsellor for children and young people. However, the course is an additional qualification that builds on the "Great Basic Qualification" (M.I.T. Institut, 2020a). As such, it is a very comprehensive and costly course, much of which covers topics less relevant to everyday professional life in the school context in relation to accompanying bereaved adults. More suitable for the school context seems to be an in-house measure offered by M.I.T., which is based on the "Small Basic Qualification" according to BVT standards. The further training is a training that is only carried out on request and is put together according to the needs of the respective target group (for example, educators) (M.I.T. Institut, 2020b).

The Deutsche Kinderhospizakademie also offers training seminars for school staff, in which advice is given on how to deal adequately with death and grief within the school (Deutscher Kinderhospizverein e. V., 2020).

In addition, the Deutscher Hospiz- und PalliativVerband (DHPV) e. V. has been offering training for teachers and other school staff on the topic of "Life, Dying, Death and Mourning in Schools" since 2004 (DHPV e. V., n.d.). The main focus of the training is to sensitise and support teachers in accompanying pupils in bereavement situations. Among other things, participants learn about mourning processes in children and adolescents, supportive rituals and symbols that can be used in schools, and skills for working with parents (DHPV e. V., n.d.). The seminars offered can be conducted within schools or across schools (forms) in educational institutions. According to the DHPV, the participants felt much more confident in dealing with death and mourning after the seminars and reported that they were confident in accompanying children and adolescents in their mourning (DHPV e. V., n.d.). However, it is not clear from the documents whether these findings stem from a well-founded evaluation or are based on individual reports of experience.

As in the German-speaking world, there are hardly any well-evaluated, evidence-based training programmes for teachers on how to deal with grieving children and adolescents at the international level. According to Smith (2009), it is essential that teachers are provided with sound knowledge about grief processes in children and adolescents and are made aware of how these grief processes can affect the experience and behaviour of their students. This knowledge forms the basis for further interventions, which should be individually designed depending on age, gender and a variety of other factors.

> **Infobox**
> In summary, it can be stated that the offer of training courses for teachers in dealing with grieving students is low, both in the German-speaking countries and on an international level, and that there is a complete lack of scientifically evaluated, evidence-based programmes, despite the great need for them.

5.4 Conclusion

In the event of an unexpected death at school or in the personal environment of one or more pupils, teachers need to consider a number of points when breaking the news and dealing with grieving pupils, which have been outlined in this chapter. Following the breaking of the news, individual interventions, for example from the fields of art and music therapy, or group interventions can be carried out at class level or, depending on the number of pupils affected, across school classes. In order not to be unprepared for this great challenge when a sudden death occurs, it is advisable to deal with the topic in advance in order to be able to react quickly and competently in an acute case. Specific training courses and advanced training seminars for teachers, which are already offered by some associations and institutes in German-speaking countries, are suitable for this purpose.

References

Becker, U., Shah, H., Mock, G., Wiese, A., & Ehlert, C. (2008). *Vom Umgang mit Trauer in der Schule. Handreichung für Lehrkräfte und Erzieher/innen*. Koelblin-Fortuna-Druck.

Blatner, A. (1997). Psychodrama: The state of the art. *Art in Psychotherapy, 24*, 23–30.

Brown, A. C., Sandler, I. N., Tein, J., Liu, X., & Haine, R. (2007). Implications of parental suicide and violent death for promotion of resilience of parentally-bereaved children. *Death Studies, 31*(4), 301–335.

BVT e. V. (n.d.). *Qualifizierung*. Accessed Jan 18, 2020, from https://bv-trauerbegleitung.de/standards/

Christ, G. H., Siegel, K., & Christ, A. E. (2002). Adolescent grief: 'It never really hit me...until it actually happened'. *Journal of the American Medical Association, 288*, 1269–1278.

Clark, M. (1997). *The tomorrow's children face when a parent dies [motion picture]*. Aquarius Productions.

Cullinan, A. L. (1990). Teachers' death anxiety, ability to cope with death, and perceived ability to aid bereaved students. *Death Studies, 14*(2), 147–160.

Dalton, T. A., & Krout, R. E. (2006). The grief-songwriting process with bereaved adolescents: An integrated grief model and music therapy protocol. *Music Therapy Perspectives, 24*(2), 94–103.

Dellanima. (n.d.). *Berufliche Fortbildungen, Seminare*, Vorträge–Termine. Accessed Jan 18, 2020, from https://www.dellanima.de/angebote/fortbildungen-und-vortrage/

Deutscher Kinderhospizverein e. V. (2020). *Angebote für Lehrer/innen, Pädagoginnen und Pädagogen*. Accessed Jan 19, 2020, from https://www.deutscher-kinderhospizverein.de/

deutsche-kinderhospizakademie/veranstaltungen/angebote-fuer-lehrerinnen-paedagoginnen-und-paedagogen/

DHPV e. V. (n.d.). *Hospizlernen.* Accessed Jan 18, 2020, from https://www.dhpv.de/tl_files/public/Service/Broschueren/FACHGRUPPEN_2/Broschuere_Hospizlernen_Ansicht.pdf

Duffey, T. H. (2005). A musical chronology and the emerging life song. *Journal of Creativity in Mental Health, 1*(1), 141–147.

Eppler, C. (2008). Exploring themes of resiliency in children after the death of a parent. *Professional School Counseling, 11*(3), 189–196.

Gladding, S. T. (2003). *Group work: A counseling speciality* (4th ed.). Prentice-Hall.

Gladding, S. T. (2005). *Counseling as an art. The creative arts in counseling* (3rd ed.). American Counseling Association.

Gladding, S. T., Newsome, D., Binkley, E., & Henderson, D. A. (2008). The lyrics of hurting and healing: Finding words that are revealing. *Journal of Creativity in Mental Health, 3*, 212–219.

Hayes, P. M. (2009). *Art therapy for grief and loss.* Cross Country Education.

Kahn, B. B. (1999). Art therapy with adolescents: Making it work for school counselors. *Professional School Counseling, 2*, 291–298.

Lawhon, T. (2004). Teachers and schools can aid grieving students. *Education, 124*(3), 559–566.

M.I.T. Institut. (2020a). *Trauerbegleitung Kinder und Jugendliche.* Accessed Jan 18, 2020, from https://www.mit-institut.de/trauerbegleitung-kinder-und-jugendliche.php

M.I.T. Institut. (2020b). *Trauerbegleitung Basisqualifikation.* Accessed Jan 18, 2020, from https://www.mit-institut.de/trauerbegleitung-basisqualifikation.php

Moreno, J. L. (1959). *Gruppenpsychotherapie und psychodrama.* Thieme.

Moreno, J. J. (1999). Ancient sources and modern applications: The creative arts in psychodrama. *Arts in Psychotherapy, 26*, 95–101.

Morganett, R. S. (1990). *Skills for living: Group counseling activities for young adolescents.* Research Press.

Naierman, N. (1997). Reaching out to grieving students. *Educational Leadership, 55*(2), 62–65.

Noppe, I. C., & Noppe, L. D. (2004). Adolescent experiences with death: Letting go of immortality. *Journal of Mental Health Counseling, 26*, 146–167.

Schroeter-Rupieper, M. (2018). *Trauer-Seminare für Lehrer und Schulen.* Accessed Jan 18, 2020, from https://www.familientrauerbegleitung.de/angebot/seminare/lehrer.html

Sharp, C., Smith, J. V., & Cole, A. (2002). Cinematherapy: Metaphorically promoting therapeutic change. *Counseling Psychology Quarterly, 15*, 269–276.

Sheperis, C. J., Hope, K., & Palmer, C. (2003). Family ties: Uniting systems theory and practice through cinematherapy. In *Paper vorgestellt auf der "annual convention of the American counseling association".* Anaheim.

Slyter, M. (2012). Creative counseling interventions for grieving adolescents. *Journal of Creativity in Mental Health, 7*(1), 17–34.

Smith, L. A. (2009). *Children and parental death: Effects and school-based interventions.* Accessed Jan 18, 2020, from https://www.semanticscholar.org/paper/Children-and-Parental-Death%3A-Effects-and-Smith/8abf6f60d8e23eb7dc455cbc9b67ce9e1502bfa5#citing-papers

Weber, H. (2020). *Was ist psychodrama?* Accessed Jan 18, 2020, from https://www.psychodrama-netz.de/content/psychodrama

Winter, E. (2000). School bereavement. *Educational Leadership, 57*(6), 80.

Limits of Grief Work

Sam Bernard and Mario Scholer

6.1 Limits of Grief Work by Teachers and Pedagogical Professionals

Children and adolescents are entrusted to the institution of school for many years and parents usually rightly regard it as a safe place for upbringing and education. Teachers and educators, on behalf of these institutions and thus indirectly on behalf of society, take on the general care and guidance of the pupils, whereby they become important reference and trusted persons for them over time (Hinderer & Kroth, 2005). The class teacher/confidence teacher is the deputy authority with a role model function, who is undoubtedly the first contact person for the children and young people within the institution.

Even though teachers should be aware of the fact that in the course of their professional life they will most likely come into contact with grieving children, adolescents and possibly also parents and colleagues (Hinderer & Kroth, 2005), it should not be forgotten that even teachers, depending on their resilience and general personal situation, have their individual limits and are confronted with these more or less regularly in everyday life.

When dealing with death and mourning, teachers should first of all be clear about their own emotional and professional limits and to what extent they are willing and able to deal with the topic of mourning or to deal with the mourning process (Krause, 2013). Grief counselling and dealing with grief must at all times correspond to the extent and scope of the teacher's own will and cannot and should not in practice be demanded by other teachers or ordered and prescribed by the school management. In addition to the social and specific competencies, the nature and character of the current personal situation is certainly also decisive, especially with regard to one's own consternation and the resulting fact that the

---

S. Bernard (✉) · M. Scholer
Department of Behavioural and Cognitive Sciences, University of Luxembourg, Esch-sur-Alzette, Luxembourg
e-mail: sam.bernard.001@student.uni.lu

supposed grief counsellor may himself be in a grief situation caused by the grief event, and as a result of this direct and subjective consternation, a rational-empathic handling of the emotional needs and reactions of others may become difficult or even impossible (Hinderer & Kroth, 2005).

In this context, it must be emphasised that teachers, of course, also have a right to a personal stress limit and overload threshold and, just like the persons concerned themselves, must be regarded as "experts" of their own needs and sensitivities and taken seriously. No one knows the individual situation, the inner life of a person better than the person him/herself, and so this right must not be questioned or denied by anyone, regardless of expectations and external requirements. If personal stress limits have been reached and acute overload situations are possibly threatening, corresponding support requests and overload notifications should be taken seriously under all circumstances and corresponding assistance and solution offers should be made or offered as promptly and unrestrictedly as possible. In order to recognize such crisis situations at an early stage and to avert possible complications, concrete assistance and support from "outside" is of course required. Accompanying persons also need accompaniment. Accompaniment not only, but also in the form of talks and offers of talks, a more or less formal "monitoring" adapted to the situation, if necessary close-meshed, in order to be able, among other things, to recognise symptoms of stress and excessive demands in good time and to be able to adapt constructively. Grief counselling and the processing of grief are a process that should be shared between several shoulders.

▸ **Infobox: Pathological Stress Reaction** Stress does not represent an illness in the medical-therapeutic sense. However, stress can lead to stress consequences if it is not adequately managed and processed. The most important of these are acute stress reaction (ICD-10-2020: F43.0) and adjustment disorder (ICD-10-2020: F43.2). Furthermore, various somatoform disorders can occur in connection with persistent stress.

If the support of mourners within the social network of schools can be provided by reference and contact persons almost without any special expertise, the adequate and controlling design of mourning processing and mourning treatment requires the application of specific and targeted methods. On the one hand, these presuppose the existence of explicit specialist knowledge and thus prior competence building within the framework of appropriate qualification measures, but on the other hand they also place high demands on space and time, which cannot be implemented into in the classroom or integrated into everyday school life (Hinderer & Kroth, 2005).

Even if the personal and social competence as well as the corresponding motivation of the teaching staff are available to a sufficient and promising extent, the latter is often a reason in practice to place grief counselling in the professional hands of external experts and thus to locate it quite concretely outside the "everyday classroom life" in terms of space and time. Experts who are either available [...], in the optimal case, [...] within the school context or who can be called upon in the immediate environment of the institution.

6.2 Limits of Grief Counselling in the Institution School

In the life context of school, the most diverse experiences of loss of the people active there with their challenges and the resulting need to adapt to new, changed life situations have an impact. The death of a friend, a close family member, a classmate or a member of the teaching staff confronts the entire school community as well as people from the immediate school environment with borderline situations. These situations make it necessary for the school as an institution to deal with the issues of dying, death and mourning, and in view of its holistic responsibility for the students entrusted to it, this is inevitable and without alternative. Being a companion in the time of mourning is not only the responsibility of professional mourning counsellors and crisis intervention teams, support should also be provided by people from the social environment. School as a central living space for children and adolescents not only imparts learning content, school is more than an educational "unit", a place where knowledge is imparted. School is an important social living and interaction space and thus also teaches, as a representative of the state and society, the importance of solidarity and community, a living community in which dealing with death, suffering and loss can be learned, but does not necessarily have to be endured and borne alone (Witt-Loers, 2015).

Institutional limits of grief counselling often already lie in the first phase of dealing with the complex of topics. Fear of contact, helplessness and insecurity in connection with death and mourning often lead to ignoring what has happened and to prematurely relinquishing or rejecting one's own responsibility and accountability in a kind of protective reflex (Witt-Loers, 2015). If the institution has not considered and planned in advance, for example if responsibilities and tasks have not been distributed, those affected in the acute situation often inevitably remain alone with their worries and needs and can hardly be reached by representatives of the school and its measures at a later point in time. If the school organism, for whatever reason, sees itself unable to cope with these undoubtedly diverse and extraordinary challenges and demands, it should, true to the principle "more harmful than the wrong help is just no help", establish contact with competent, professional agencies at an early stage in order to obtain immediate but also longer-term help and support.

> **Infobox:** *Grief and Crisis Intervention: Institutional Structure*
> An essential prerequisite for professional crisis and grief intervention is a structured and coordinated approach. To this end, it is necessary to define appropriate institutional structures in a formally binding manner with regard to the following aspects, among others, and to communicate them within the institution (Witt-Loers, 2015)

1. Information processing
2. Competence and distribution of tasks (if necessary external interfaces)
3. Contact with the relatives concerned
4. Meet, inform and accompany affected pupils and colleagues
5. Shaping the school's internal farewell
6. Parents' evening
7. Enable places and times of remembrance, find rituals

However, if schools have recognised their responsibility in good time and have consistently considered the possibilities of support, a "space" for mourning can be constructed and made available (Hinderer & Kroth, 2005), which enables an intensive examination of the topic and leads to a jointly supported, shared and lived culture of mourning. This culture of mourning is able to guide and support all participants in their actions, but above all to make the context of school even more lifelike and reality-competent. Equipped with this increase in competence, schools can, in addition to the space for mourning and processing grief, also create spaces which can be used by all those involved, first and foremost the students, the teaching staff, the employees of the institution, but possibly also neighbouring educational institutions, for joint and creative reflection. Equipped and integrated in this way, the school, aware of its responsibility for all those involved—here, explicit reference must once again be made to the group of pupils and their needs and world of experience—can preserve its autonomy and find viable paths and form constructive alliances in a self-determined manner. In this way, schools learn to know and recognise their limits "from the inside out", are able to identify weak points and to counteract them in a targeted and appropriate manner.

In addition to the acute reaction to crises and borderline situations, school as an institution should first and foremost, mediated by internal competence bearers such as social workers and appropriately qualified pedagogues, proactively and steeringly shape the medium-term processing of grief and the confrontation with grief consequences and the effects in the context of the living environment of school. In a further step, in close cooperation with external partners and expert networks, it should also become active in a moderating function with regard to non-school concerns, challenges and psychosocial well-being and develop concrete support potential. In this way, schools and, through them, pedagogy can comprehensively fulfil their task and mission in the area of dying, death and mourning and, if necessary, mediate, advise and accompany on the basis of knowledge and experience (Maywald, 2013).

The responsibility of schools and pedagogy naturally ends where mourning processes, dealing with the consequences and effects of death, take on pathological manifestations and, fundamentally and without exception, whenever the circumstances of death are violent and/or suicidal in origin (Maywald, 2013). In this sense, school as an institution must not primarily be understood as a place of therapeutic intervention or assume and claim this role for itself on its own initiative. School inevitably reaches its limits where it is demanded and expected to go beyond its original mandate, where it may possibly treat and heal, where it is no longer only a school but also an unrestricted problem and conflict solver, where it may even have to take over educational and custodial tasks on behalf of others, where its actions come into conflict with its very own function, where the tension between society's idea and conception of it and its actual activities increases and expectations can sometimes only be fulfilled to a limited and inadequate extent.

▶ **Infobox: Pathological Grief** Also referred to as complicated grief or persistent grief disorder. In pathological mourning, the mourning reaction is significantly more intense and, in contrast to "normal" mourning, considerably prolonged. Diagnostically, this form of "grief complication" is defined as an adjustment disorder resulting from severe, possibly traumatic stress (ICD-10-GM-2020: F43.2). The emotional experience as well as the social life of the affected persons are partly considerably impaired. Symptoms appear in both the psychological and physical spheres. People with an adjustment disorder do not always require therapy.

School always reaches its limits where school is no longer allowed to be or no longer wants to be school, i.e. a place of knowledge transfer, education and generative and social encounters. It inevitably reaches its limits where competencies are insufficient and resources are exhausted or not even available or provided for in the first place, where functionaries are overburdened and social systems are brittle and no longer sustainable due to overstrain.

6.3 Limits of Grief Work with Affected Persons, Relatives and Fellow Sufferers

Apart from specific cases, those affected and their relatives are primarily responsible for themselves and are entitled to accept help and support from the school and its representatives in whole or in part or to refuse it, even without stating their motives (Hinderer & Kroth, 2005). The right to self-determination applies in full, even in stressful exceptional situations, and can neither be overridden by events nor by the, albeit possibly justified and comprehensible, will to intervene on the part of outsiders. Fundamentally, parents and guardians are responsible for the welfare of their children; spouses and family members have the right to their "own" grief and how they deal with loss. Grieving individuals may not want to be reduced to their grief and perceived as "intact," may not want to share their grief, their sorrow, or yet, may not want to make or allow their loss to become the loss of others. Here, school must be sensitive, seek dialogue with those affected as soon as possible, initiate personal contact immediately, make very concrete, binding and unbiased agreements, find an appropriate, balanced relationship of closeness and distance, accept boundaries if necessary and then also maintain these towards third parties. School must make transparent what it wants to achieve and how, what it is capable of and what it is not capable of, where it can and wants to be active and where it can and may only act as a mediator. Expectations become tangible and become agreements, expectations are made visible and communicated. Hunches and assumptions become knowledge for all. Recognizing the wishes and needs of those affected, directing and regulating information flows, offering support services and coordinating different, independent support services, bringing them into contact with each other and making them effective.

The same applies, of course, to all those "uninvolved and involved". How much mourning, how much accompaniment and "compassion" can be expected and trusted from the pupils of a class, the staff of a school, the class teachers and liaison teachers? When does compassion become pain and bearing it become a burden, what are the effects and "side effects" of mourning processes? Which boundaries are crossed unconsciously and unintentionally or deliberately and intentionally, how can classmates signal when their individual limits have been reached, when their emotional resistance is exhausted and how can they avoid too much, too long and too intense without turning away from school and falling into self-doubt? Mourning work must not produce victims or turn empathy into antipathy, it must be turned towards everyone, be careful and cautious, act considerately and keep an eye on the mourning environment and all those involved.

6.4 Limits of Bereavement Work by Carers

Partly independent of the theories and models presented so far on the course of grief, or also interventions in school areas in cases of bereavement, one should also look at the topic of grief work from the other side. Also the carers, be they psychologists, therapists, social workers, carers, or any other helping force, are equally exposed to such an event and should be aware of the potential distress attached to it (Knight, 2013). In such a situation, it is not sufficient to worry only about the welfare of the affected persons, but one should also always look after oneself—this has nothing egoistic, but is rather a call to all the persons who work in such areas to also worry about themselves. Those who work in such areas are regularly confronted with traumatic events, and for a healthy approach it is essential to have the appropriate psychological hygiene, not only that which is imparted to those who are grieving, but also precisely that which is often too rarely claimed for oneself (Reddemann, 2003).

6.4.1 Compassion Fatigue and Secondary Traumatic Stress

When it comes to supporting others in the form of psychological assistance, it is important to consider the resources of the person helping. As long as a person has the energy, this support can be provided without any problems, but this energy is finite, and in various circumstances this energy may be lacking; this is then referred to as *compassion fatigue* or, in more severe cases, even *secondary traumatic stress* (Bride, 2007; Hensel et al., 2015;

Zeidner et al., 2013). Supporting, sustaining, or assisting a person in their grief in those first moments when those very first impressions are grasped and realized can be unimaginably stressful. This circumstance is only further potentiated when the person involved is a young person or even a child. Grief work in schools can be all the more stressful because, as an adult, it is not uncommon to try not to let children bear some of this heavy burden alone at first. This is all the more so because children and adolescents often do not yet have the cognitive maturity to deal with such situations on their own or are powerlessly at the mercy of fate (McCann & Pearlman, 2015).

Compassion fatigue is the term used by professionals to describe the inability to fully empathize with a person, often resulting in indifference or apathy on the part of the caregiver. However, this phenomenon should not be misinterpreted as malicious intent, but is often the result of physical and mental fatigue that can result from "too much" empathy (Adams et al., 2006; Figley, 1995). A recent review of studies (Van Mol et al., 2015) shows that the upper limit of possible compassion fatigue affected individuals working in professions where they are in frequent contact with traumatic content is somewhere between around 35% and 70%—this prevalence may not translate directly to a psychologist working in bereavement work with children, but is a very strong indicator of the impact such work can bring. Caring for traumatized persons can be a heavy emotional burden for the psychologist, not least because one tries to assist the person in his or her fate and, if necessary, also puts oneself, even if only partially, into his or her position in order to be able to understand him or her better. Comparable to the more familiar diagnosis of burnout (Figley, 1995), caregivers or psychologists are thus also capable of burning out and using up their "supply" of compassion. An important difference to burnout, however, is the process: what in burnout is often a slowly creeping condition, in compassion fatigue can arise very quickly and in isolated cases can even be triggered by a single exposure to trauma (Conrad & Kellar-Guenther, 2006).

These symptoms of fatigue can also be found in the secondary traumatic stress (STS) mentioned earlier. In the case of secondary traumatization, however, not only is too much selfless devotion a risk, but this goes a bit further. In the case of regular and/or intense emotionally demanding contact with traumatic content, even someone who is only indirectly (secondarily) affected by it (such as a therapist or psychologist) can feel a serious strain (stress). If one does this regularly and with great dedication over a longer period of time, or within a short period of time to a high degree (both in terms of volume, but also in terms of content), this can lead to the emotional burden exceeding the personal bearable limit (Bride, 2007). It is at this point that the aforementioned fatigue can occur and the empathy capacity of the carer flattens, but beyond this, other health consequences become apparent. The lifetime prevalence (the probability spread over the whole life) of people working in this field coming into contact with traumatised persons at least once and being confronted with their trauma is between 40 and 80% (Bride, 2007). Similarly, as one can compare compassion fatigue with "classic" burnout for a better understanding, one can draw the parallel with post-traumatic stress disorder to secondary stress (Breslau, 2002; Hensel et al., 2015). Accordingly, the consequences in more severe cases are characterized by depressive moods, irritation, up to increasing anxiety states and can even manifest as intrusive flashbacks (Cieslak et al., 2013, 2014). In individual cases, it can even have such far-reaching consequences that these memories and arbitrary "witnessing" are perceived so strongly that those affected become seriously ill (Figley, 2002a, b).

6.4.2 Relevance of Self-Care

Now the question arises whether the consequences such as compassion fatigue or secondary traumatization are inevitable, or whether it is possible to prevent them—to which the answer is a very clear "yes": you can do something. The magic word in this case is *self-care*. The practice of self-care is not a panacea that will make all these risks null and void, but its relevance is now hard to deny (Dahl, 2017, 2019), here several aspects need to be distinguished.

On the one hand, there is resilience (De Terte & Stephens, 2014; Luthar et al., 2000), a construct that describes a person's personal disposition, the extent to which a person is able to cope emotionally and mentally with experiencing a crisis, or how quickly they can recover to a pre-crisis state. At this point, the literature is not entirely conclusive as to what resilience is defined as. For example, Zautra et al. (2010) take the approach that resilience is a product of many different other factors, whereas other authors often classify and operationalise it as a developmental process or a personality trait (Luthar et al., 2000; Zautra et al., 2010). The approach advocated here follows the approach of seeing resilience as a product of many other elements and, related to this, the possibility of strengthening and supporting personal resilience through other pathways.

The American Psychological Association (2011) states a handful of factors that are indicative of strong resilience: first and foremost, it is important to have a healthy and supportive environment, both family and friends. Furthermore, the ability to make and execute realistic plans, a healthy view of self and a positive confidence in one's strengths and abilities, clear communication with one's environment, and the ability to deal with strong emotions and impulses are all elements that go hand in hand with strong resilience. Admittedly, that these sub-elements contribute to being better able to deal with difficult situations (both as a therapist and as a sufferer) is probably obvious in most cases; the question is rather how to achieve these attributes. Again, there are a number of recommendations (American Psychological Association, 2011; Siebert, 2005; Radey & Figley, 2007; Reich et al., 2010):

1. *Exchange and contacts with others*—the direct environment can often be a valuable source of help and even a sympathetic ear can make a big difference.
2. *Avoiding the view that crises are insurmountable events*—these events happen, there is very rarely anything that can be done about them, but you can direct your own vision into the future and even small elements of improvement can help with the heavy lifting.

3. *Acceptance of change*—Change is part of life, accepting change that you can't change allows more focus on the circumstances that can be adapted.
4. *Making clear decisions*—even if it's hard, making clear and decisive decisions in difficult circumstances inevitably moves you forward, letting go of problems and hoping they will go away is giving up your freedom of action.
5. *Seek opportunities for self-awareness*—often, as a person, you grow from situations and experiences from which you expect less; noticing such growth can help you become more aware of your own strengths.
6. *Looking after yourself*—what could generally be classed as *self-care* is also noticeable in the little things in life; paying attention to your own feelings and needs, pursuing activities you enjoy, exercising or simply taking time for yourself.
7. *Keeping a realistic perspective*—generally keeping a long-term view of the future can help maintain that perspective in difficult situations and not make the problem seem bigger than it really is.

Especially for professionals in areas in which contact with more difficult topics is frequent, supervision is added. The supervision outlined here differs from that provided for in basic psychotherapeutic training (Bundesamt für Justiz, 2019)—the latter describes here the accompaniment and consultation with a psychotherapist authorised to train and not necessarily the pure processing of difficult cases. For professionals who often find themselves in contact with and caring for victims, beyond the resilience described above, it is important to repeatedly work through these experiences in supervision sessions in order to avoid consequences such as compassion fatigue or secondary traumatic stress. Personal supervision is not legally required at any point, but the recommendation stands loudly, even as a professional, not to take this burden lightly and to take care of yourself now and then and work through this experience (Dahl, 2017, 2019; Radey & Figley, 2007; Reddemann, 2003), as this has been shown to reduce the risks associated with this delicate activity (Knight, 2013; Hensel et al., 2015).

6.5 End and Closure of Grief Work

Even though the range of possible assistance and interventions that can be used in the context of accompanying a grief reaction is broad, a very elementary and non-negligible point remains the question of closure. It is possible that at first such a question may seem rushed, even understandable that a question "When will we be done?" may strike the wrong note. Nor can the question at hand be so heavy-handed. What is at issue here is the ambiguity of where to go as a companion; where does grief work stop? To trust and enable children and young people to grieve and to experience the feelings and limits associated with this creates trust, trust in an adult world that accompanies competently, mediates and suffers within the limits of mature consternation, but above all shares sincerely and courageously. Dealing with dying, death and mourning is part of the spiritual and mental development of children and contributes optimally to the formation of a self-confident attitude towards life, but also an emphatic and subsidiary way of dealing with those affected.

If we look more into this question, we can see that such a mourning work cannot last forever, but that the aim of such an intervention is to support a mourning reaction and that this reaction is of a finite duration. In this framework, it is therefore not unimportant to have an idea from the very beginning of where the guided mourning work should go and how the point is defined at which this work is finished—knowing that the end of such work also plays an important role.

Consequently, such closure can be illuminated and defined from different perspectives. On the one hand, closure can be a clearly defined state and step of a chosen intervention; on the other hand, grief work and support can also follow a natural process and coping can thus be achieved via a different, free-flowing path.

6.5.1 Closure as Part of a Defined Intervention

Many of the interventions already presented are clearly structured in their application and provide a clear framework for application. The possible individual interventions presented in Sect. 4.2.4.2 *Individual and group interventions* provide a clear framework. In the art-oriented intervention presented by Kahn (1999), there are 3 clearly specified stages, which should culminate in the student defining a goal for him/herself and dealing with it artistically and reflecting on it. After this task, this specific intervention is completed with what it may achieve, and thus the grief work directly associated with it. Similarly, Sharp et al.'s (2002) *Cinematherapy* involves open discussion to help process what has been seen and felt. In this form of intervention, it is therefore primarily a matter of absorbing the initial grief reaction, dampening it somewhat if necessary and helping to find a direction for the coming period; it is not so much a matter of taking over the feelings of grief of the person affected, or even taking them away, but rather of supporting them in this first phase.

Similar to these clearly defined interventions, which are about catching an initial grief reaction, there are also offers such as grief groups, which are about dealing with the feeling of grief in a group and learning to better understand this dealing. These may differ in form from one another, but should still not be without purpose. Samide and Stockton (2002) report that such longer forms of groups should not be shorter than 8 weeks, but the possibility of an extension up to a year is not a problem as long as the appropriate framework can be given; however, the conclusion is also important here. One must be aware that the dissolution of such a group can also be an experience of loss for a child, this may also be felt as such, however, it is advised to arrange such a last session in such a way that the view is directed to what has been achieved, without suppressing a possible arising feeling of grief.

However, it should be explicitly pointed out that clinically relevant knowledge about the long-term effects of such groups is still relatively limited, and thus it is also not clear in what form such a bereavement group should be conducted in the best possible way. What is certain, however, is that the conclusion of this form of grief work should be clearly defined, communicated as such and also processed (Samide & Stockton, 2002).

6.5.2 End of Grief Counselling as a Natural Process

Allowing children to grieve also means giving them the opportunity to understand and say goodbye. Grief can be integrated, can create a connection, if it is a generative event, if it is allowed to oscillate between the world of children and young people on the one hand and the world of parents and grandparents on the other, if the reality of the other is not kept silent, avoided and denied in demarcation from one another, but is viewed, experienced and endured with one's own eyes. The process of mourning thus proceeds without external intervention in a natural process along the phases of processing appropriate to development and competence, which, under the influence of the time dimension, channels the overwhelming stream of impressions and feelings, drains tributaries, reduces the speed of flow and finally releases the view of the shore and solid ground again. At some point it seems possible for the bereaved to refocus their sense of life, to slowly turn to the world as it is now in distinction to what it once was, and to develop a new, updated world-view. Old tasks and social roles are resumed, new ones must be added. The self is updated and redefined differently according to the circumstances; there is an adaptation to the changed situation, a reality without the deceased. Patterns of thinking, feeling and acting that were inseparable from life before the loss event must now be discarded so that innovations can emerge and positive growth is possible.

In line with this, Verena Kast (2018) describes the last of the four stages of mourning as the phase of new self and world reference. The deceased has become an inner figure and there is an awareness of the significance of the relationship with the deceased. Perceptions are adjusted, one's own position in the grief structure is possibly adjusted. The loss is accepted, new patterns of life are developed without the deceased being forgotten.

> **Infobox:** *Stages of Grief According to Verena* **Kast (2018)**
> This model of the stages of grief was developed by the Swiss psychologist Verena Kast with the aim of being able to better understand oneself in one's own grief or other people who are grieving.

This model is based on the assumption that grief, like any other processual event, is characterized by a clear beginning and a clear end. The beginning of the grieving process is the loss of the loved one. The end of the mourning process is to be seen through the reorientation of the entire life structure.

The four phases of the mourning process according to Verena Kast

- the phase of denial
- the phase of bursting emotions
- the phase of searching and separation
- the phase of the new reference to the self and the world.

Under no circumstances should the impression be created that stages of grief proceed in a linear fashion. Less so than with adults, nor do they do so with children and adolescents. But our mind is not least designed for this process, this development. A natural process which inevitably, as far as not pathologically deformed and distorted, leads to a phase of adaptation and reorganization: a "somehow it must and will go on". Attention is gradually directed to everyday things. The past, depending on its severity, loses its salience and presence in thought, feeling and action. A physiological forgetting process sets in and the traumatic event is transferred into memory. Certainly, the real extent of the inner involvement of the persons involved comes into play here. How directly, indirectly or remotely does what has happened affect them and what influence does it exert in different worlds of experience and perception. Affectedness gains form and shape with an actual, reflected reference to reality. Loss acquires a face, a form, a body.

It may not be possible to process grief and come to terms with it conclusively.

But perhaps it is not supposed to do so.

Grief and loss can be a protracted, sometimes lifelong process. Companions with many faces and a long breath. The stream becomes a river, perhaps a trickle. It flows steadily, its roar receding into the background. Perhaps pools form that lie hidden and whose bottom cannot be guessed. It is important here to have functioning and healthy strategies for dealing with memory. The "what do I allow when, to what extent and within what framework" is of immense importance for the individual. Memory needs its time, its space and its rituals. Memory must therefore be successfully anchored and located both internally and externally. Here, fixed structures in the form of memory rituals help those affected. Just as mourning and the experience of sadness have been guided and supported, targeted support should now also be provided at this stage in the form of joint discussion and finding solutions.

The end of grief counseling defines the beginning of memory work.

6.6 Conclusion

The question of the boundaries of grief work and grief counselling cannot, as already indicated at the beginning, be answered in a universally valid and satisfactory way for all actors within the grief process. The border areas, border zones, border spaces, more or less tangible and graspable thoughts and ideas about borders presented here should rather be understood as suggestions and impulses for concrete border finding and border definition. The topic must be considered and analysed in a differentiated way and with the necessary care and conscientiousness within the institution, but above all discussed and reflected upon in an open and constructive dialogue with all those concerned. Boundaries can be explored, adapted, expanded and respected, but should in no case be ignored or disregarded. This applies to those affected, as well as to those in the immediate environment or outside carers; everyone should be aware of their own limits and not shy away from accepting, signalling and, if necessary, dealing with them accordingly. Grief counselling ends where it is instrumentally planned or where it arises naturally.

References

Adams, R. E., Boscarino, J. A., & Figley, C. R. (2006). Compassion fatigue and psychological distress among social workers: A validation study. *American Journal of Orthopsychiatry, 76*(1), 103–108.

American Psychological Association. (2011). *The road to resilience*. Accessed Jan 15, 2020, from https://www.apa.org/helpcenter/road-resilience

Breslau, N. (2002). Epidemiologic studies of trauma, posttraumatic stress disorder, and other psychiatric disorders. *The Canadian Journal of Psychiatry, 47*(10), 923–929.

Bride, B. E. (2007). Prevalence of secondary traumatic stress among social workers. *Social Work, 52*(1), 63–70.

Bundesamt für Justiz. (2019). *Ausbildungs- und Prüfungsverordnung für Psychologische Psychotherapeuten (PsychTh-APrV)*. Accessed Jan 15, 2020, from https://www.gesetze-im-internet.de/psychth-aprv/BJNR374900998.html

Cieslak, R., Shoji, K., Douglas, A., Melville, E., Luszczynska, A., & Benight, C. C. (2014). A meta-analysis of the relationship between job burnout and secondary traumatic stress among workers with indirect exposure to trauma. *Psychological Services, 11*(1), 75–86.

Cieslak, R., Shoji, K., Luszczynska, A., Taylor, S., Rogala, A., & Benight, C. C. (2013). Secondary trauma self-efficacy: Concept and its measurement. *Psychological Assessment, 25*(3), 917–928.

Conrad, D., & Kellar-Guenther, Y. (2006). Compassion fatigue, burnout, and compassion satisfaction among Colorado child protection workers. *Child Abuse & Neglect, 30*(10), 1071–1080.

Dahl, C. (2017). Ein Plädoyer für mehr Selbstfürsorge. *Prävention Und Gesundheitsförderung, 13*(2), 131–137.

Dahl, C. (2019). Warum es sich lohnt, gut für sich zu sorgen. *Prävention und Gesundheitsförderung, 14*(1), 69–78.

De Terte, I., & Stephens, C. (2014). Psychological resilience of workers in high-risk occupations. *Stress and Health, 30*(5), 353–355.

Figley, C. R. (1995). Compassion fatigue as secondary traumatic stress disorder: An overview. In C. R. Figley (Ed.), *Compassion fatigue* (pp. 1–20). Brunner/Mazel.

Figley, C. R. (2002a). Compassion fatigue: Psychotherapists' chronic lack of self care. *Journal of Clinical Psychology, 58*(11), 1433–1441.

Figley, C. R. (2002b). *Treating compassion fatigue*. Routledge.

Hensel, J. M., Ruiz, C., Finney, C., & Dewa, C. S. (2015). Meta-analysis of risk factors for secondary traumatic stress in therapeutic work with trauma victims. *Journal of Traumatic Stress, 28*(2), 83–91.

Hinderer, P., & Kroth, M. (2005). *Kinder bei Tod und Trauer begleiten: konkrete Hilfestellung in Trauersituationen für Kindergarten, Grundschule und zu Hause*. Ökotopia Verlag.

Kahn, B. B. (1999). Art therapy with adolescents: Making it work for school counselors. *Professional School Counseling, 2*, 291–298.

Kast, V. (2018). *Trauern: Phasen und Chancen des psychischen Prozesses*. Freiburg im Breisgau.
Knight, C. (2013). Indirect trauma: Implications for self-care, supervision, the organization, and the academic institution. *The Clinical Supervisor, 32*(2), 224–243.
Krause, K. (2013). *Trauer in der Grundschule: Der Umgang mit trauernden Kindern im Schulalltag*. Diplomica Verlag.
Luthar, S. S., Cicchetti, D., & Becker, B. (2000). The construct of resilience: A critical evaluation and guidelines for future work. *Child Development, 71*(3), 543–562.
Maywald, C. (2013). Der pädagogische Umgang mit sterben, Tod und Trauer: Unterrichtung. *Beratung und Begleitung*. Hamburg: disserta Verlag.
McCann, L., & Pearlman, L. A. (2015). *Psychological trauma and adult survivor theory: Therapy and transformation*. Routledge.
Radey, M., & Figley, C. R. (2007). The social psychology of compassion. *Clinical Social Work Journal, 35*(3), 207–214.
Reddemann, L. (2003). Einige Überlegungen zur Psychohygiene und Burnout-Prophylaxe von TraumatherapeutInnen. Erfahrungen und Hypothesen. *Zeitschrift für Psychotraumatologie und Psychologische Medizin, 1*(1), 79–85.
Reich, J. W., Zautra, A. J., & Hall, J. S. (2010). *Handbook of adult resilience*. Guilford Press.
Samide, L. L., & Stockton, R. (2002). Letting go of grief: Bereavement groups for children in the school setting. *Journal for Specialists in Group Work, 27*(2), 192–204.
Sharp, C., Smith, J. V., & Cole, A. (2002). Cinematherapy: Metaphorically promoting therapeutic change. *Counseling Psychology Quarterly, 15*, 269–276.
Siebert, A. (2005). *The resiliency advantage: Master change, thrive under pressure, and bounce back from setbacks*. Berrett-Koehler Publishers.
Van Mol, M. M., Kompanje, E. J., Benoit, D. D., Bakker, J., & Nijkamp, M. D. (2015). The prevalence of compassion fatigue and burnout among healthcare professionals in intensive care units: A systematic review. *PLoS One, 10*. https://doi.org/10.1371/journal.pone.0136955
Witt-Loers, S. (2015). *Trauernde Jugendliche in der Schule*. Vandenhoeck & Ruprecht.
Zautra, A. J., Hall, J. S., & Murray, K. E. (2010). Resilience: A new definition of health for people and communities. In J. W. Reich, A. J. Zautra, & J. S. Hall (Eds.), *Handbook of adult resilience* (pp. 3–34). Guilford Press.
Zeidner, M., Hadar, D., Matthews, G., & Roberts, R. D. (2013). Personal factors related to compassion fatigue in health professionals. *Anxiety, Stress & Coping, 26*(6), 595–609.

Index

A
Accidents, 9, 94–103
Accompaniment, 148
Accompanying young people in their grief, 59–61
Adolescent grief in the school context, 53–56
Anger, 44
Annual deaths, 5
Application, 156
Art-oriented intervention, 156

B
Bereavement, 18
Boundaries, 151
Bowlby model, 41
Bullying, 108
Burden, 153
Burnout, 153

C
Caregivers, 153
Causes of death, 5
Child's understanding of death, 33–34
Chronic disease, 69
Cinematherapy, 156
Closure, 155–158
Compassion, 152, 153
Compassion fatigue, 152–154
Competence, 148
Complicated grief, 118
Compulsive behavior, 84
Concrete operational period, 33
Coping with grief in adolescents, 50–52
Cultural differences, 48–49
Culture of mourning, 150
Cyberbullying, 109

D
Death, 2
Delivery of the message, 135–137
Depression, 114
Development, 156
Difficulties, 45
Dissociations, 113

E
Emotional needs, 148
Empathy, 153
Extended suicide, 103

F
Fatigue, 153
Fear, 44
Female coping strategies, 20
Formal operational period, 33

G
General death rates, 5
General model of grief and loss, 40
General prevalence data, 5–10
Grief, 2–5, 17
Grief among adolescents, 49–61
Grief counselling, 147
Grief groups, 156
Grief in children, 29–49
Grief like no other, 117
Grief reactions, 43–46
Grief via social media, 56
Grief within the family circle, 56–59
Grief work, 46, 147–149
Grieving intensity, 17

© Springer-Verlag GmbH Germany, part of Springer Nature 2022
M. Böhmer, G. Steffgen (eds.), *Grief in Schools*,
https://doi.org/10.1007/978-3-662-64297-9

Grieving norms, 18
Group interventions, 137
Guilt, 43

H
Healthy and pathological grief, 4–5
Homicide, 105

I
Idealization, 44
Individual intervention, 137
Infantile mourning process, 40
Inpatient hospices, 74
Institution school, 149–151
Intervention, 156–157

K
Kast's model, 41–42

L
Leaking, 107
Limits, 147–149

M
Male coping strategies, 20
Memory, 158
Mobbing, 108
Model concepts, 40
Mourning, 2, 18, 147
Mourning period, 17
Mourning processes, 2
Mourning rituals, 22
Multiplier training, 77

N
Natural process, 157–158
Normal grief, 47

O
Opposing views, 36
Outpatient hospice services, 74

P
Palliative care, 74
Parents, 147
Pathological grief, 47

Physical diseases, 6
Piaget's view, 34–36
Post-traumatic stress disorder (PTSD), 114, 153
Pre-operational period, 31–32
Prolonged grief disorder, 118
Protective factors, 93–94
Psychologists, 153

R
Regression, 43–44
Relatives, 151–152
Resilience, 154
Responsibility, 149
Reunification, 43
Risk factors, 88–93

S
School, 45
School environment, 149
School shootings, 105
Secondary traumatic stress, 152–154
Self-care, 154–155
Sensorimotor period, 30–31
Sleep disturbances, 45
Somatic symptoms, 44
Somatization in the grieving process, 52–53
Specialized outpatient palliative care (SOPC), 74
Stages and processes of grief, 4
Stages of mourning, 157
Sudden death, 96
Suicides, 6, 85–94
Supervision, 155
Support, 152
Symptoms, 153

T
Theory of cognitive development by Jean Piaget, 30–33
Therapist, 153
Training of teachers, 142–145
Trauma, 153
Traumatic experience, 112
Traumatic grief, 117
Trust, 155

V
View of Fleck-Bohaumilitzky, 36–39
View of Nagy, 34
Violence, 103

Printed in the United States
by Baker & Taylor Publisher Services